ASPEN

ASPEN

*The History
of a Silver-Mining Town,
1879–1893*

MALCOLM J. ROHRBOUGH

New York   Oxford
OXFORD UNIVERSITY PRESS
1986

Oxford University Press

Oxford   New York   Toronto
Delhi   Bombay   Calcutta   Madras   Karachi
Petaling   Jaya   Singapore   Hong Kong   Tokyo
Nairobi   Dar es Salaam   Cape Town
Melbourne   Auckland

and associated companies in
Beirut   Berlin   Ibadan   Nicosia

Published by Oxford University Press, Inc.,
200 Madison Avenue, New York, New York 10016

Oxford is the registered trademark of Oxford University Press

Library of Congress Cataloging-in-Publication Data
Rohrbough, Malcolm J.
Aspen: the history of a silver-mining town, 1879–1893.
Bibliography: p.   Includes index.
1. Aspen (Colo.)—History. 2. Silver mines and
mining—Colorado—Aspen—History. I. Title.
F784.A7R64   1986   978.8'43   85-30099
ISBN 0-19-504064-3

9 8 7 6 5 4 3 2 1
Printed in the United States of America

FOR

Elizabeth

Justin

Peter

with respect and love

Acknowledgments

Mining starts out as an individual prospector with basic equipment confronting a harsh landscape that presumably holds great riches. It becomes an increasingly complex exercise, involving partners, assayers, lawyers, and a parallel growth in the significance and size of technology to include a railroad, a smelter, and eventually a mint. The line from streak of mineral to mint is hardly a straight one; rather, it is surrounded by twists and turns of talent, judgment, and luck.

The history of a mining town is remarkably parallel in its many variations. It begins with an idea on the part of an author, but it rapidly escalates in complexity to include a wide range of partners in the form of librarians, archivists, colleagues, and institutional and individual financial supporters. And it also becomes an exercise that needs its own technology in the form of microfilm, Xerox machines, and the counting and word-processing mechanisms of the computer.

This history of Aspen is no exception. From the beginning of this project, I have benefited from the interests and professional skills of librarians and archivists in the Colorado Historical Society, the Western History Department of the Denver Public Library, the Western History Collections of the University of Colorado in Boulder, the Western History Research Center of the University of Wyoming, the Aspen Public Library, and the Aspen Historical Society. I have also conducted profitable correspondences with the American Jewish Archives in Cincinnati and the Cincinnati Historical Society. I am grateful to all these institutions.

Several present and former graduate students at the University of Iowa have assisted in the preparation of this manuscript. They are William N. Silag, Jerry Harrington, Fred Bjornstad, Kendall Staggs, and Kimberly Porter. Judy N. Lensink of the University of Arizona offered constructive editorial criticism. I am also indebted to John Kolp of the Laboratory for Political Research of the University of Iowa. John N. Schacht and Robert McCown of the University of Iowa Library have provided a continual stream of references about Aspen and mining.

Of the people and institutions who have provided financial help in carrying this project to its completion, I especially wish to acknowledge the assistance of my father, the late George Irwin Rohrbough, who was a source of never-ending interest and support. The University of Iowa provided a semester's leave through a University Developmental Assignment that forwarded my work. The Graduate College of the University of Iowa helped to defray the cost of preparing the photographs for inclusion in this book.

Two members of the staff of the Iowa State Historical Department at Iowa City have contributed much to the completion of this manuscript. Mary K. Fredericksen spied out useful materials in distant depositories and offered insightful editorial advice. Steven J. Fuller performed high feats of technology on short notice. He continues to be the only computer doctor I know who makes house calls. Both helped immeasurably to bring this book to completion.

Two colleagues in the Department of History, H. Shelton Stromquist and Linda Kerber, have offered wise counsel on a wide range of questions. I am also under heavy obligations to my colleague Sarah Hanley, for her support and advice.

All errors, of whatever size and shape, are mine alone.

North Scituate, Mass.   M.J.R.
August 1985

Contents

Contents

I

THE CAMP
Aspen, 1879–1883

1

Into the Valley
of the Roaring Fork

On July 4, 1879, a party of four prospectors reached the crest of the
Continental Divide some thirty-five miles southwest of the young
silver camp at Leadville, Colorado. Independence Pass was in the
midst of its summer, and the four men crossed at the most hospitable
time of year, but at twelve thousand feet the summer season was brief
and carried then—as it does today—a sense of the harshness of this
place and its climate. On the arctic tundra a few wildflowers bright-
ened an otherwise stark landscape of lichen, moss, and rock outcroppings. Early afternoon temperatures had risen to almost sixty degrees,
but large patches of snow and the constant chill wind served as a
reminder that summer comes late to the high mountains and that the
summer season is short.

Charles E. Bennett, the party's leader, and his prospecting companions, Walter S. Clark, A. C. Fellows, and S. E. Hopkins, did not pause
to admire their natural surroundings. Theirs was a business trip. They
were three days out of Leadville in search for mineral wealth. That
professional prospectors should penetrate west of the Continental Divide was understandable, for the great silver strikes in Leadville only
two years before were the talk of the mining world. Visions of similar
bonanzas inspired determined men to risk their lives in remote mountain valleys acquired from the Ute tribe by treaty only the preceding
year. The Bennett party was physical testimony to this determination.
In addition to the usual food, clothing, and tools that formed the staple
of every prospecting trip, Bennett and his companions carried copies of

the Hayden surveys. With the grudging acquiescence of the Ute Indians, Hayden had mapped the geographic and geologic features of the region during the season of 1873–74. Hayden's party had also named many of the prominent landmarks, mountains, and watercourses. Bennett and the others had carefully examined these published documents while waiting for negotiations with the Indians to open up the area to exploration and settlement. They had noted the similarities between the geologic formations west of Independence Pass and those in the Leadville area, site of the recent bonanzas. So Bennett, Clark, Fellows, and Hopkins rode across the mountains with the lead rope of a pack horse in one hand and Hayden's surveys in the other.

The Bennett party camped for one night at the pass and at first light started down the steep slope on the western side. A short distance below the crest, the prospectors came upon a swift mountain stream appropriately named the Roaring Fork, and they turned to follow the twisting watercourse down the valley. The Roaring Fork River originated in melted snows high on the western side of the Sawatch Range. Volcanic uplift and the weather erosion of a thousand years had shaped its course. This first group of American entrepreneurs wasted no time gazing at some of the most spectacular mountain scenery in the world. Instead, their eyes searched the surrounding rock formations for marauding Utes, while their inner attention focused on the prospective mineral wealth that they sensed on all sides. As they moved down the valley to lower altitudes, life around them changed, tundra gave way to pine, and pine in turn yielded to aspen groves.

At the end of some twenty miles, the land leveled out and the mountain stream ceased its headlong rush. A small mountain park now lay before them, meadows and limpid pools that contrasted sharply with the rock outcroppings and rushing streams higher up the valley. Moving forward at a businesslike pace, the adventurers passed through a gap in the mountains. At this point, the Roaring Fork swung sharply in an arc to the north, and a valley floor spread out before them. Four mountain landmarks immediately captured their attention. On the left hand, its sides scarred by snow slides, loomed Aspen Mountain. Just beyond lay West Aspen (now Shadow Mountain). Behind them, Smuggler Mountain guarded the entrance to the upper Roaring Fork Valley. Farther down the valley on the right lay Red Mountain.

Charles Bennett and his party turned away from the Roaring Fork to ride along the base of Aspen Mountain. Negotiating the two high-banked swift watercourses of Castle and Maroon creeks, they made their way through a meadow . . . and found themselves face to face with another prospecting party. Philip W. Pratt, Smith Steele, and

William L. Hopkins were also based in Leadville; their equipment, guidebooks, and maps were the same. So was their purpose in visiting the valley of the Roaring Fork. Bennett balanced the disappointment of finding a rival group against the consolation of added strength in case of Indian attack. The valley, the river, and the mountains had long been the hunting ground of the Utes. After the discovery of gold near the present site of Denver in 1858, and, more recently, the silver strikes in nearby Leadville, the federal government had forced the Utes to accept a series of treaties that moved the tribe west of the Continental Divide.

Bennett sensed that the valley offered opportunities for mineral wealth great enough to accommodate both prospecting parties. He was right. Pratt and his two colleagues had been locating mineral claims for almost a week, using the Hayden reports as their guide. These three early arrivals had already laid off the Spar and the Pioneer, two claims that would later achieve considerable prominence in the Aspen mining world. Around a blazing campfire that evening, the two parties exchanged news in the style of the endless verbal poker games that often characterized communications among prospectors. The Pratt party spoke confidently of the riches to be found and exploited in the valley of the Roaring Fork. Bennett, Clark, Fellows, and Hopkins were quickly caught up in the fever of discovery. Secure in the knowledge of their strength against Indian attack and buoyed by visions of mineral wealth that obsessed so many who penetrated the lofty mountain ranges in the last half of the nineteenth century, the pioneering prospectors slept soundly that night.

The following morning, Philip Pratt and his companions departed for Leadville, while the Bennett party began the systematic exploration of the eastern end of the valley. Guided by the geologic findings of Hayden, occasionally enlightened by the guarded conversations of the preceding night, and supported by their own professional instincts, the four men moved over the land. Altogether, they stayed five days, examining the ground minutely, crisscrossing the valley and the surrounding mountainsides. They found exactly what they had sought: several rock formations and outcroppings that corresponded to the geologic characteristics of the Leadville area. After lengthy consultation, the prospectors carefully laid off seven claims, each a rectangle 1,500 feet long and 300 feet wide, placed on the ground in such a way as to contain within its boundaries the largest number of silver vein outcroppings. These claims corresponded to no natural boundaries and bore no logical relationship to one another, but the seemingly random rectangles laid the basis of future mining fortunes. The entrepreneurs then gave to their newly marked claims those names that would in future years be alternately consigned to oblivion or splashed across the front pages of mining journals throughout the western world: the Durant and the One-Thousand-and-One on Aspen Mountain; the Monarch, the Iron, the Hopkins, the Mose, and the Steele on West Aspen Mountain. They also took over an abandoned claim on Smuggler Mountain, christening it the Smuggler.

The laws of the United States and of the state of Colorado were specific with respect to the making and protecting of a mining claim. They needed to be. As in this case, prospectors often laid out their claims in the most remote places and then departed, leaving their claim stakes unprotected. The federal law of May 10, 1872, under which these claims were made specified that rights to such claims would be preserved in absentia, provided that the claimant made improvements worth at least $100 each year. These improvements were designed to ensure that the locator was a claimant intent on working his claim, not simply in laying out rectangles on a mountainside for quick resale. In order to comply with the law, the prospector had to sink a shaft to the depth of ten feet, and he had to make other improvements of at least $100 each year to preserve his rights. The members of the Bennett party spent much of their time in the valley of the Roaring Fork satisfying these requirements for their claims. Then, filled with visions of future wealth founded on the work of a single week, Bennett and his business partners packed their horses and retraced their steps toward the high mountain passes to the east. They were returning to Leadville, where they would perform a final official step by registering their claims with the clerk of Lake County.

The return trip through the upper valley of the Roaring Fork, across Independence Pass, into the valley of the Arkansas River, and thence north to Leadville, was a time for canvassing prospects. A legally valid mining claim offered many opportunities for profit. The Bennett party had staked eight such claims. The next step was to decide the best way to maximize profits and minimize risks. What should Bennett, Clark, Fellows, and Hopkins do with their claims and when? Should they sell out over the ensuing winter? Should they do more development work, which would cost money (albeit probably not a lot at this stage) and might enhance the value of their claims? Or, alternatively, might further development work reveal them to be less valuable than originally supposed? Or should Aspen's early entrepreneurs carry their mines into production? The decision to mine and process ore would involve great expense and enormous risk, but the rewards could be correspondingly great.

If the prospectors chose to sell, they had to face the question of identifying the most-appropriate buyers. The savvy mining men in Leadville were easily accessible and strongly under the spell of the Leadville bonanzas, but they were wise in the ways of mines and mining. Or they could take their claims to capitalists in Denver, who might be more gullible, but the new strikes were inaccessible and might be difficult to sell to the bankers on Broadway. And what of the international market? The phrase was synonymous with fabulous sums paid by rich foreign investors for indifferent mines. These new discoveries were probably too recent to appeal to New York or London markets, but the new mineowners could not help thinking in such grandiose terms.

The staking of mineral claims in the valley of the Roaring Fork raised the possibility that a town would emerge on the site. A large, stable mining camp would open up chances for profits in many areas besides mining. Did the prospectors wish to participate in the economic opportunities of an urban experience, with town lots, subdivisions, and false storefronts? In short, did they wish to become "town fathers" as well as mining-claim owners? Or did they wish to leave the founding and direction of the mining camp (and the risks and profits) to others? The possibilities were numerous.

Finally, how should they report what they had seen and done west of the Continental Divide? What had Pratt, Steele, and Hopkins said of the mining prospects in the Roaring Fork Valley on their return to Leadville? And how had their reports been received? Publicity increased the value of a mining site, but large numbers of new arrivals brought confusion, conflicting claims, and inevitable litigation. Eight claims in a mountain wilderness were only the first steps in the fortune that every mineowner saw on the horizon. Bennett and his colleagues did not lack significant issues to discuss on their return trip to Leadville.[1]

Bennett, Pratt, and the scores of other prospectors who later came to the valley of the Roaring Fork and participated in the founding and growth of what would become the city of Aspen could trace their entrepreneurial ancestry to the early Spanish conquistadores. The European exploration of the New World began in the mid-fifteenth century with a rising interest in commerce that led to the search for trade routes to the Orient. To this end, the sovereigns of the competing nations of Italy, Spain, and Portugal financed voyages to seek out shorter and safer trade routes to China. The discoveries of Christopher Columbus and other oceangoing adventurers at the close of the fifteenth century led England and France to join the hunt, and soon European nations had established colonies in the New World, first in the islands of the West Indies and then on the mainland of South and North America.

Spanish colonization of the New World began with the search for trade routes and expanded into an effort to save the souls of heathen native peoples. When the Aztec king Montezuma sent the invading Hernando Cortez a gift of gold in 1519, however, the ambitions of Spaniards and the direction of Spanish colonization changed. Adventurers to the New World and their rulers quickly forgot about trade and thought only of gold. The riches plundered by Cortez in Mexico (1518–21) and by Francisco Pizarro in Peru (1524–28) transformed the colonization of the New World into its first great gold rush. The legends of the Seven Golden Cities of Cibola and Quivira, where a king reclined under a tree with golden bells, had carried Francisco Coronado into the Great Plains of the American Southwest by 1540. By that time, the Spanish had developed silver mines around Mexico City and Zacatecas. The exploitation of the New World soon included silver as well as gold.

Over the second half of the sixteenth century, gold production in Mexico doubled and silver production increased twentyfold. The opening of the great mines of the New World transformed Spanish life in many ways. It created new opportunities for wealth among the Spanish nobility by colonial service and established a tradition of quick exploitation of mineral resources that would carry over to the American West. Spain translated these riches into heightened political, economic, and military influence throughout Europe. Gold and silver from the New World enabled Spain to hire armies to fight on the Continent and to finance the construction of the Great Armada, which was annihilated in 1588.

Spanish mineral riches in the New World and the personal fortunes and obvious political consequences that flowed from these discoveries attracted the attention of the other western European nationstates. Occasional allies (the French) and rivals (the English) tried to imitate Spanish successes. Although they failed to find gold and silver, the French established a great empire in North America based on commerce in furs. The stolid soil-bound English also exhibited a powerful interest in mineral wealth. At the founding of the first permanent colonies in Virginia, in 1607, the new colonists refused to work in the fields and instead searched for treasure in the woods. But the English colonists found no gold or silver, and hunger forced them to depend on the soil for their survival. The English settlements slowly expanded inland over the next century and a half. By the outbreak of the American Revolution, the Anglo-Americans had achieved a substantial presence in the New World, with a population of more than 2.5 million in permanent agricultural settlements stretching from Massachusetts to Georgia, from the Atlantic seaboard inland to the foothills of the Appalachians.

With the close of the Revolution, Americans crossed the Appalachian Mountains into an agricultural Garden of Eden, but they showed continued interest in minerals. Several thousand citizens of the Republic participated in a gold rush to mining camps in Georgia in the 1830s, and lead-mining operations in Missouri (1820s) and portions of Iowa, Wisconsin, and Illinois (1830s) confirmed the appeal of mineral wealth.

The great American mining experience of the nineteenth century began in January 1848 at John Sutter's mill on the American River in California. In the spring, the San Francisco newspapers raised the cry "GOLD," which immediately spread through the rest of California in the summer, reached the East Coast by autumn, and soon echoed from street corners and housetops across the nation. It was a message of hope and expectation that led people everywhere to lift their heads from the daily drudgery that was nineteenth-century American agriculture and to look toward the Golden West.

Gold brought a new dimension to the lives of Americans. For 250 years, the vision of fertile lands had dominated their dreams. Generations of the landless poor of Europe and, later, from the exhausted stony lands of the East Coast had found the fertile lands they sought by immigration to the American West. The dream of agricultural independce was real, but it involved unending labor in all seasons by all members of the family. From year to year, such pioneer families and even farmers in the long-settled areas of rural America saw little cash. They lived in a world of hard work and limited economic expectations. The end product of a lifetime of such labor was a modest landed estate that could be passed on to the next generation, which would then repeat the process.

Gold in California changed the dimensions of this world in a dramatic way. At a time when agricultural laborers earned $1 a day for twelve hours of backbreaking labor, farm laborers-turned-prospectors panned $20 a day in gold from California's streams; those with skill and luck in the right proportions could pan $100 a day. The most fumbling of these argonauts was likely to see more money in a month than the average family saw in a year. The expectation of the frontier experience had been transformed. Gold and silver dramatically enlarged the concept of wealth for nineteenth-century Americans.

The response was the greatest transcontinental migration in the history of the young Republic. It was the more striking in view of the vast distances to be crossed, for the forty-niners and the subsequent annual waves of immigrants had to endure eighteen hundred miles by wagon and horseback over primitive tracks, with the natural obstacles of rivers without bridges, vast treeless plains with new flora and fauna, bright deserts and dry water holes, and two ranges of mountains with peaks fourteen thousand feet high. Spurred by restlessness, ambition, and youth, Americans did not seem deterred. The two hundred thousand who came overland and by sea to California in the first three years of the gold rush became known as the forty-niners; in numbers, distance traveled, and influence, they represented a new benchmark in the national experience. They burst through the last barriers to the Far West, colonized California virtually overnight, and submerged the ancient cultures of the native Americans and the Hispanics by their sheer numbers.

The search for gold in California began with single men, burros, picks, and pans. Miners appeared in numbers in the summer of 1849 on the streams that flowed down the western slopes of the Sierra Nevada, where they prospected for gold on a small scale, commensurate with their equipment and skills. Individuals or a few men in partnership panned for gold in swift-flowing streams. The water flowing through the gravel in the pan filtered out the "dirt" and left a residue of heavier gold nuggets or flakes at the bottom of the pan.

These first argonauts of 1849 found wealth reminiscent of the discoveries of Cortez and Pizarro three centuries earlier. Yet the differences were more important than the similarities. Unlike the gold of the Spanish colonial experience, this gold would go not to support kings and their armies but to the individual citizens of the American Republic. The democratic nature of the experience was the more complete because the first gold was readily accessible to individuals without special knowledge, capital, or technical skills. The only requirement was a willingness to perform manual labor, a trait present almost universally in the nation of farmers that was America at mid-nineteenth century. The early waves of prospectors profited accordingly, taking gold worth $10 million from California's streams in the summer of 1849, and by 1852 the annual output had reached the extraordinary figure of $81.3 million. In the period from 1848 to the opening of the twentieth century, California's mining output exceeded $1.3 billion.

Between 1848 and 1852, the population of the new state (admitted to the Union in 1850) ballooned from 14,000 to 223,000, and the most accessible of the rivers and streams began to play out. The answer to this problem was a series of new discoveries—or "strikes" as they were known—across the West. Prospectors in search of the Mother Lode followed the call to the new El Dorados in high valleys or on desert floors—to Colorado in 1859, to Nevada in 1859, and to Montana in 1862. Thousands of prospectors and their supporting cast of merchants, saloonkeepers, and townsite boomers carried the mining frontier throughout the West in rushes that by the close of the century stretched from the Canadian border to Mexico, from the front range of the Rocky Mountains to the Alaskan Klondike.[2]

As it established new levels of wealth, so mining also created on a large scale a different kind of frontier society: young, single, wandering males rather than extended family groups tied to the land. The universal nature of the mining exercise in its first stage—a man needed only a pan and shovel to join the game—produced a mixture of ethnic groupings as random as that in any large eastern city. Miners came from the United Kingdom (the Welsh and Scots were particularly well represented), France, Germany, Italy, Norway, Sweden, Denmark, and the other nations and principalities of eastern and western Europe. To these should be added two other groups: Mexicans and Chinese. The Europeans—whatever their claims to the term "American"—joined the resident Americans in discriminating sometimes against the Mexicans and, by 1860, almost always against the Chinese.

These diverse peoples who gathered at a mining strike characteristically formed compact urban rather than dispersed rural settlements. As the miscellaneous claims stretched out along innumerable streams, a tent city to shelter the prospectors unfolded on the hillsides. The streets ran parallel to the stream bed or mountain ridge that formed the focus of the claims. Eventually a mining camp emerged. The camp had wooden shanties for lawyers' offices, hotels, restaurants, and stores.

Mining camps had their own species of entrepreneurs, with talents distinct from those of mining promoters. The experiences and accumulated knowledge of townsite boosters may be thought of as running parallel to technological advances in mining techniques. To make or to help make a successful mining camp was an achievement of skill and luck no less difficult than and almost as profitable as bringing a mine into production. Both required talents of a high order. The evidence for this statement lies in the large number who tried and failed at both mining and town building and in the small number who succeeded at either.

The new mining society also created new institutional forms to establish ground rules by which men would seek wealth and, once achieved, protect it. Forms of local government and law fashioned for the agricultural world of the East did not work well in this transient world, where rumors of a mineral strike could establish a camp with a population of five thousand men in three days. Pioneers who went west in 1849 or participated in later mining rushes over the next half a century sometimes found themselves in places lacking the institutional structure of government and law. Or, if government had been organized, it did not function effectively, and law and the court system poorly controlled the mass of single young men intent on fortunes that might be found in highly contested small plots of ground.

When these diverse groups came together at a placer diggings, their proximity to one another and the intensity of the competition for wealth in a restricted space often produced friction. To prevent violence and to protect their interests, the first miners convened themselves in a sovereign body to establish the legitimacy of their claims. This unit of organization they called a mining district. At such a meeting, they adopted and published regulations to govern their new society and to lay down rules under which the search for wealth would be conducted. These rules—eventually standardized throughout the mining West—conferred advantages on those who first staked claims in the district. The United States mining law of 1866—the first major legislation for the mining West—imposed federal order on the mining frontier by a simple expedient: it recognized these informal bodies and made their deliberations the law of the land.

The economic implication of mining were far-ranging. The army of prospectors campaigning in the field required elaborate and continuous supply services. There was a demand for food and equipment—from flour to candles, from shovels to stamp mills—and everywhere enterprising men moved to meet these needs. Merchants proliferated as rapidly as claims on the surrounding hillsides, and they charged all that the market would bear. And, like others who lived in urban settings, miners rapidly required professionals such as lawyers, doctors, and, not least, entertainers.

Mining gradually evolved into a complex, large-scale corporate industry, using the latest in technology supported by innovative financing. This meant more technical and sophisticated means of extracting gold and silver, with machinery, chemicals, and trained professionals. But such advanced techniques were expensive, far beyond the means of individuals. Small miners soon found themselves superseded on the mining frontier by financiers, industrialists, and their agents. Heavy financial investment, company towns, and corporate boardrooms in San Francisco and eventually New York replaced the burro, the pick, and the pan. Mining became a corporate enterprise. As early as 1852, mills and smelters to crush and refine ore had become a prominent part of California mining. Mining also grew specialized. As the mines developed into large industrial complexes, consolidated mining companies (as they came to be called, because they consolidated several claims) employed professional miners, wage earners who labored deep underground. In its structure, large-scale investment, and stock manipulation, mining became an extension of changes taking place elsewhere in America with the large-scale organization and integration of the steel, petroleum, and transportation industries.

California was the first chapter in the story of the search for gold and silver throughout the mountain West. The second was the silver-mining district in Washoe, Nevada, better known as the Comstock Lode. The rush of miners to the Washoe District began in July 1859. California capitalists quickly bought the most promising silver claims from the early prospectors, transforming the site from a series of placer camps into a city in the desert. They invested huge sums of money in what would become the largest, most highly capitalized, and most technically advanced mining enterprise in the world. By 1865, as the Civil War came to a close at the other side of the continent, Virginia City, Nevada, had a population of nine thousand. That year, its professional miners raised to the surface 430,745 tons of ore that translated into silver bullion worth $15,833,000. Between 1860 and 1880, the mines in the Comstock Lode produced $300,000,000 worth of gold and silver and attracted the attention of the mining world.

Virginia City became a late-nineteenth-century American industrial city along the lines of Lowell, Massachusetts, or Homestead, Pennsylvania. Population, investment, and production gave it stability. The Comstock mines pioneered in the science of mining low-grade silver ore deep underground, meeting challenges of flooding and cave-ins with new technology. In 1870, men mined at the 1,300-foot level; ten years later, they were down to 3,000 feet. The urban stability associated with Virginia City, its great investment and fabulous dividends, the technology that made possible the recovery of a fortune from huge quantities of low-grade ore, laid the groundwork for the great silver-mining industry in Colorado.[3]

The third and most immediate antecedent of Aspen was Leadville. Leadville influenced Aspen by its proximity, for it lay only forty miles distant, albeit across some of the highest mountain passes on the continent. Leadville's great silver boom began in the summer and autumn of 1877, when its population was scarcely two hundred and its business directory listed one general store and two saloons. The silver bonanzas generated enormous immigration, as thousands of men rushed to reach the highest incorporated town in the country. By 1880, Leadville had almost fifteen thousand people and was the second-largest city of Colorado.

While Leadville's growth produced a degree of vice and violence that horrified and repulsed, it also generated great profits. The fortunes rivaled those found anywhere else in the mining West, and the characters who made them were among the most colorful in all of mining history. Take the case of Horace A. W. Tabor, a storekeeper from Maine, who with his wife, Augusta, came west in the first Colorado gold rush of 1858. The Tabors tried and failed in several mining camps before arriving in Leadville with the first miners. There, as was their custom, they opened and managed a general store, where they grubstaked impecunious prospectors. Two of the Tabors' ne'er-do-well customers discovered what would become the Little Pittsburg mine in May 1878, and by honored custom they received a one-third interest. Horace Tabor went on to make millions in a few years. His name became a household word, invariably mentioned in the rags-to-riches stories associated in the popular mind with the American mining experience. His divorce and remarriage to the exotic Elizabeth ("Baby Doe") McCourt symbolized the breakdown of moral values in the face of overwhelming wealth. Leadville, for all its rowdiness, dirty streets, and short summer, was an inspiring place to make money. And making money was what mining was all about.[4]

The arrival, exploration, and departure of the first prospectors in the valley of the Roaring Fork over a fortnight in the summer of 1879 was only the first step in Aspen's founding and growth. They were immediately followed by town builders. It was their business to lay off streets, establish government, provide minimum services for citizens, and, above all, to publicize their creation.

The business was a chancy and imprecise one. Technical tests would show that a ton of ore from the surrounding mountainsides would produce a specific quantity of silver, and this information would form the basis of a business decision whether mines might be developed or discarded. Building a camp offered no such specifics. The intangibles of individual leadership, outside influences, and good luck were impossible to measure.

The town builders arrived before the end of the summer of 1879. They passed a long and lonely winter in the valley of the Roaring Fork, surrounded by tall mountain peaks, six feet of snow, and rumors of a

Ute uprising. Men continued to arrive throughout the late winter; with the coming of spring, heavy immigration began. These early Aspen settlers became the nucleus of a mining camp, a camp still without form or official status. Theirs was a commitment to a most uncertain future. For the first settlers, it took a special leap of faith to see a future town where mountain wilderness now stretched forth all around them. They cut their ties elsewhere and staked their futures on the camp at the junction of the Roaring Fork and Castle Creek. They had to convice one another and eventually others east of the mountains—first in Leadville, then in Denver, and finally across the nation—that their camp would endure.

The two log cabins and the dozen inhabitants of the summer of 1879 changed into a town, and the town grew into a city. The whole process took less than fifteen years. By 1893, Aspen was the third-largest city in Colorado, exceeded in size only by Denver and Leadville, and in expectations for the future by none. The city had paved streets, gas streetlamps, a municipal streetcar system two miles long, two electric light and power companies, a municipal water system, three banks, a post office, an opera house, a courthouse, a city hall, a jail, a luxury hotel, a hospital, and three daily newspapers. It also had a stable and effective city government.[5]

This story of chance turned into astonishing success drew to Aspen a collection of striking personalities who made it home, business, and sometimes playground. Aspen also had thousands of ordinary men and women and children who made homes there and who did the daily work. What these people together created was a monument to their energy, industry, and ambition.

2

"We Could Make Our Fortunes":
The First Arrivals Establish
a Mining Camp

Nature abhors a vacuum. So does a good mining strike. Scarcely had the first wave of prospectors disappeared up the valley toward Independence Pass and Leadville than others moved toward the site of the recent discoveries. Indeed, so rapid was the appearance of the second set of people to replace the first, they almost seemed to step in the same tracks, to tread on the same blades of grass, to startle the same wildlife. This second group of entrepreneurs had camped on the banks of the Roaring Fork by the fall of 1879.

They had come in response to the mysterious stream of rumors that flowed in ripples, eddies, and sometimes raging torrents through every mining camp. Stories of the new strikes circulated almost before the first prospectors had dismounted from their horses in Leadville. Men responded instinctively, as they had since the California gold rush in 1848. By the time the aspens turned yellow on the sides of the surrounding mountains, perhaps as many as thirty-five people had camped on the level ground at the foot of the Aspen Mountain between Castle Creek and the Roaring Fork. A dozen tents with various levels of housekeeping testified to their presence. It was a familiar backdrop for a mining site. This second generation, all of sixty days older than the first, openly exploited opportunities in the new district—selling townsite lots, food, clothing, and supplies to prospectors who swarmed over the colorful sides of Aspen, West Aspen, and Smuggler mountains to stake out their claims.

Into this idyllic autumn scene of sunny days and crisp nights combined with the heady atmosphere of fortunes to be made came word of an Indian uprising. The boundary line of the Ute Reservation lands that the treaty of 1868 guaranteed the tribe ran close to the Roaring Fork Valley. Ouray, the Ute chief, had granted permission for Frederick V. Hayden's surveying party to enter the region and map the geographic and topographic features, but by the autumn of 1879 the Utes were convinced that the United States government had deceived them. A group of them killed the Indian agent they regarded as the symbol of this betrayal and left the reservation. Colorado's governor, Frederick Pitkin, in the tradition of a frontier politician confronted by an Indian uprising, immediately dispatched messengers with instructions that the inhabitants of the new mining district were to return across the Continental Divide for their safety. Many of them did so—going to Leadville, to Buena Vista, and, in some cases, to distant Denver, surely spurred by the imminent arrival of winter.

A few stayed in the Roaring Fork Valley, standing guard at night, venturing out only in groups and then heavily armed. The game of town building at the site of the new strikes had begun. It was still a wide-open exercise, but it was also a game with rules. These first settlers knew what the rules were, and they resolved to abide by them as the best way of protecting their interests. The dozen men still there in November 1879 organized a camp. Meeting in solemn conclave, they passed a resolution to respect the claims of those who had retreated east of the divide, for whatever reasons. It went without saying that the claims of those still on the site had the same protection. These intrepid first citizens made no survey. Thus, their camp had no legal standing in Colorado law, but with the law east of the mountains in distant Leadville, those on the spot could claim much authority for their actions. Even more than in the agricultural lands in the Ohio and Mississippi valleys, sovereign authority in a mining district belonged to those on the site.

Their coming together in the form of a deliberative and legislative body transformed them into a "sovereign" body in the eyes of the state of Colorado. The concept of the "sovereignty" of mining districts had begun in California with the first gold strikes and received statute recognition under the federal mining law of 1866, which opened the mineral lands of the public domain to citizens of the Republic and recognized the rules of local mining districts.[1]

The second group of entrepreneurs to visit the Roaring Fork Valley had the same objective as the first prospectors: to profit from the presence of minerals in the surrounding mountainsides. These town builders who followed so closely on the heels of the prospectors were a diverse group. Some were businessmen—merchants, outfitters, mining assayers; others were petty-office holders and bureaucrats; still others were the wives and families of these men. In origin, they included urbane easterners (the terms used loosely then as now) and rough-and-ready figures from earlier western mining camps; in condition, those with money to invest and those fleeing debts elsewhere. They had as many different ideas about how to build up a camp as there were veins of silver in the surrounding mountains. Many had almost certainly played parts in the town-building experience before. Probably they had failed, at least to the extent that the unknown camp on the Roaring Fork offered more and better prospects than the ones they left behind. They quickly found themselves united by a common destiny. From the moment the embryonic camp emerged, these men and women pledged their allegiance to it—in good times and bad, in cold winters and pleasant summers, and in sickness and health.[2]

With remarkable rapidity, these town builders created three mining camps—Ute City (later Aspen), at the junction of the Roaring Fork and Castle Creek; Independence, high in the upper valley of the Roaring Fork toward Independence Pass; and Ashcroft, ten miles up Castle Creek. The early circumstances of the three camps favored Independence and Ashcroft. Independence was a gold-mining camp, and the immediate profits that came with gold mining gave it a strong initial boost. Independence also had the backing of a company. Two prospectors had discovered gold on the site on July 4, 1879, calling their claim the Independence in honor of the national holiday. The tent city that immediately sprang up took the same name. Within a year, a group of Leadville entrepreneurs bought up most of the claims and incorporated the Farwell Consolidated Mining Company. The business directory for 1881 listed four grocery stores, three saloons, and four boardinghouses.

Ashcroft's early development depended more on promotion than on a profitable mining enterprise. Townsite promoters, whose moving force was T. E. Ashcraft (pronounced Ashcroft), laid out a site on the upper reaches of Castle Creek, ten miles up the valley from the site of Ute City. The camp grew rapidly, with good claims and skillful promotion. Its original name of Chloride was soon changed to Ashcroft to honor the pronunciation if not the spelling of the founding father. In the summer of 1881, Ashcroft had a population of five hundred people.

High altitudes handicapped both Independence and Ashcroft—the one at eleven thousand feet and the other at nine thousand. Ashcroft enjoyed some compensation in its favorable location (comparatively speaking), for those coming to the Roaring Fork Valley from the south passed Ashcroft on the way to Ute City. In the end, Ute City (soon renamed Aspen), the slowest to organize and the last to begin mineral production, won out. It triumphed through a series of geographic and economic accidents. At eight thousand feet, it was at a lower altitude than its rivals; it mined silver rather than gold; it had many entrepreneurs rather than one. Its selection as temporary county seat in 1881 marked its triumph, a first step on the road to permanence.

The first age of the Rocky Mountain mining camp belonged to the promoter. The age might be short—anywhere from a few weeks to a few years—but a camp achieved life and grew in response to the ministrations of an interested party or parties, who lavished tender care on their new urban creation, which in reality was very likely nothing more than an elaborate campsite. The first such figure (of what would be many) to attach his fortunes to the camp at the site of the Roaring Fork was Henry B. Gillespie.

A native of rural Cooper County, Missouri, Gillespie had graduated (with high honors) from Kansas State University in Manhattan and immigrated to Colorado. In 1874, he settled in Boulder County, where he worked as a bookkeeper for a Cincinnati capitalist named Abel D. Breed. Breed had large mining interests in the area. Gillespie later followed a surge of people to Leadville. From his office on Harrison Avenue, he saw the first prospecting parties return from the Roaring Fork Valley in mid-July 1879, and, sensing an opportunity, he followed it.

Gillespie was a model of the second generation of mining entrepreneurs who followed prospectors with an instinct for town building and mining enterprise, who knew how to mix the two in proportions that maximized profits, and who had sufficient capital (albeit in small amounts) to prime the investment pump, while appealing to others with larger bankrolls. He now proceeded to act in all these capacities with customary energy and aggressive confidence.

From the original Leadville prospectors, Gillespie immediately purchased options on the Spar and the Galena claims on Aspen Mountain for $25,000, payable at a future date. He then rounded up a dozen or so willing miners and led them across the Continental Divide to begin developing his properties. Snow had already fallen on the high passes, and the party had to make a part of the trip on snowshoes. Once established in the camp, Gillespie persuaded the score or so squatters on the site to hold a meeting to organize the camp. Most of those in the valley of the Roaring Fork were prospectors, and they seemed content to let Gillespie take the lead. Besides, it was agreeable to hear someone in their wilderness campsite speak confidently of a post office, telegraph lines, paved streets, and railroads.

Gillespie organized a camp, named it Ute City, and drew up a petition, willingly signed by the wintering prospectors, asking the federal government to establish a post office there. This would be a first step in official recognition. He then left for Washington, D.C., to press for the establishment of a post office. On the way, he stopped off in Cincinnati and sold a half interest in his properties to his old employer, Abel D. Breed. Breed was every mining entrepreneur's vision of an ideal partner. He had made a fortune in patent medicines and had branched out into the coffin business, where he had also prospered. (That there existed a connection between the consumption of his medicines and the growth of his casket business was rumored but never proven.) Breed had invested in mines before with great success, especially in the celebrated Caribou property in Boulder County. Breed could provide the capital that Gillespie required to develop his mining properties on the sides of Aspen Mountain.

Confident that he had been successful in Washington, Gillespie went home by way of Philadelphia, where he persuaded other capitalists to organize the Roaring Fork Improvement Company, a corporation that would construct a toll road from Buena Vista to Ute City. Gillespie had now put together the requisite ingredients for success in a new mining camp: he had mining claims and a partner with capital; he had a townsite plan that would let him control the future development of the camp; and he had organized a corporation to provide needed facilities for the new campsite and, at the same time, to profit from them. It was a thoroughly professional performance by a man who had been around mining camps long enough to know the several avenues to profit. Unfortunately for him, these several arrangements meant that he had been absent from the campsite for several months. Much had happened in his absence.[3]

In February 1880, while Gillespie sought official status, capital, and partners in the East, the stillness that surrounded the wintering pioneers on the banks of the Roaring Fork was disturbed by the arrival of B. Clark Wheeler. It was the first of the hundred or so trips that Wheeler would make to Aspen, and the manner of his arrival—on skis after crossing the mountains from Leadville in the dead of winter—befitted a style that alternately inspired, entertained, and irritated, but never bored. Wheeler, or B. Clark, as he would be remembered by many, was a professional boomer of grandiose proportions. He had made a marginal career on the mining frontier of the Far West for more than fifteen years. A native of Tioga County, Pennsylvania, Wheeler trained for a career as a teacher, serving as principal of several high schools in Pennsylvania, and all his life he retained the style of the pedagogue instructing backward pupils. He eventually left teaching to study law and then departed the East for the mining West in 1864. His travels took him up and down the backbone of the Rockies, from Canada to Mexico, in and out of endless mining camps. To teacher and lawyer he now added the self-conferred title of mining engineer. His final and most lasting title, that of professor, nicely suggested all three professions to which he laid claim.

Yet Professor Wheeler was not a scientific man, either by training or by inclination; rather, he was a promoter. He threw his boundless energy into promoting the mineral resources of the Rocky Mountain West for capitalists from the East or for anyone who would listen to him. Affecting the dress of a mining explorer, which matched his aggressive stride, black beard, loud voice, and ever-present cigar, Wheeler praised empty tunnels, salted claims, and bonanzas impartially. For him, the mining West was the reincarnation of the early Spanish search for gold and silver, updated to match the values and expectations of late-nineteenth-century Protestant America.

In the winter of 1879–80, Wheeler found himself without steady employment, dividing his time between Denver and Leadville. In both places, he picked up news of the strikes on the Roaring Fork and, acting with the interest of the promoter and an instinct for the expanding opportunity associated with a new mining district, determined to seize the moment. That he did so in the dead of winter was typical of his energy and determination. His skiing trip combined risk, adventure, and action in a way characteristic of his future relationship with the camp of Aspen.

Wheeler and his three companions brought more than a few Leadville newspapers to the news-starved wintering prospectors. They knew how to transform the campsite on the Roaring Fork into a legal urban entity, carrying with it the force of Colorado townsite law. Unlike those on the site, Wheeler did not intend to wait for spring to stake out claims or improve town lots. He, like other professional town builders, knew no season for his work. He intended to "jump" Gillespie's claim to the site on the Roaring Fork, and to this end he carried with him an order for the survey of the site signed by the surveyor general of Colorado. In crisp, sunny winter weather and floundering about in three feet of snow, Wheeler made a line-of-sight survey, laying out the boundaries of the camp.

21

The older settlers watched quietly, not venturing too far from the warmth of their cabins. Gillespie had been gone three months, and no one could say with certainty that he intended to return. Wheeler's mysterious rites of compass, chain, and paper represented progress to them. They knew that well-established custom would protect their squatter's rights. Wheeler did the hard work, but they, too, would profit. As a last act, Wheeler had to give the camp a new name to establish an identity independent of Ute City. With the casual flourish of an artist signing his work, he scrawled ASPEN across the face of his sketch. A founding father has certain prerogatives.

The grinning prospectors who waved good-bye to B. Clark Wheeler and his companions as they struggled up the valley toward Independence Pass with skis perched atop packs would have been less pleased had they known Wheeler's ultimate purpose. He represented a group of eastern investors, and on the basis of the townsite survey supplied by him his employers organized the Aspen Town and Land Company, incorporated in March 1880. This second Philadelphia corporation (Gillespie's was the first) intended to control the development of the townsite, or at least to control it insofar as Wheeler's survey—sanctioned by the surveyor general of Colorado—gave the company the legal authority to do so. But the Aspen Town and Land Company carried the new camp forward in a great leap from being a sketch on the wall of a mining shack to being a corporate entity with legal standing. Furthermore, the camp now had the interest of eastern capitalists who had invested money with the intention of realizing a profit. For some, at least, the mining camp of Aspen was now a business.[4]

Henry B. Gillespie and B. Clark Wheeler, Aspen's first town builders, represented eastern capitalists responding to an investment opportunity. Hundreds of others with humbler resources came in response to spring. Theirs was an annual ritual that might have been patterned after ancient tribes that migrated in pursuit of game. Americans who followed the mining frontiers had moved in the same seasonal cycles since the days of the California gold rush. With the snow melt of spring, miners hurried out to the "diggings" in the high mountains, where they joined in the search for mineral wealth over the summer months; in the autumn, they gradually drifted back to more hospitable climates and closer to the necessities of life. The surest gauge of the permanence of a mining camp was its year-round population, a number that reflected the degree of commitment to it.

In the spring of 1880, Aspen now experienced its first such cycle. Varieties of peoples, from grizzled cynical veterans to eager greenhorns, came over the mountains. The common denominator among them was the desire to begin anew, to forget the failures of the past, the dry holes, and the unpaid debts, to seize the chance of renewal in which a few moments of dazzling success could wipe out the memories of endless failures. The earliest of the spring arrivals came on snow-shoes, skis, or sled, and by mid-March they came steadily, on horse-back or on foot, in parties of half a dozen or more.

Many came from Leadville, where the silver bonanzas of 1878 had produced fabulous riches for a few, but where prosperity and growth had reduced the prospects for those without capital or influential friends. It was one of the cruel and perpetual ironies of the mining frontier that success narrowed opportunity from the many to the few, from the prospector to the capitalist. The only exception was the op-portunity offered the professional miner who worked underground in the deep shafts and remote drifts for three dollars a day. Miners and prospectors were not interchangeable. Each was a professional in his own way, and the ways were different. Prospectors now headed over the Continental Divide to the new camp of Aspen. With them came their support groups and camp followers: merchants, millers, builders, blacksmiths, wagon masters with teams, saloonkeepers, assayers, drummers, and confidence men.

Among those who came in Aspen's first summer of youth were H.P. ("Grandpap") Cowenhoven, a merchant from Black Hawk, Colo-rado, his wife, Margaret, his daughter, Katherine, and his young clerk, David R. C. Brown. Cowenhoven and Brown would both play promi-nent parts in Aspen's early history. Yet their route to the new camp on the Roaring Fork and the character of their decision making were pro-bably as accidental as those of scores of others who came with them. Henry P. Cowenhoven, born in East Prussia in 1814, immigrated to America in 1841. After a brief stay in New York, he moved to Indiana; in 1849, in response to the gold strikes, he crossed the plains with the forty-niners. In 1852, he was back in Indiana managing a general store, but the lure of the mining frontier was strong, and in 1859 he joined the second generation of gold seekers in Colorado.

Brown was a native of New Brunswick, Canada. He immigrated to Black Hawk in 1877, at the age of twenty-one, and found employment as a clerk in Cowenhoven's general store. In April 1880, Cowenhoven decided to leave Black Hawk. The prospects of that camp had faded. He sold his store and loaded the stock on two wagons. After quickly canvassing his prospects, Brown agreed to drive the second wagon. Perhaps he had already received assurances from Katy Cowenhoven, whom he had been courting for some time. The party departed Black Hawk on June 5. The trip was a slow one because Cowenhoven stopped at several camps to collect debts that were not easily collectible. They stayed briefly in Leadville, where they must have marveled at the vibrancy and liveliness of a booming camp—now a city—whose mines, stores, and saloons ran twenty-four hours a day.

After four days in Leadville, they resolutely set out down the valley of the Arkansas River, as Brown remembered Cowenhoven's plans, "for nowhere in particular, but he thought he would go to Arizona." At Twin Lakes, an outfitting place with fresh provisions and horses, Cowenhoven and Brown met a man named Blodgett, who told them the Indians were hostile in Arizona and New Mexico. "Why don't you go to the Roaring Fork country?" he asked. Blodgett showed some ore samples and an enthusiasm for his adopted camp that would have done honor to B. Clark Wheeler at his most expansive. With an insight that he would later bring to bear on his several economic enterprises, Brown noted that Blodgett "handled the truth carelessly." Yet, for all their skepticism, Brown and the hardheaded Cowenhoven were halfway convinced. The little caravan changed course for Buena Vista, the logical route to Aspen, where Cowenhoven and Brown made further inquiries. Whatever their questions, the answers must have been satisfactory. They would go to Aspen on the Roaring Fork. Brown summed up his own decision in these words: "I saw so far as I was concerned I wanted to go where Blodgett told us we could make our fortunes."

To make the decision to go to the Roaring Fork was simple; to get there with two loaded wagons was extremely difficult. Cowenhoven immediately saw the opportunity for profit in a new mining camp in a new mining district, where growing numbers of spring arrivals would quickly outrun available supplies. Here lay the contradiction. Aspen was poorly supplied because there was no road across the Continental Divide suitable for wagons. With his two wagons loaded to the tops, the Cowenhoven party followed the road out of Buena Vista toward Taylor Pass. In two and a half days, they reached the top of the pass, where their troubles began.

From a vantage point far above the timberline, Cowenhoven and Brown looked down a slope so steep that the question was whether it was passable for men and horses, let alone wagons. Determined to take their cargo with them, they started down the impassable slope with two loaded wagons, but they measured progress in terms of yards, sometimes only a few hundred in the first days. On reaching the cliff edges, they unloaded the supplies, disassembled the wagons, and lowered them in sections by ropes and chains, pulleys and winches, to the next level ground below. There they reassembled the wagons, while Margaret and Katy Cowenhoven brought the mules,

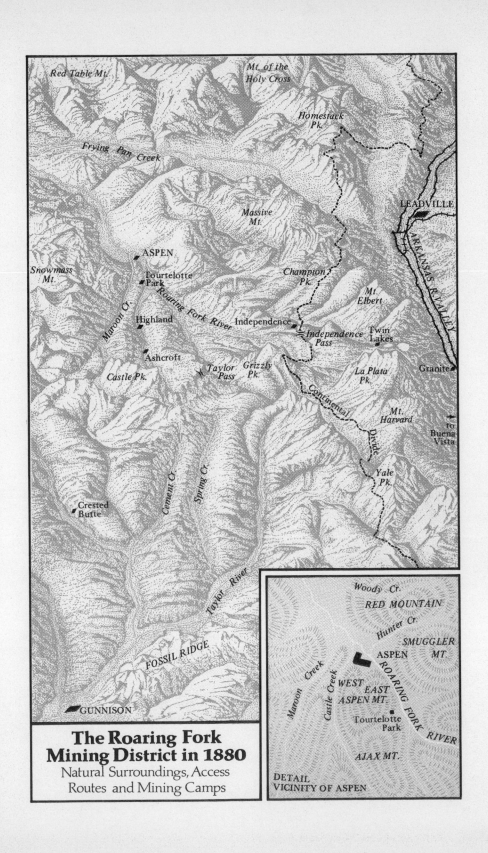

Red Table Mt.

Mt. of the Holy Cross

Homestack Pk.

Frying Pan Creek

LEADVILLE

Massive Mt.

ARKANSAS R. VALLEY

ASPEN

Snowmass Mt.

Tourtelotte Park

Champion Pk.

Mt. Elbert

Maroon Cr.

Roaring Fork River

Highland

Independence

Independence Pass

Twin Lakes

Ashcroft

Taylor Pass

Grizzly Pk.

La Plata Pk.

Granite

Castle Pk.

Continental

Mt. Harvard

to Buena Vista

Divide

Cement Cr.

Spring Cr.

Yale Pk.

Crested Butte

Taylor River

FOSSIL RIDGE

GUNNISON

The Roaring Fork
Mining District in 1880
Natural Surroundings, Access
Routes and Mining Camps

Woody Cr.

RED MOUNTAIN

Hunter Cr.

SMUGGLER MT.

ASPEN

Maroon Creek

Castle Creek

WEST ASPEN MT.

EAST ASPEN MT.

ROARING FORK RIVER

Tourtelotte Park

AJAX MT.

DETAIL
VICINITY OF ASPEN

loaded with the goods, by a more roundabout way to the new site. Then they reloaded the wagons and rehitched the mules. As they descended down the valley, the slope was less steep and they progressed faster.

In two weeks, they covered ten miles. At last they came in sight of the camp of Ashcroft, still a thousand feet below them in the valley of Castle Creek. Brown rode into town and hired two men with axes and chains to clear for the wagon caravan a path into the valley. Resisting the blandishments of Ashcroft and its prospects—"they thought they had the greatest mines in Colorado," Brown remembered—Cowenhoven and Brown pushed down Castle Creek to Aspen. They reached the camp on July 21, 1880. Brown recalled, "It was the most wonderful sight I ever beheld." The next morning, Cowenhoven bought a corner lot at Cooper Avenue and Galena Street for $75 and began building a house and store.[5]

In the spring and summer of 1880, the merchant, his family, and his clerk had lots of company. The trickle of people and supplies in the early spring had become a flood by midsummer. Some thought as many as eight hundred had come across the range; others said a thousand. Not all these people were at the camp on the Roaring Fork, of course, for many of them had scattered into the high mountain parks and valleys to prospect for new claims. The first serious building in the camp had begun, spurred by the arrival of businessmen and other professionals who needed places to transact business. Men bought, bartered, or seized town lots as opportunities presented themselves or as necessity demanded. Cowenhoven and Brown's store was the fourth to open for business. In addition, the camp had a hotel, a sawmill, a restaurant, an engineering and surveying firm, law offices, and several saloons. Such a listing might convey a sense of physical order and progress that the reality of Aspen belied. The camp was a hodgepodge of tents, cabins in various stages of completion, false-front stores, and vacant lots. It was, in short, like other mining camps in the Rockies at the age of twelve months.[6]

Another early arrival, William M. Dinkel, pronounced himself disappointed in Aspen's appearance. His description of the business section probably nicely captured the circumstances under which Cowenhoven began his work. "The merchants had their stocks of goods in tents with rough board counters, and a few board shelves were put up," wrote Dinkel. "The stock consisted chiefly of the necessities of life in the grocery line—sugar, coffee, sale-side (a kind of green bacon or salt pork, as some called it) and flour, tea, and canned goods, when they could get them. There were a few things in the way of wearing apparel—shirts, stockings, overalls, hats and shoes—but never much of a choice." Dinkel supported himself by working on one of the toll roads that connected Aspen to the world across the mountains and by cutting wood to sell to Aspen residents.[7]

These business transactions and signs of progress took place amid considerable confusion about who or what actually owned the townsite on which these miscellaneous structures appeared. B. Clark Wheeler returned in early May 1880, and with him came J. W. Deane. Deane may or may not have been the first lawyer in the camp—this was later a matter of considerable dispute—but there was no disputing that he was the Aspen Town and Land Company's legal representative. Deane and Wheeler now laid out Aspen's first subdivision, Deane's Addition, a tract of land between the original townsite and the foot of Aspen Mountain. It was an expansion undertaken under the auspices of the Philadelphia company, and it further strengthened its claim to title to the campsite.

The growth of the camp's population and the arrival of businesses and professionals who needed lots in the town were paralleled by a growth of hostility toward the townsite company. In early June, a group of original settlers with the support of newer arrivals proposed to seize several of the company's townsite lots by force, a popular movement that Deane quelled only with the greatest difficulty. He did so by appealing to other leaders in the camp to respect property rights. After all, he argued, if the townsite company's lots could be seized this week, then privately claimed lots with improvements might be taken next week. His logic carried the day, but the lull was only temporary. The "jumpers" organized an association to protect their interests against the company. The question of townsite ownership quickly became Aspen's first political issue.[8]

The Aspen Town and Land Company, well aware of the confusion and hostility surrounding its claim, tried to provide order and compromise within the context of its self-interest. To give a greater degree of order, B. Clark Wheeler did a finished survey of the campsite. The final plat named the streets for company officials—Hallam, Hyman, Cooper— names that have survived to the present day. The compromise proved more difficult. Through its resident agents, Wheeler and Deane, the company argued that the interests of the camp were best promoted by a corporation rather than by individuals or even a collection of individuals like the "jumpers association." The company gave substance to its argument by offering to finance improvements for the camp. If the squatters would cede their claims to the company, it would guarantee possession for the nominal charge of ten dollars. In addition, the company would finance construction of roads and a smelter. For the camp to survive, it needed improvements—and it needed them immediately, for it was isolated from the east by high mountains and threatened by local rivals in Ashcroft and Independence.

Some lot holders accepted the compromise, and during the course of the summer months the company cut a road through Taylor Pass to Buena Vista. Cowenhoven and Brown actually passed the construction crew on their way to Aspen. The route that Cowenhoven and Brown had traversed with such difficulty was now open for regular wagon traffic—in season, of course, for everything in the high mountains had separate rules for winter. The road over which the wagons passed was primitive—like other roads that Aspenites would build over the next several years—a cleared track with tree stumps still a foot high, streams unbridged, only marginally usable for wagon traffic. Still, it represented a declaration of the company's interests, interests now shared with hundreds of immigrants in the mining camp called Aspen.[9]

The existence of a portion of a state free from Indian claims and with an influx of white settlement was a situation that no responsible state official could condone. Such an area must be organized in accordance with Colorado law, and in view of its small transient population and its isolation, it was customarily attached to an existing political unit. In such a practical spirit, Colorado legislators sitting in Denver in the summer of 1880 attached the settlements in the valley of the Roaring Fork to Gunnison County. Gunnison County officials took their responsibilities seriously; pursuant to the legislature's wishes, they formed the Roaring Fork settlements into the county's Twelfth Precinct. Their actions also reflected a petition from the early settlers in the valley, asking for some provision for law and order. Those who intended to make fortunes in minerals, townsite promotion, merchandising, or any of the other innumerable opportunities associated with a growing mining camp took pains to preserve such fortunes even before they had been won.

The Gunnison County commissioners now appointed Warner A. Root justice of the peace for the Roaring Fork District. Root, a Leadville newspaperman, had come to the Roaring Fork Valley in November 1879. He came impelled by the same force as other immigrants: the desire to match ambition with opportunity. Root remained in Aspen for the first winter, sharing deep snows, bright days, and depressing isolation. He also shared in the pioneer reputation that accrued to those first Aspenites who cast their resources and presence with the new and fragile camp. As peace officer, Justice Root exercised his very considerable authority—the laws of the state of Colorado spelled out the duties and responsibilities of a justice in great detail—over the summer of 1880. In carrying out his duties, he had the support of a deputy sheriff appointed by the Gunnison County commissioners in May. Root held court in a one-story log cabin with one window of four panes and a brush-dirt roof.[10]

With a justice of the peace to interpret the law, a deputy sheriff to enforce his decisions, a connection to an established county, and large numbers of new immigrants, Aspen had achieved the appearance of permanence. As it turned out, the appearance was deceptive. With the onset of winter, the bustling mining camp of summer vanished. The hordes of people who had arrived with such clamor and tumult were sucked back across the mountains as surely as they had been propelled into the valley six months earlier. The reasons for this were the same practical considerations that dominated life in every remote mining camp: great distances, poor roads, the demands of a mountain winter. Winter supplies would be scarce and expensive, for the camp would be isolated for four months from anything except individuals on skis or snowshoes. The inventory of the camp did not permit heavy stockpiling. So those who were not assured of support returned as they had come.

The winter emigration left some thirty-five souls out of a summer population of several hundred to hibernate on the site of the camp for a second winter encampment. Among the wintering residents were Mr. and Mrs. Cowenhoven, Katy Cowenhoven, David Brown, Mr. and Mrs. Henry B. Gillespie, and Mr. and Mrs. Warner A. Root. By all accounts, they turned out to be a lively, active, inventive group. The men passed their days in skiing, planning, and making minor improvements. The women—there were at least thirteen, including Mrs. Cowenhoven and her daughter, Katy, and Mrs. Gillespie—established Aspen's first cultural institutions: a literary society, a literary paper, a Sabbath school, musicals, dances, and elaborate, creative meals from limited supplies. Society and ceremony helped to make up for isolation.[11]

Through the long winter of 1880–81, the trapped residents of the camp held meetings to debate their future. A consensus emerged that the camp should seek legal status as a county and "town" under Colorado law. First came the county. It was a logical step. The legislature would need to establish several new counties in the Ute Cession. The growing numbers of new settlers around Independence, Ashcroft, and Aspen provided justification for immediate action. The leaders of the camp left nothing to chance, however, and lobbied vigorously. The legislature and Governor Frederick Pitkin responded by laying off the new Pitkin County on February 23, 1881. The law specified boundaries, designated Aspen the temporary county seat pending an election, and made arrangements to transfer the relevant records from the Gunnison County courthouse to whatever would serve as the courthouse of Pitkin County. The law also set elections for the office of county commissioners.

The organization of the town was more personal. With a decision that the camp should seek legal status as a "town" under Colorado law, Justice Root, in his capacity as the leading public official of the camp, drew up the appropriate documents and conveyed them to the commissioners of Gunnison County. In March 1881, the commissioners granted the petition and scheduled an election. Aspen's first municipal election took place in May 1881, when qualified voters chose a mayor, four trustees, and a city clerk. The trustees subsequently selected a police magistrate and a city attorney. With its newfound authority, based on Colorado law for such officially recognized municipalities, Aspen now took control of its own affairs.[12]

The thirty-five wintering Aspenites rejoiced in the news. They saw it as evidence of the permanence of the settlement and as justification of their faith in the camp. In this celebration, they were premature. Aspen and its supporters had taken a first step in what would be a long and precarious journey. Armed with statutes of urban authority and supported by energetic and ambitious boosters, the young camp now ventured forth into the world. At the same time, the alliance among its supporters was an uncertain one. Crowded on every side by declarations of permanence and fidelity, but internally surrounded by doubts, questions, and feuds, the new camp had to move energetically forward to reassure its supporters and convince its doubters. The chance for success was a narrow edge. No one wanted to be the last person to leave a dying mining camp. The more ambitious and energetic the followers, the greater their expectations.

With the first signs of spring, the camp began to stir. The warming sun drew off the snowy mantle to reveal a mining camp with six streets laid out east and west along the axis of the Roaring Fork Valley, and another half a dozen north and south. The whole camp covered perhaps two and one-half acres. But people were still few and improvements even fewer. Empty lots outnumbered buildings. Streets—if the term may be used—had stumps, potholes, and no sidewalks. Aspen had made a beginning, but it was only a beginning, nothing more.

3

"A Thrifty Mining Camp"

The incorporation of the mining camp of Aspen in May 1881 gave legal status to the collection of buildings, improvements, and people that lay within the boundaries of the townsite. The few Aspenites who had passed the winter there had drawn up the articles of incorporation, and the Gunnison County commissioners had acceded and called for an election. The result of the poll—overwhelmingly favorable to the organization of the new county, with Aspen as its temporary county seat—was never in doubt. What was astonishing was the number of voters who turned out, some 332. The number reflected the strength of an early spring immigration. New arrivals began to appear in camp with snow still deep on the ground and the temperatures still below zero. By the end of March, sleighs ran on a regular schedule between Twin Lakes and the gold camp of Independence, where immigrants hired horses or walked to Aspen. Others came from Buena Vista by way of the Roaring Fork Improvement Company's toll road over Taylor Pass. Construction in the camp kept pace, and by the time the mountain spring arrived, a new, three-story hotel on the southeast corner of Mill and Durant streets stood ready for paying guests.[1]

Aspen also filled another need for the new and ambitious mining camp—a newspaper. The *Aspen Times* began publication in April 1881, with the words "A newspaper, in a rich and growing mining camp like Aspen, is more than an advantage; it is a necessity." The editor went on, "The necessity is two fold . . . the one being to furnish the camp with news of the outside world and the other to furnish the outside world with a knowledge of the production and of the strikes in the camp." He spoke from the experience of a generation of camps on the mining frontier. A newspaper's importance exceeded that of any mining claim, and a printing press was often the first piece of machinery brought into a new mining camp. So it was in Aspen. With the appearance of the *Rocky Mountain Sun* in July 1881, Aspen was never without at least two papers. Although the editors frequently disagreed among themselves, especially as they became more politically partisan over the next several years, they united in defense of the camp. To promote the growth of the camp was their principal objective; they never lost sight of it.[2]

The incorporation of the camp represented more than a post office and a signboard. It endowed the land, buildings, improvements, and residents with a new and significant legal status under the laws of the state of Colorado. The state law of April 4, 1877, laid down the groundrules for "towns and cities." In brief, incorporation created machinery for establishing a government, and the government could make rules for the conduct of individual citizens, appoint public officials, and provide services for its residents. And with these powers went the authority to levy and collect taxes—to support the government, the bureaucracy, and the improvements.[3]

The organization of the mining camp of Aspen moved forward in accordance with the law. At the election in April 1881, voters chose a mayor (George W. Triplett), four trustees (John Adair, R.C. Wilson, Angus McPherson, and George Elrod), a city clerk (Newton J. Thatcher), and a city attorney (J. H. King). The character of Aspen's first public officials might be described as professional, mildly southern, and nonpartisan. They included two mining superintendents, a lawyer, a merchant, a stockman, a prospector, and a contractor. Six of the seven were born in states loyal to the Confederacy, including four in Kentucky. The seventh was a native of Canada. Four of the seven were Democrats. Their ages ranged from twenty-five to forty-one, which supports the generaliztion that mining camps were, initially at least, places for the young.[4]

The general laws of Colorado for the organization of new towns provided that the elected town officials establish a bureaucratic structure to preserve order and record necessary documents, promulgate rules of conduct, and organize the services that every mining camp (or any town, for that matter) required. The selection of appointed public officials was the first order of business. The officials so chosen must fill several needs. To begin with, they should be recognizable names, men who inspired confidence and support among the citizens by their known long-standing association with the camp. They must be known for competence and efficiency. In his inaugural address to the council, Mayor Triplett referred to the need for a "thrifty mining camp." Finally, they must be prepared to work for modest wages, because their salaries would be paid by their fellow Aspenites. Among the first officials to be selected were the recorder and the marshal, who received a salary of $60 a month plus expenses. Both of their jobs were considered part-time.[5]

The trustees also enacted a series of ordinances for the camp. In subject and wording, these ordinances were generally interchangeable with those in other Colorado mining camps and closely followed the guidelines of the state law. The first official acts in every mining camp set out basic regulations for physical order and the safety of its citizens by banning false fire alarms, the discharge of firearms, and the use of explosives within the city limits. Another group of regulations dealt with moral issues: drunkenness, vagrancy, and loitering. Town fathers everywhere, from colonial New England to late-nineteenth-century Aspen, vigorously discouraged idleness. Even more abhorrent was what the ordinance referred to as a "house of ill fame," or the saloon-keeper who employed "a lewd woman or any woman having the repu-tation of a prostitute." Confidence games, nudity, and graffiti also caught the attention of the trustees, who took a firm stand against all such manifestations.[6]

The raising of revenue involved less consensus, for the tax and li-censing fees affected the various elements of the community unequally. The standard targets of the licensing fees were those in revenue-produc-ing businesses. Merchants were the most obvious. There was also a question of whether immoral trades should be subject to a "moral tax" to discourage their practice. Saloons were a good case in point. Because their acknowledged profitability was an affront to some citizens, they became the logical targets of a tax against sin as well as a revenue-pro-ducing measure. Yet such businesses were part of the entertainment industry of mining camps, and necessary to some part of the camp's population. They met the needs of single men who would come to the camp in numbers, serving as a combination social club and entertain-ment center. Licensing fees also had to be paid by pawnbrokers, liquor dealers, "shows and establishments" ($50 for three months or $10 for a single show), billiard tables, bagatelle tables, bowling alleys, peddlers, and public carriers.[7]

Taxes and licensing fees paid for services. The services that citizens had a right to expect were also standard, and the town trustees' first budget enumerated them: streets, sidewalks, crossings, bridges, ditches, and culverts were allotted $500; town printing, $500; stationery, furni-ture, books, and meeting rooms, $1,000; the camp jail, $1,000; the fire department, $200. Throughout the spring and into the summer of 1881, the trustees sifted bids, contracted, inspected, and paid for the improvements. But they paid grudgingly, as befitted a "thrifty mining camp" and a treasury that was always on the verge of being empty. On October 15, 1881, the trustees announced that the town's debt stood at $1,262.59.[8]

If Aspen's permanence and prosperity were sure things in the long run—and officials, entrepreneurs, and editors continued to insist that they were—its immediate future was beset by financial difficulties. Ambitious plans by civic leaders, who saw themselves laying the foundation for a town of several thousand, could not be supported by the tax base of a few hundred residents with a barter economy. Aspen needed public improvements and services, and these plans rapidly outran the receipts in the town's treasury. The result was the decision to issue city scrip, notes of indebtedness that formed an underground circulating medium—underground because no one wanted to accept them, certainly not at face value, and preferably not at all. In an economy in which cash was scarce, however, such notes increased the circulating medium, and they had a certain credibility beacuse they were receivable in payment for debts due the town—notably, taxes. The problem was simply that few people paid taxes and that those who did spent much time contriving to reduce their obligations to the camp to the vanishing point. It was this cycle that had made scrip necessary in the first place. By the summer of 1882, the cash value of the camp's scrip had sunk to thirty cents on the dollar.[9]

Many Aspen businessmen and contractors found the camp an uncertain business proposition, but, in the tradition of mining camps almost everywhere, it was still the largest employer around. A leading contractor and trustee of the camp, R. C. Wilson, knew firsthand the opportunities and hazards associated with a client that printed its own money. Wilson contracted to build the jail. Soon after its completion, he petitioned the trustees for a liquor license and asked that the license fee of $25 be deducted from the sum owed him for work on the jail. He did not add, although he might have, that the town proposed to pay him in depreciated scrip for his work and to collect cash for the license fee. His fellow trustees objected, and in response Wilson read them a lecture on the mining-camp economy. He had built the jail for no profit, he told them, and had furthermore taken scrip supposed to be worth seventy-five cents on the dollar when in reality it was not worth over forty cents. The trustees backed down. Wilson received his license, a commodity far more negotiable than town scrip. Another contractor presented a bill for $60 in cash or $120 in scrip, and a reporter for the *Rocky Mountain Sun* noted that "the novelty of the demand struck the worthy councilmen in a tender spot."[10]

At the trustees' weekly meetings, the principal topics—aside from indebtedness and the sinking value of camp scrip—were improvements and services, especially streets, water, and schools. The streets remained potholed and dusty in summer—when they were subject to heavy traffic, particularly in the form of wagon trains of goods from across the mountains—and rather more passable in wintertime, when successive layers of snow served to hide their primitive condition and give them an even (if temporary) surface. The campaign to build sidewalks moved by fits and starts, proceeding at the pace dictated by local abutters. Pollution from sawmills on the Roaring Fork and on Castle and Maroon creeks threatened the purity of the water supply. Progress had its price even in young Aspen. The water supply remained a constant concern because of the perceived direct relationship between a readily available supply of water and protection against fire.[11]

Surrounded by such practical matters, trustees, editors, and other prominent citizens still proposed to provide for some form of public schooling. The discussion summoned up images of the future character of the camp. Aspen would be a great camp in the sense of mineral deposits and mining profits, the trustees affirmed, but it would also be something more. It would not be a mining boomtown, with honky-tonk saloons, accustomed to hard men and hard language, where the gentle refinements of education and religion languished in the drive for individual and civic success. No, Aspen would be a camp for families. As early as the summer of 1881, the *Aspen Times* explained that Aspen was not simply a place "where a man camps till he has made his pile." To the contrary, it had "all the essential elements of home," a quality that tended to make its "population more permanent" and its prosperity "broad and deep." A school, accordingly, was a major priority in the scheme of things.[12]

As early as May 1881, the *Aspen Times* reported twenty-five school-aged children in Aspen, twenty in Independence, and perhaps as many as a hundred elsewhere within the limits of Pitkin County. The numbers suggested, among other things, that Aspen's population was still a minor part of the whole. The dispersion also bespoke the problem of distance in providing schooling facilities to a widely scattered population. Moreover, the elected officials of the camp did not distinguish themselves by their leadership in solving the problem. Members of the school board, including Henry B. Gillespie and H. P. Cowenhoven, did nothing. The editors charitably excused them on the ground that they were too occupied with their own affairs. In July, the cause of education suffered yet another setback when the newly appointed county superintendent of education vanished. The long-awaited school opened on Monday, September 19, in Judge Root's log building.[13]

While the town trustees did not seem to feel any great need for haste in regard to schools, streets, sidewalks, or water, one issue seized their immediate and continuing attention: the question of who or what owned the townsite. At stake was the question of authority over the town, or at least of sufficient authority to influence the growth of the camp in the strongest possible way. On this issue, and this one alone, the town fathers lavished their attention and most of their scarce tax dollars. Indeed, they threw into the struggle whatever slender resources the camp could command at this early stage in its history.

The initial enthusiasm for the Aspen Town and Land Company quickly turned into indifference and then hostility. This early support had been based on the primitive and disorganized condition of the camp and on the company's promise to undertake improvements that individuals could not finance. With the incorporation of the town and the establishment of the county, civil authority and the powers of taxation seemed to promise a solution to early problems that now rested within the camp itself. So many citizens rejected cooperation with the company in favor of a policy of independence and self-help.

In mid-May 1881, Mayor Triplett gave official form to this discontent—and perhaps a boost to his young political career—by calling a meeting to mobilize popular support against the townsite company. In response to the mayor's appeal to protest the company's earlier application for a townsite patent from the federal government, citizens assembled and voted to levy an assessment on each lot holder to pay attorneys' fees. With a vociferous popular mandate behind him, the mayor directed the city attorney to draw up a legal document in support of the camp's position. The issue of the townsite patent was not a simple one, whatever elected officials told their constituents at public meetings. It was at once utilitarian, personal, and legal. The utilitarian aspect revolved around the presence of the company and its shadowy absentee directors in Philadelphia. Eastern capitalists might do much for the struggling mining camp that the camp could not do for itself, but they had done little or nothing, at least not in its first official year of life.[14]

The Aspen Town and Land Company now offered to sell lots for $10 each to those already on the site, provided that it received confirmation of its title to the vacant lots. Aspen businessmen wondered how they should respond. Whatever the popular outcry, perhaps it was better business to pay the $10. Suppose the camp officials lost their appeal? Then the company might substantially increase the price of the lots—even for the earliest settlers. Or, consider the risk of running a business dependent upon popular patronage and appearing to side with the company against the camp. It was not an easy decision for the lot holders. Most of them hoped to placate both sides, while keeping profits high.

Added to this question was that of personal aggrandizement. Were some men using the townsite question as an issue to promote their young public careers? The company so charged. Some observers agreed. Finally the question of communal benefits invariably arose. Would the town's officials or the company do the most for the camp, especially in these early years, when all joined in the quest for outside capital? The Philadelphia corporation represented just such capital, and it was certainly outside. Still, it was hard to oppose the popular argument that the citizens of the camp should have title to it and the authority to control their civic destiny.[16]

The second absentee company, the Roaring Fork Improvement Company, had constructed a toll road from Buena Vista to Aspen by way of Taylor Pass. The appointment of a resident manager, Mr. William Balderston, was tangible evidence of its presence. When Balderston brought criminal court charges against some citizens for failure to pay tolls on the toll road and won, he provided additional proof of the company's power. The company also worked energetically behind the scenes to protect its own vested interests. With the receipts of the toll road running from $60 to $75 a day, paid mainly by teamsters who carried freight into camp, Balderston lobbied against the construction of public roads that would provide an alternative to the company's toll route. He also considered bribing public officials to reduce the company's tax assessment, but after extended discussion he and the company treasurer decided against this step. Balderston indicated that nothing could be done with the trustees except by dispersing "*lots* of cash," and in the end, the company rejected bribery.[15]

Beyond the limits of the struggling mining camp lay the county. Pitkin County was a significant influence in the life of its citizens. County government was an independent and powerful force. It was designated by statute to carry out or at least set in motion many programs that lay beyond the capacity of individual citizens and beyond the sphere of the state. The constitution of the state of Colorado and other laws gave counties authority to help themselves rather than to come to the state for assistance. Pitkin County, however small and dispersed its population, had this same authority, and the governor had appointed men to exercise the powers conferred by statute. Among the first appointed officeholders were the county judge, recorder, sheriff, treasurer, coroner, surveyor, assessor, and three commissioners. Of the ten appointees, two were residents of Independence. The rest were

Aspenites. Those selected included the most prominent men in the county, probably to no one's surprise. The tradition of putting county authority in the hands of the leading economic and political figures went back to colonial Virginia and stretched in an unbroken strand for 250 years—through the Revolution and the Civil War—to the valley of the Roaring Fork in 1881. Presumably, such men represented stability and commitment to the new camp; they would probably also be the largest taxpayers.[17]

The institutional needs and forms of the county seemed to parallel those of the camp, but on closer examination the spheres were seen to be different. The camp served what people had or needed in an immediate way; the county responded to what they hoped to have. The camp dealt with the present; the county, with the future. In the eyes of the residents of Pitkin County in 1881, the future meant contact with the outside world. The ultimate means of contact was the railroad, but until the arrival of the iron horse, plain roads, supplemented by a telegraph line, would do. Although the county had other needs—a courthouse, jail, care for the poor and insane—the commisioners spent almost all their time on the issue of roads.

The mining camp of Aspen lay at the end of a horseshoe, with the open end facing west down the valley of the Roaring Fork. Contact with the world of capital, supplies, technology, and people (in the form of immigrants) lay toward the east, however, across the axis of the horseshoe, by way of mountain ranges more than fourteen thousand feet high. The centers of logistical support were Leadville and Buena Vista. The camp could be approached from only two directions: west from Leadville by way of Independence Pass; north from Buena Vista via the Taylor or the Cottonwood Pass. The Roaring Fork Improvement Company had already opened a toll road to Buena Vista, and now that a road to the south was in operation, the county commissioners found themselves without options for routes, because however distasteful the toll road, a second road to Buena Vista would be superfluous, not worth the investment of tax monies. At the same time, the county had no control over the company's toll road, its fees, or its maintenance.[18]

Over the next two years—until the spring of 1883—the county did build roads, and in this publicized area its accomplishments were real. In addition to a road to Leadville, to be completed by November 1881, it undertook to build a road or series of roads from the camp of Aspen to the mines on the surrounding mountainsides. Under the direction of the county commisioners, one hundred men employed by the county built the road in brisk autumn weather at a cost of $9,000. Called the

Aspen Mountain Road, it was extended in the spring to ever-more remote mining claims—at ever-greater cost. In the spring of 1882, the commissioners, with the assistance of ranchers, laid out a road to the western boundary of the county. The Pitkin County road network was complete. Road communication led to regular stagecoach service with Leadville. The first coach crossed the mountain passes in November 1881, with the coach company advertising "a fine lap robe and heavy wolf robe for every seat." By the spring of 1882, the coach service was on a regular basis, including two daily stages from Leadville, and there was the promise of a daily mail.[19]

Road construction as practiced by Pitkin County requires some explanation. It was a labor-intensive process, designed to create what might be termed a "road" by the standards of a mountain environment. It made use of the large pool of unemployed laboring men in the camp, and it did so at little cost to taxpayers. The commissioners first considered the priority of a road, on the basis of its usefulness to the community and of the popular demand for its construction, as measured by petitions and personal appeals. The route agreed upon, the commission let the road out to bids. The contract let, the construction crew went to the site. Axmen, or "wood choppers" (as they were often known), led the way, followed by the "graders." Upon notification of a road's completion, the commissioners would designate one of their number—or another trusted citizen—to inspect the work. If it was judged satisfactory, the contractor was paid.[20]

Over the two years from spring 1881 to spring 1883, the commissioners increasingly served as their own contractors. They would advertise for laborers in the newspapers, offering payment at the rate of six dollars per day in county warrants. Under the direction of a superintendent of construction hired by the commissioners, the workers assembled on the designated day and walked to the site, where they not so much built as leveled a route. The topography in Pitkin County ran to extremes—from level ground, where the workers scraped a wide pathway, to tumbling streams and valley escarpments, where the men, sometimes numbering a hundred or more, might require several days to go a mile or less. Bridging remained rare, and spring flooding regularly washed out bridges. The well-marked ford sufficed for most roadwork.

Roads meant people, animals, and wagons, and the net effect was growth for the town and county—and wear and tear on the road surfaces. By summer of 1882, the condition of the toll roads to Leadville and Buena Vista, open for scarcely twelve months, was the subject of endless complaints. In short, roads that were expensive to build needed continual maintenance as soon as they were put into use. Thus, the contours of the land shaped road building in Pitkin County as they did elsewhere in the Rocky Mountain West.[21]

A telegraph, symbol of immediate contact with the world across the mountains, became an item of great importance to Aspenites. But a telegraph could not be had cheaply, or at least not as cheaply as people wanted it. In the face of a $3,800 bid from Western Union that outraged the local citizenry, the county decided to build its own telegraph line by means of volunteer materials and labor. Several citizens contributed telegraph poles, and a committee assumed responsibility for placing the poles and stringing the wires north to Ashcroft. Like other aspects of Aspen's communications network, the telegraph encountered delay, greater than anticipated cost, and endless recriminations about who was responsible for these sins. Still, the silver wire held a deep significance, and when the line went into operation, in June 1882, a newspaper column described it as the "electric spark connecting us with the busy multitude across the range."[22]

These very considerable achievements of the new county—roads built and maintained, a substantial work force put into the field, and a telegraph connected—came at a very considerable price: debt. Almost from their first meeting, the county commissioners planned and executed projects they could not pay for—at least not in cash on a continuing basis. As a result, the Pitkin County debt grew with its road network. In the first ten months of road construction, from December 1881 to September 1882, the county's debt rose from $37,299 to $176,636.[23]

Although the size of the debt worried Aspen's leaders, they did not propose to curtail it by ending the construction of needed improvements. Quite to the contrary, much of the debt circulated in the form of county warrants, which were invariably quoted at a fraction of their face value. In July 1882, Denver brokers quoted Pitkin County warrants at fifty-three cents on the dollar. It was not a strong showing for an ambitious new mining camp, desirous of impressing the outside world with opportunities for investment. The debt had become a kind of barometer of the county's financial condition that local forecasters feared to read. They felt that an impoverished county offered few attractions to potential eastern investors. The twin answers were reduced expenditures and increased taxes.[24]

In order to finance improvements, county officials had legislative authority to levy taxes. Their experiences here testified that taxes were as uncertain and liable to detours as road construction was. The first set of county taxes came due in December 1881, payable immediately, with a penalty added on January 1, 1882. If we are to believe the collection figures, those taxed took scant notice. On January 7, 1882, the commissioners reported that of $8,000 levied (the county debt already exceeded $37,000) only $926 had been paid. And, accompanying their pleas for the payment of taxes came the outraged cries from those who thought they had been overtaxed. The commissioners spent much time hearing appeals. Despite modifications, the collection of taxes did not improve.[25]

In addition to building roads, the county commissioners also created a bureaucracy, a cadre of officials who benefited from the business of government. To some extent, the state law mandated the structure of the county. But such legislation could hardly lessen the resentment aroused by the knowledge that a few Aspenites benefited in the form of salaries and fees from the hard-earned and begrudged tax dollars of the many. Salaries represented a substantial portion of the costs of county government each year. Did the commissioners themselves pass from the stage of public servants to that of public beneficiaries? Some critics thought so. Furthermore, the costs of road construction sometimes seemed curiously proportioned. In the summer and fall of 1881, for example, laborers who worked on constructing the Twin Lakes Toll Road received $6 a day in county warrants, then quoted at fifty to sixty cents on the dollar. At the same time, the commissioners examined and approved a bill for attorneys' fees submitted in connection with the toll road in the sum of $1,369, payable in cash.[26]

Beyond roads, salaries, and debt, Pitkin County progressed through its infancy amid a panoply of adult problems. The environment shared by all of Aspen's citizens was already under assault. As early as the summer of 1881, a grand-jury report noted that the tailings of the sawmill polluted rivers and streams and so endangered the water supply of the camp. The jurors also recommended that the camp prosecute fishermen who used explosives to catch trout. Within the first year of the new camp's existence, the *Sun* complained, "Our town, like all first class towns, is infested with tramps." The poor and insane needed assistance even in the newest communities, but they found little help in Aspen. In the spring of 1882, the commissioners appropriated $400 to return one citizen to an insane asylum in Jacksonville, Illinois. Removing the indigent and mentally ill to a distant place was an inexpensive and painless social remedy. Assistance for the poor, if such existed, was the array of volunteer institutions so familiar to late-nineteenth-century American life.[27]

After a year of planning and expenditures, the commissioners cataloged their achievements. The improvements included a road up Aspen Mountain to the mines, repair of a toll road over Independence

Pass, a county road to the agricultural section of the county, a road to Ashcroft, and a small courthouse.[28] The list was simultaneously a defense of those in office and an appeal to investors in Boston, Chicago, and New York City to take note of this ambitious, but hitherto little-noticed, mining camp on the western slope of the Rockies. Between 1881 and 1883, the first elected officials created "a thrify mining camp." The facilities and services were delayed, expensive, and sometimes broken—as they were in virtually every other mining camp of the same age.

In the spring of 1883, Aspen was two years old and home to perhaps eight hundred people. What kind of place was it? Its residents proclaimed it the perfect place to live. In the words of the *Times*'s editor, "The weather surprises everyone by its mildness, and its perpetual sunshine is not equalled in Italy's sunny clime." The physical appearance of the town was equally appealing: "laid out in squares, the streets are broad and clean, with sparkling mountain streams running at the side of each, irrigating shade trees and gardens." To these advantages could be added its population: "the pretty cottages, the palatial stores, and neat church and public buildings, attest to their energy, prosperity and cultivation." Other structures of note included "two first class hotels." Of course, Aspen had its drawbacks: "every fellow cannot have a girl, nor can anyone go to the opera."[29]

To such physical, civic, and social attractions must be added the potential of wealth beyond dreams. This little mining camp was surrounded by some of the richest mining claims in the world. They lay in the sides of the mountains visible from the center of the camp. The mines were Aspen's ultimate claim to permanence and fame.

4

The Mining Camp of Aspen Grows and Divides

From its beginnings, Aspen took the form of an urban settlement. In appearance and character, it was descended from a long line of frontier towns. In spite of variations in time and place over 250 years, from the early seventeenth century to the opening of the Civil War and across a continent from Boston harbor to San Francisco harbor, these towns had their own special quality. They provided few services of the kind customarily associated with urban areas, for the simple reason that their citizens needed few and refused to pay for any. They were characteristically unfinished, unsanitary, malodorous, and preeminently designed for the making of money.

Whether they were on the James River or in the foothills of the Rockies, such towns had generally served an agricultural population. They provided a center for trade, professional life (such as it was), and sooner or later, social and cultural activity. The discovery of gold in California in 1848 and the subsequent spread of the search for mineral wealth across the West in the next half-century made the "mining camp" a standard urban form for a third of the continent.

Early mining settlements were called camps because men had literally camped out on the site of the strikes. As the name implied, these collections of people were generally temporary and always seasonal. Spring brought immigration and movement to the high mountains; summer brought camps in more or less urban form; by late autumn, traces of such human habitation had disappeared, as the summer residents had taken down the camp, packed it up, and scattered, like the

Bedouins of the Sahara or the Indians of the Plains. By the time winter spread its silence across the high mountains, the land had returned to its original, deserted condition.

Even where the claims were deep and rich, the character of mining camps remained temporary. Their residents—generally male, young, and ambitious—came together for a short time in their lives to make money, not communities. They thought of themselves as transient. Their camps lay in some of the most inaccessible places on the continent. Here, they came to make their fortunes—and leave. Such mining camps offered legal and sometimes medical services; almost always gambling and prostitution; supplies of food and mining equipment; and, in some camps, rough boardinghouses. Mining camps of any size had an entertainment industry in the form of saloons and bordellos. These were designed to make sure that those who did prosper in mining (at whatever level) would not take it all with them when they departed.[1]

Aspen's experiences were variations on these themes. In the beginning, the camp was temporary and seasonal, as befitted the intimidating isolation and the sporadic economic enterprise being pursued. In the two years from 1881 to 1883, there took place a gradual shift toward permanence, and those who had wintered on the Roaring Fork—initially only a handful—became the seedlings of a permanent settlement. This change was exemplified by the physical growth of the camp through construction of public and private buildings, by efforts of local government to provide necessary services, and by the gradual emergence of social institutions like churches and schools. Throughout this period of growth, Aspenites congratulated themselves on the quality of the community they were building to go along with houses and stores. Yet even as this community emerged, it divided and subdivided.

First came physical growth in the form of business buildings, private homes, and sidewalks. Construction in Aspen, like so much else, was seasonal. The construction season began in spring and early summer. At that time, carpenters, builders, and mechanics found their skills in demand. Contractors did a good business in the spring and summer of 1881. From the beginning of May to the end of August, Andy McFarlene's sawmill ran fourteen hours a day to keep up with the demand for boards, shingles, and timbering.

But Aspen aspired to more than houses and business buildings. It wanted to create an impression of cultural as well as physical growth. Churches testified to the permanence and high moral tone of a prospering community. Civic leaders watched the organization of the first Protestant and Catholic churches with an air of self-satisfaction. Re-

43

ports of the first wedding in the Congregational church in September 1881 sent a thrill through the camp. Two weeks later, the second celebration of matrimony coincided with the first snowfall of the season. A Roman Catholic priest said the first mass in late November, an event that caught the attention of local editors. The Congregational church was still seeking a regular minister in November 1882. "Such a man could redeem the camp from stud-horse poker and kindred schemes," wrote one editor, diplomatically refusing to be more precise.[2]

The camp also needed basic facilities for its single men. Hotels, boardinghouses, and restaurants appeared to provide a variety of such services. Hotels housed and fed short-term visitors to the camp. A quality hotel also made a favorable impression on a prospective businessman or investor. Hotel ballrooms served as sites for social activities. The boardinghouse met the needs of laborers and miners for more-modest accommodations. Restaurants became social centers, renowned for good company as well as for good food. The Chloride Restaurant was the most important public eating place. Calling itself "the Delmonico of the West," after the famous New York City restaurant, the Chloride had a menu that included fresh trout, venison, and elk steak.[3]

Aspen's newly chosen government issued minimal ordinances for health and sanitation. The camp planted shade trees in 1882, and the newspaper editors urged that property owners do the same. An expression of sentiment for a waterworks soon emerged, as it did at about this time in every mining camp. In Aspen, readily accessible water meant attractive lawns and gardens. When the city fathers built no sewage system in 1882, the council passed an ordinance instructing residents to dig a deep sinkhole on each property. Aspen wanted to smell nice as well as look neat. There was already much to be concerned about. The snarling saw at McFarlene's busy mill spewed waste that fouled the waters of Castle Creek, but for the moment no one seemed to mind. The polluted waters swept downstream, while new buildings remained to celebrate Aspen's growth. The dispute over land titles and the uneven rate of improvements left Aspen—like other mining camps—in a perpetually half-finished condition. Tent stores alternated with solid wooden buildings, and everywhere lay vacant lots, some unclaimed, others simply unoccupied and unimproved. Rank weeds and pools of stagnant water decorated these eyesores.[4]

Civic leadership in Aspen involved a consensus decision making among various groups. The mines were the most important enterprise, and the mineowners were the dominant figures. They included a dozen men who spoke for the largest and most prominent mines.

These people did not hold elective office. Officeholders tended to be merchants and professional people, especially lawyers. Mineowners could always find officeholders to look out for their interests. Indeed, in a town that would rise and fall on the reputation and production of its mines, all elected officials (or those aspiring to election) supported mining interests. These circumstances did not indicate corruption. They simply suggested the reality of a silver-mining camp: namely, that in the long run the permanence of the camp and the fortunes of its citizens would directly depend on the success or failure of the mines around it.

Politics moved rapidly from the traditional frontier contests of personality and consensus on issues to political parties. The Republicans and Democrats ran noisy campaigns for camp and county offices as early as the fall of 1881, each aided by party organization of a kind and by the support of a local newspaper. Of the Republican gathering in mid-August, the editor of the *Times* remarked, "To liken this convention to a circus would be using a mild comparison." The circus-like atmosphere carried over into the campaigns for local office, which were carried on as if the fate of the nation depended upon the outcome. Yet the vigor of the campaigns—around such issues as economy in government and efficiency in road building—obscured a broad consensus on the sources of the camp's prospects. These were intimately bound up with the mines.[5]

The growing mining camp of Aspen gradually established a broad range of social and cultural institutions. The types represented included reform, social, cultural, and practical. The term "social" is somewhat imprecise, for virtually every aspect of Aspen life had its social side. The best-publicized reform institution was the Temperance Union. Founded in April 1881, coincidentally with the incorporation of the camp, it was an extension of the growing national campaign against alcohol in every form. The inevitable entertainment patterns of a mining camp—established in California in 1848 and continued throughout the mining West—made a temperance society a logical institution for the reform minded who wished to create a moral and upright community. Another reform organization was the Relief Society, organized by the Master Masons. Especially active around the winter holidays, the Relief Society focused on good works directed toward the less fortunate and indigent of the camp. It kept alive a nineteenth-century American tradition of voluntary assistance that relieved government of any suggestion of responsibility for the poor and that kept the tax rate, accordingly, low.[6]

A volunteer fire company, a necessity in a growing and expanding town of wooden buildings, was also an important social club. The leading merchants of the camp sponsored the volunteer fire companies by underwriting the cost of uniforms, competitions, and the entertainments that followed. The list of officers of the volunteer companies contained the names of the most prominent citizens of the town, men like Henry B. Gillespie and H. P. Cowenhoven. That they served in an honorary capacity should not lead us to diminish the influence of the fire company as a common feature of life in Aspen and other mining camps. Spirited competitions between fire companies became a highlight of holiday celebrations, and the social affairs that accompanied them were among the camp's best known and most popular.[7]

The Ladies' Aid Society had its charitable side, as the name suggests, but it was also largely a social affair. The society raised money for charity through organized social and cultural functions. The meeting of January 1882, for example, featured a production of the drama *The California Uncle* by the members. Songs and musical selections supplemented the drama. Among the star performers were Mr. and Mrs. Henry B. Gillespie. The whole affair raised more than $100 for charitable purposes. Like other such institutions, the Ladies' Aid Society was most active in the winter season, presumably the season of the greatest need and also the social season. The most prominent cultural institution was the Aspen Literary Society, founded by Mrs. Gillespie in the winter of 1880–81, in which literary (and socially) minded people gathered together weekly for public presentations. In a camp completely isolated from the outside world, the society offered the most important scheduled social and cultural events. Attendance was high and participation almost universal. With the coming of spring, the Literary Society assumed more modest forms, and other social and cultural notices thinned out in favor of outdoor activities—picnics, sporting events, and public holidays.[8]

Aspen's theater—or opera house, as it was known in mining camps—was the scene of its principal all-season form of cultural life. The theater provided more than simply a series of public entertainments. It was a symbol by which the camp established its identity and documented its growth. The "Theater Comique" of Aspen opened in temporary quarters in the summer of 1881. Its early presentations included "a wrestling and sparring match." The term "theater" referred to a building as much as to dramatic performance. The structure itself became a benchmark in the town's progress and permanence. The construction of a permanent building transformed the theater from a vehicle of entertainment (some of doubtful content) into a symbol of civic pride. The new hall, under the direction of Messrs. Corkhill and

Smith, opened in December 1881. A local editor called it a theater "any town of 5,000 inhabitants might be proud of." With the camp's population at only one-tenth that figure—when one counted itinerant prospectors in for the day to stock up on supplies—the theater might be numbered with the mineral claims as among Aspen's most important resources.[9]

The theater connected the camp to the outside world in a specific way. Touring shows of varying kinds stopped there to entertain and profit. Only rare and unambitious camps confined presentations in the opera house to local talent. To do so was an admission of inability to attract name entertainment from such distant cultural meccas as Leadville and Denver. By summer 1882, Corkhill's Opera House (it had changed names) had established itself as a stop on the touring circuit. The first large extravaganza featured musicians from the Denver Opera House in performance. Their program involved fourteen musical numbers, concluding with the "Grand Anvil Chorus by the Entire Company, with glasses, instruments, and anvil combined." A capacity audience went home well satisfied, thinking that it had seen the best that Colorado's cultural scene had to offer. It probably had. Equally important, those who attended might take satisfaction in the fact that their camp could offer such entertainment.[10]

Social interaction among Aspen's socially conscious families was frequent, involving endless rounds of dances, parties, and balls. Sometimes participants combined such entertainments with an earlier musical performance or lecture. The fertile imaginations of Aspen's socially minded citizens generated innumerable reasons for social gatherings. Among the occasions were surprise parties, birthday parties, private parties, masked balls, and prominent weddings. That a camp of five hundred could support such social functions on a regular basis was a tribute to the socially minded few who invented, supported, and reported their activities.

Most of these regular social functions featured dancing. Private parties with dancing took place as early as July 1881. A large dance in August of that year prompted the observation that, among other delightful features of Aspen's climate, it was "never too warm" for dancing. At the "Grande Soirée Dansante" that climaxed the fall social schedule, "the elite of the city" danced in the Grand Ballroom of the Clarendon Hotel until midnight, at which time they adjourned to the Chloride Restaurant for supper. A local reporter confessed himself "dazzled by the richness of the gentlemen's costumes." He concluded, "Gunny sacks and ducking are not used as much as last season and flour sacks are something of the past for Aspen underwear."[11]

Over the long winters, Aspen's social life seemed to revolve around dances and balls. The "Firemen" held three "socials" in consecutive months. A surprise party at the home of Mr. and Mrs. John Teller in honor of her visiting sister, Mrs. Ferguson, included dancing to an orchestra. The entertainments at the skating rink—a center of winter social activity—featured music by a string band of homegrown talent. Social functions grew more elaborate with the passage of time. The Second Firemen's Ball featured displays of the "terpsichorean art." Singled out for special mention were the "Dick Sliter style," "a rollicking, vigorous jig," and "the Boston Dip."[12]

Masquerade balls found great favor. As early as January 1882, a "Grand Masquerade" took place at the skating rink. Masquerades provided economic bonanzas for merchants who stocked and aggressively advertised costumes. The climax of the masquerade motif was the Aspen Club's Great Ball of January 1883. Descriptions of the costumes emphasized their diversity and elaborate character. Among the ladies, examples included a Spanish lady, a Greek lady, a Mother Goose, a snow storm, a Martha Washington, a lady fireman ("dress ornamented with hook, ladder, trumpet, &c."), an Aurora ("the Goddess of Morn"), a goddess of liberty ("in natural colors and a fine representation"), and a jockey ("this lady was richly and beautifully dressed, with riding whip, spurs, and ornaments appropriate to the character"). The gentlemen produced representations of a convict, a chimney sweep, an English officer, a Turk, a man in yachting costume, a clown, a King Louis XVII, and a Highland chief. The prize went by acclamation to a "Just-Over Irishman" whose costume included "a hungry-looking grip-sack" in one hand and, in the other, a banner with the messages "I am waiting for the boom (?) in Aspen" and "The advance guard of the spring rush."[13]

A striking feature of the young camp's social life was the elaborate parties for children. Birthday parties were especially noteworthy. Reports of such celebrations appeared regularly in the newspapers and listed the names of those in attendance and the presents brought by each child. Nellie Corkhill, whose father owned and managed the celebrated opera house, had a full-scale celebration on her sixth birthday. On the occasion of Dale Osman Jacobs's birthday, his parents sent out fifty invitations. "Gifts for young Master Dale" included a gold finger ring, a gold pin, a box of blocks and toy chariot, a horse and cart, a dog, a bottle of perfume, and a lace collar and pin. Gift giving was not anonymous, and the lists published in the Aspen newspapers must have provoked a certain anxiety among parents whose daughters and sons received invitations to such affairs. Merchants in the young camp did a good business in luxury children's toys, freighted across the mountains from Leadville by jack train for these occasions.[14]

The many social notices at all seasons of the year—complete with names, costumes, dances, menus, and children's gifts—conveyed the sense of an active social life. It also suggested the existence of a group of men and women for whom such an active life was important, who were willing to invest time and money to make such an environment for themselves, and who wanted such activities reported to the public and in full detail. It revealed, too, something about the people's pride in their new mining camp. These individuals and families proclaimed to themselves and to the world a quality of life that made the new mining camp of Aspen a place where progressive people could lead civilized, cultured lives. Whatever the condition of the muddy streets, irregular water supply, and vacant lots overgrown with weeds, this camp had other standards and values to which it aspired.

Aspen intended to prosper socially as well as economically. The economy may have dictated the range of its ambitions, but society was a second and almost equal partner. Editors engaged in the work of camp promotion constantly glorified Aspen society as among the virtues of the adolescent camp. Writing in the summer of 1882, one observer could speak simultaneously of the improving architecture of the town and the educational achievements of its leading citizens: "Many of our business men have had collegiate education and traveled in many European countries, speaking several languages." It is not recorded whether he was refering to, among others, the German immigrant Cowenhoven, already one of the community's leaders, who spoke German like the immigrant that he was. As for Aspen society, the commentator continued, its principal qualities were "refinement" and "superior literary tastes." To the question "What kind of a place is Aspen?" its promoters could respond in the spring of 1883 that Aspen was a place where one could make a fortune and where one could live surrounded by social and cultural graces of the highest order.[15]

A second camp that emerged in Aspen was less visible but equally vigorous and certainly larger in numbers of inhabitants. It included dozens of upstanding, honest families not invited to the elaborate New Year's Day "open houses" of the social elite. It contained scores of single men who worked during the week with their hands: in the mines, prospecting on the hillsides and in remote valleys of the high mountain ranges; on the roads, for county warrants; in construction, to make the brick commercial blocks, opera house, and frame houses that drew the admiration of editors and visitors alike; in the service industries, such as the freighting business with Leadville and Buena Vista that supplied the camp with necessities (including costumes for fancy-dress balls) and carried ore samples to the smelters across the range; or in the simple but necessary duties of clerking, carrying, waiting on tables, and doing the laundry. These hundreds of men took their social ease at their own clubs—the Toledo Bar and Billiard House ("a quiet game of billiards or to quaff a delicious drink") or the Pioneer Saloon ("Billiards! Wholesale and Retail Wine, Liquor, Cigars"). They patronized Aspen's twelve saloons and enjoyed a glass of beer while they gazed across a green cloth at a game of five- or seven-card stud poker. At night, they slept in boardinghouses and hotels. They were a real part of Aspen, despite their anonymous character and their absence from the newspaper social columns.[16]

The two Aspen communities intersected on only a few occasions. Holidays were the most universal, for they engaged all Aspenites, whatever their economic condition or social pretension. For both groups, two great holiday seasons dominated the year: the Fourth of July and Christmas. Independence Day remained the universal national holiday—characteristically American in its manifestations and celebrations. All Aspen joined in. For the social elite, a picnic hamper at Red Butte served as a focal point of the day. For the ordinary citizens of the camp, horse races and baseball sparked celebrations that lasted all day. "We had horse racing, foot racing, and good humor and whisky galore," wrote one observer.[17]

The winter holiday season offered much diversity. Independence Day and Thanksgiving–Christmas–New Year's differed in part because in winter several of the most socially prominent families left town for long periods. Those who remained found themselves more intimately involved, with smaller numbers, indoor activities, and the threat of winter's isolation hanging over them. Beginning with Thanksgiving, the winter holidays meant varieties of entertainment, celebration, and dining, starting with a Thanksgiving ball at the courthouse. The Christmas–New Year's holiday brought the same range of activities, in which distinctions between the two societies of Aspen became ever-more apparent. The differences were not entirely economic, for Thanksgiving and Christmas were preeminently family holidays. Part of the distinction was thus between those with families and those without. Those with families celebrated in them; those without who could afford to do so went to a restaurant or a hotel—generally the Chloride or the Clarendon—for a fancy meal. Those who could not afford such luxury made do. Sometimes they had a little help. Aunt Mary's Restaurant offered a free Christmas dinner, and on that special day, during serving hours, the single men in the camp thronged to its tables.[18]

The holiday season ended on New Year's Day with a clear-cut manifestation of the two worlds of Aspen. The ordinary citizens of the camp rested from the celebrations of the night before; the camp's social elite held "open house" for one another. What had begun as a universal holiday season six weeks before, at Thanksgiving, had evolved into a holiday season of ever-growing distinctions. The differences involved not only financial status but also a sense of what was right and proper. For a few, a social display—including an account in the newspaper—was appropriate. Indeed, such public notices might be found across the nation, in large city and small town. Such individuals wished to emulate these examples, so from the very beginnings, some individuals and families adopted standards making them a social elite. There is no evidence they felt any uneasiness about social distinctions. Such distinctions were part of American life. In this sense, Aspen simply reflected the values of the nation as a whole. What was striking was the rapidity with which such social differences appeared in a new and isolated silver-mining camp.

The "other Aspen"—the larger, hidden Aspen of beer, billiard halls, and stud poker—entered the public eye through sports. Sporting events involved a high degree of public participation—of which footraces, target shooting, and boxing were good examples. The most popular Aspen sport was baseball. Only twenty years old, baseball had already spread across the nation—even, if Aspen was any yardstick, to its most remote areas. The Aspen season was short, because of the climate, but the camp did not lack for enthusiasm and interest.

Organized baseball began in Aspen in the summer of 1881 when a few energetic citizens organized a team to challenge nines from Ashcroft and Independence. The games involved much civic pride, and baseball games became the focal point of a weekend's activities. Leagues appeared, and teams with names like the "Frontiers" and the "Duffers" met one another in spirited competition. Visits to other camps became highlights of the season, which saw local contests every weekend. Merchants began to stock and advertise baseball equipment, including gloves, bats, and shoes. The next year, the newly organized Aspen Baseball Club arranged for sponsorship of teams by several merchants.[19]

Baseball remained preeminently the participatory and spectator sport of the miners, mechanics, teamsters, carpenters, and draymen. Some played and other watched, but all groups talked, joked, ate, and drank. Baseball's celebratory aspects made every weekend a Fourth of July without fireworks. If one waited long enough into the evening, one might also hear explosions; newspapers reported the results. Aspen's workingmen and -women—those who worked with their hands—had their unifying social activity. And, in a sense, the accounts in the press were their society columns. Yet differences in values had already begun to intrude. By the summer of 1882, complaints appeared about the profanity and drunkenness associated with baseball games. Sporting contests had become social gatherings—but, for some, gatherings of the wrong kind.[20]

The minor excesses of games mixed with whiskey reminded all Aspenites—if they wished to be reminded—of the thin veneer of social order that coated mining camps. Protection in the form of an armed city marshal was visible evidence of the enforcement of the law and the preservation of order. Jimmy Magee carried "two big six-shooters," and he had the reputation of being a man who could "eat out of any trough." Yet nowhere in the nation did people of wealth and those in marginal financial circumstances come into such close proximity. In Aspen's drive for order and stability, its civic leaders faced the options that confronted people in mining camps everywhere. A sometimes large, restless, mobile, male population had to adjust itself to a life circumscribed, on the one side, by hard physical labor and, on the other, by complaints against physical displays, whether of approval or of outrage. The provision of absolute physical controls to enforce ordinances and laws cost money, more money than even the most confirmed supporter of order wanted to pay. So a compromise had to be found that produced good order amid the trappings of tangible enforcement at a reasonable price. The compromise provided for the customary daily circumstances—enforced in part by the rigors of the season—but not for all contingencies.[21]

On occasion, a degree of disorder touched Aspen. The docket of the police court reflected the excesses of Saturday night: fights, brawls, drunkenness, disorderly conduct. The magistrate's court usually imposed a fine of five dollars and lectures on future conduct. Theft plagued the camp, but it was petty theft. Thieves generally ransacked the cabins of those at work. The nature of the plunder—firewood, books, provisions, cooking utensils—attests more to the standard of living than to the existence of a crime wave. Still, it was a sobering and continuing reminder of the presence of a degree of human depravity in the Garden of Eden that was Aspen. There is no record of larger-scale theft involving the houses and residences of Aspen's well-to-do.[22]

Many aspects of life in Aspen even in the first few years—social order and disorder, social ambition and display, social institutions and reform, indigenous and imported culture—necessarily reflected the economic prospects of the camp. Social and cultural life at all levels was built on a foundation of prosperity, progress, development, and growth. Social order was more easily maintained when economic advantage spread to all corners of the camp. After a period of auspicious growth—estimates of the population reached one thousand in the summer of 1881—Aspen's expansion slowed and then stopped. For the first time in the short history of the camp, its supporters exhibited a concern about its present state and its future.

During the spring of 1882, no great rush of population came with the melting of the snows in spring. By the middle of the summer, this matter was a subject of open discussion. Reasons came readily to hand in the form of a general economic depression in the state of Colorado— in which Aspen was something of an unfortunate and innocent victim. Or so ran the reasoning of the day. Actually, Aspen managed to avoid most of the impact of hard times for the simple reason that its economic development was so primitive. Promoters saw an unusually early exodus from the camp that fall but consoled themselves with the thought that modest construction continued and that most of the merchants had laid in goods for the winter season.

Yet nagging doubts persisted over the winter months. From small beginnings, Aspen had made great strides, but only up to a point. Although roads had been built toward the outside world at enormous expense, the camp seemed as isolated as ever. The telegraph line came only after great delay and endless charges of mismanagement. Most important, all the promoters, capitalists, editors, mining engineers, and entrepreneurs of every stripe could not bring about the construction of a smelter to process Aspen's ores. That necessary ingredient of every mining camp eluded the grasp of Aspen and its friends and supporters. Even Independence and Ashcroft had smelters by the summer of 1882, and Aspenites scorned these rivals as beneath notice. Smelter plans appeared with the regularity of the changing seasons, only to fade into oblivion within a few months. Aspen's original burst of energy had dissipated by the summer of 1882, leaving behind a sense of disillusionment and a variety of uncompleted civic tasks. Business had stagnated; mining had never begun.[23]

In spite of its unfinished air—the vacant lots, the silent mine shafts, the paper smelters—Aspen had in many ways become a middle-class town. Its sense of order and propriety and the suggestion of firmly set class lines testified to public values that were similar to those of a hundred other small towns. What distinguished Aspen was the pretension that this small camp contained the germ of a future great city. Social Aspen therefore continued its round of balls, musicales, masquerades, amateur theater, and the attractions imported into the opera house. Behind this burst of activity lay an undefined air of watchful waiting. Watching, waiting—for something to happen that would give substance and permanence to all the dreams of wealth from silver that lay so near and yet so undeveloped.

5

A Mining Camp without Mining: Aspen, 1879–1883

When Aspen entered into the world of mining, in 1880, it joined an experience that was already a generation old. Aspenites did not need to do anything new or different; they simply needed to repeat what others had done in many successful mining camps, from California in 1848 to Leadville in 1878. It was not an easy task. With the stakes so high, Aspen was born into a highly competitive world. Many embryonic mining camps raised the flag of mineral wealth and proclaimed themselves a new El Dorado. Few made it to a second birthday. Successful camps needed good claims, good management, and good luck. By 1880 the many mining camps throughout the mountain West fell into three basic groups: the great success stories—Leadville, Virginia City, Lead (South Dakota), and Butte (Montana), to name only four of the most prominent; those with a few prosperous seasons, followed by decay, of which Ashcroft and Independence were good examples; and the hundreds of ambitious camps that were born with bright hopes and that expired unmourned. In Colorado alone, one might easily identify a score of such silver ghost towns by 1880.

Silver mining—like all other mining enterprises that came under the law of 1872—started with a claim. Having laid out the claim in a rectangle 1,500 feet by 300 feet, with the principal vein or ledge outcropping running down the backbone, the prospector sank stakes or made other markings to identify the limits and did the necessary development work to satisfy the requirements of the law. He then had to file a location certificate within sixty days in the office of the nearest county clerk.[1]

The story of Aspen mining began with ten claims located by two prospecting parties in the summer of 1879 and duly recorded with the county clerk in Leadville, county seat of Lake County, Colorado. Within a few months, the cast of main characters underwent a change, as a second generation of entrepreneurs replaced the first prospectors. In November 1879, Philip W. Pratt and his associates sold the Spar, for $25,000, to Henry B. Gillespie and Gillespie's partner, Abel D. Breed, a Cincinnati capitalist. Initially, Gillespie was also interested in the camp-site, but during his absence in the winter of 1879–80, B. Clark Wheeler skied across the mountains, surveyed the site, and changed the name from Ute City to Aspen. Henceforth, Gillespie would devote himself to mining.

Wheeler represented a second group of eastern investors. The early prospectors on the Roaring Fork had registered their claims in Leadville and then dispersed throughout the West for the winter. Some went to Denver. In 1880, Denver had a population of thirty-five thousand and an impressive array of banks, smelters, railroads, and investors. It was a beehive of mining activity. In January of that year, Wheeler—the wandering promoter of Colorado mining, western mining, and even Mexican mining—met Charles A. Hallam, a young Cincinnati professional man on a visit to the West for recreation and possible investment. Hallam represented a Cincinnati lawyer, David M. Hyman. Caught up in the swirl of mining speculation that was Denver and propelled by the visions of wealth conjured up by Wheeler, Hallam took an option on seven and one-half claims and on the ranch sites of the original prospectors Bennett and Hopkins. The purchase and sale agreement in January 1880 between Hallam (representing Hyman) on the one hand and Bennett and Hopkins on the other completed the cast of main characters who would play central roles in Aspen's first three years of mining enterprise.

Mining (as distinct from prospecting) began on the site of the camp of Aspen in the summer of 1880. Heretofore, the purpose of the digging, tunneling, and sampling had been to ascertain the value of the claims. Now the major claims had new owners, men who began to develop their properties. Two major investment groups dominated the scene. Henry Gillespie pressed forward work on the Spar on behalf of himself and Abel D. Breed. Hallam and Hyman concentrated on the Durant and the Smuggler, the most promising of their claims. These owners employed small numbers of professional miners to work the claims for them. Proprietors of less celebrated properties and smaller resources worked their own.[2]

The mining activities in the Roaring Fork Mining District in the summer of 1880 bore little resemblance to the complex mining operations of Leadville or Virginia City. The most that might be said of them is that they represented a first stage in the search for such stature. Mining parties of no more than half a dozen men—and sometimes of only one or two—sank shafts, drove tunnels, and planned drifts, in search of ore bodies and samples for favorable assayers' reports. Especially rich ore might be carried over the mountains to the Leadville smelters by returning jack trains. Some was, but with freight charges at four cents a pound (or $80 a ton) only the richest ore could justify the expense. No production figures emerged for the first summer of mining operations, but the total must have been small.

While a few miners labored for daily wages on the claims of absentee investors, large numbers of prospectors attracted by rumors of the strikes swarmed over the hillsides and valleys around the Roaring Fork, seeking new outcroppings of the great vein of silver ore that had emerged so sharply on Aspen and Smuggler mountains. By the close of the prospecting season in the fall of 1880, they had staked out several hundred claims over four miles. Of these, some forty major claims of sufficient importance to be listed regularly in the newspapers lay in the immediate vicinity of the camp. Local editors, eager to promote the camp, optimistically described half a dozen of these claims as among the richest in the state of Colorado.[3]

With the first mining season over and the young camp of Aspen still in its infancy, certain mining patterns had already emerged. The "mining" around Aspen was not (or only rarely) carried on to extract ore for smelting; rather, it was exploration and development work, designed to demonstrate more fully the value of individual mines and to preserve title to them by a physical presence. A few mines had established dumps, where ore was stored pending shipment, and two or three had actually shipped some ore to Leadville for testing and processing, although none had shipped more than a few tons. But by far the largest number of mines remained mines on paper only. They were really claims to mineral outcroppings, not working mines. Furthermore, mining—if that term is appropriate here—remained a seasonal occupation. Most of the camp vanished with the coming of fall. There was no mining enterprise of sufficient importance to justify mining operations in the winter.

These characteristics persisted, even intensified, over the mining seasons of 1881, 1882, and 1883. What emerged was a growing divergence between the physical expansion of the camp and the continued lack of producing mines. The year 1881 was one of notable advance in the institutional organization and physical growth of the camp. People came in large numbers—perhaps more than a thousand by midsummer—and they created Aspen's first building boom. Sawmills did a frantic business, and construction workers labored from sunrise to sunset.

Yet the character of Aspen's mining remained the same. A few mineowners—principally the Spar and the Smuggler groups—sank shafts to seventy or even eighty feet, where visitors and newspapers editors (candles in hand) might marvel at the silver chlorides winking at them from the wet walls. However, at midsummer during the height of the boom in population and construction, even the most vigorous boosters and promoters of the camp admitted that Aspen mining was dull to nonexistent. So little had been done, in fact, that some miners had not even been paid for their season's work, because some owners had insufficient resources. In an annual report of production, Independence and the Falwell Company Gold Mines dominated the statistics and the news. The silver mines of Aspen and Ashcroft did not rate a single line.[4]

Throughout Aspen's first four years, the most prominent mines were the Smuggler and the Spar. Each, in turn, was the principal mine of one or two investment groups that were simultaneously Aspen's greatest boosters and its most bitter personal rivals. Charles A. Hallam and David M. Hyman owned and operated the Smuggler group. Hyman worked in the role of adviser and financier, dividing his time among Cincinnati, New York, and Denver. His chief concern was raising capital to open the mines. To this end, he worked behind the scenes with prospective investors in principal cities. His partner, Hallam, made his headquarters in Aspen, where he served as general manager of mining operations, the spokesman of the group, active in community affairs, and one of Aspen's most prominent civic and social leaders. Hallam's ranch, some of it later subdivided for an expansion of the camp, became a center of social life. Hallam's wife and family lived in Aspen during the summers; Hyman's remained in Cincinnati.

The first work on the Smuggler began in the spring of 1881 when workmen sank a shaft to the level of forty-six feet and ran two short drifts from it. The owners shipped a ton of the best ore to Leadville in the same month. It took a train of ten jacks to carry the ore over Independence Pass to the Leadville smelter. During the summer, work on the second and third shafts began, and the main shaft reached the eighty-foot level. At the close of the season, work ceased. Over the winter, Hallam ordered machinery, especially large pumps to handle the water already seeping into the shafts. The machinery came in the spring of 1882, packed over the mountains in pieces by jack trains. With much publicity and celebration, Hallam blew the first steam whistle ever sounded in the valley of the Roaring Fork to signal the start of large-scale operations, at which point the work force of seven men trooped into the mine. It was the largest mining crew in the Roaring Fork Mining District.[5]

Although Hallam and Hyman talked publicly of sinking the main shaft to four hundred feet, their tiny mining crew in fact occupied itself in timbering the shafts at the present level of around one hundred feet. Questioned about the delay, Hallam noted that major operations had been slowed until the arrival of the steam pump, at which point a "full force" would begin work. He never specified the numbers involved, and no one pressed him to be more specific, because such vague statements formed the staple of Aspen mining news. The half a dozen or so men continued to work over the summer, but the company issued no reports of its progress. In early October 1882, amid reports of the serious economic slump, Hallam and his family left the camp.[6]

The story of the second major mine, the Spar, revealed another side of mining in Aspen—litigation. Whereas agriculture entailed large-scale landownership, mining offered the possibility of fabulous wealth based on the possession of a small tract of ground. Farmers and, later, ranchers argued over fence lines, but such disagreements involved much pride and, except where water rights were involved, little of economic consequence. A mining claim was a tiny point in the wilderness of the high mountain valleys. At relatively few places did mineral belts break the surface and form the basis of contact claims, and a claim of the maximum size allowed by the law of May 10, 1872—1,500 feet by 300 feet—covered only a little more than ten acres.

The sequence of making a claim worked against a good, clear title. Prospectors dug small holes and set stakes to outline the limits of their claims, then retired from the locale, sometimes for long periods or perhaps never to return. A likely-looking belt of mineral—such as that stretching for four miles through the heart of Aspen—became crisscrossed with hundreds of claims, scores of them inevitably conflicting. The more promising the claim, the more likely a legal conflict. To these factors must be added the endless subdivision of claims by developers who sold fractional holdings in order to raise capital for speculation, to begin mining operations, and, later, to finance costly litigation. When the mine at last began production and achieved a degree of success, entrepreneurs who had earlier sold out brought suits alleging fraud and deception. The case of the Spar provided a perfect illustration.

The Spar was the most publicized of Aspen's early mines, so it comes as no surprise that this mine became the center of early litigation. Philip W. Pratt and Smith Steele, two of the early prospectors who crossed Independence Pass in July 1879, staked out the Spar on a prominent ledge on Aspen Mountain, subsequently known as Spar Hill. They made an open cut to about fifteen feet, sufficient to satisfy the requirements of development work to ten feet as well as to extract mineral that produced favorable assays at a Leadville office. In November 1879, the two prospectors sold the claim to Henry B. Gillespie and Abel D. Breed, the Cincinnati patent-medicine–casket king. The price was $25,000.

In December, further development work under Gillespie's supervision disclosed a large body of high-grade ore. This "strike," for so it was called in the local newspapers, established the Spar as Aspen's foremost mining property, and some observers went so far as to call it one of the richest in Colorado. The description was surely an exaggeration, especially for a mine that had progressed so little toward actual production, but Aspenites needed something to talk about. The Spar was a suitable subject. Exploration work continued in desultory fashion for the next several months—in the style of other Aspen mining enterprises—until Breed himself arrived on the scene in June 1881. At this point, Breed and Gillespie planned large operations, including a tunnel up to one thousand feet long.[7]

In September 1881, the former owners, Pratt and Steele, brought suit in local court, claiming fraud in the original sale of the mine and asking for the return of the property and $150,000 in damages. The suit languished on the docket of the district court for twelve months, while lawyers for each side prepared arguments. Mining operations—never very energetic—ceased in the face of such uncertainty about ownership.

Suddenly, events took a more active turn. On March 1, 1882, in a dramatic gesture that caught the attention of all Aspen, Pratt, Steele, and several armed miners seized the mine. Posting an armed guard, the new management—so to speak—now proceeded to work the mine with a vigor that contrasted sharply with the legal owners' indifference; it extended the tunnel and took out a considerable body of ore. Silver ore is clumsy loot to make off with, and this lot was no exception, so the new claimants piled their ore on a dump near the entrance. The ore taken out by the Pratt-Steele party now became a part of the lawsuit over ownership that continued to grind its way through the court at Buena Vista. Matters continued in this vein for the next five months.

Then, in a daring raid early on the morning of July 30, Gillespie and Breed reoccupied the mine, which they then proceeded to fortify against their opponents by physical breastworks and court injunctions. The suspicion arose that Pratt and Steele did not resist the repossession assault by Gillespie and Breed, because they had run out of money, and the ore stacked at the mine entrance—whatever its psychic satisfactions—could not be used to pay their miners. Gillespie and Breed did not continue work, however; they contented themselves with awaiting the outcome of the suit. The legal conflict dragged on for another six months, as Pratt and Steele lost every round and immediately appealed to a higher court.[8]

Thus, in a perverse chain of events, Aspen's most prominent mine was the object of litigation for the camp's early years. The case became an issue of importance not only for the principals but also for the welfare of the entire camp. The new mayor of Aspen, J. W. Tanfield, made the suit the focal point of his speech on the state of the camp in the spring of 1882. "During the past year the deadly hand of vexatious litigation has seized with its withering grasp upon the richest of the mineral resources of our vicinity, paralyzing labor, benumbing our energies and spreading a dark pall of oppression over all the healthful activities of our camp," he intoned.[9] Strong words for one lawsuit, one mining claim among hundreds, and yet Aspenites had come to see that the welfare of the whole camp was at stake. Legal delays victimized all those associated with the camp. Aspen's mines and their growth could no longer be regarded as private matters. To the extent that the activities of a few men, in the mines and in the courtrooms, controlled the future of the camp, such litigation was a matter of public concern.

No mining camp—and especially no silver-mining camp—was an island of a few individuals. By the end of the nineteenth century, mining was an enormously complicated and expensive business that could be carried out profitably only with the latest in technology and very considerable capital investment. Aspen needed investors, men with surplus capital who would establish a financial basis for the camp and its mines that would permit successful exploitation of its mineral resources. The risks were high. Furthermore, mining investment and financial manipulation had an unsavory reputation by the 1880s. Too many eastern and European investors had lost money—some of them, large sums of money—and there emerged the image of unscrupulous western mining men selling worthless claims for high prices to eager and innocent easterners. The task of finding financial support would not be easy, and the alliance would inevitably have its share of quarrels and misunderstandings.

What Aspen needed was capital to develop the mines. Editors, boosters, and public officials agreed on this single point, and they sounded the theme over and over for three years. Aspen received its initial infusion of investment capital with the purchase of early mining claims by investors in the fall of 1879. By the spring of 1880, Gillespie, Breed, Hallam, and Hyman—easterners all—were the second wave of mineowners that every camp required. But this second wave did not pursue the systematic development of the mines. Gillespie and Breed encountered a crippling obstacle in the form of litigation. Breed, the man with capital, lost interest and waited to sell out at a good profit. There were no buyers. Hallam and Hyman, on the other hand, had invested all their capital in the purchase of claims. They lacked the reserves to press forward the development of their claims. In three years, Aspen's eastern capitalists had not put their claims into production.

To assist in the development of producing mines, Aspen required a smelter. The smelter was a significant benchmark in the maturing of a mining camp, for it meant an industrial capacity to process ores from surrounding mines. Modern smelting processes had their origins in Europe, where by the mid-nineteenth century the first professional metallurgists and schools of metallurgy had given European mining a technical knowledge far in advance of anything in North America. With the discovery of gold in California at mid-century and the spread of mining across the western third of the North American continent— into Canada, Mexico, and, eventually, Alaska—America developed a strong and immediate use for European smelting technology.

At the time of Aspen's founding and early growth, European techniques still formed the scientific basis of the rapidly expanding American smelting industry. Denver, Pueblo, and, recently, Leadville, all had major smelting complexes, including heavy machinery, a professional work force, and large capital investment, that smelted ore mined from places as distant as Montana and Arizona. Aspen's promoters sought something far more modest, of course: a single plant using the coke process to reduce tons of ore to silver concentrate and to discard bulk slag that would not have to be transported across the mountains. Such a smelter would give Aspen independence from the smelters across the mountains and from the jack trains that laboriously crossed the high passes with a few tons for Leadville.[10]

The search for a smelter gradually exceeded in intensity, planning, publicity, and acknowledged disappointment every other aspect of the camp's mining development. Part of this problem lay in the specific nature of a smelting operation. Aspenites, like people in other young mining camps, thrived on vagueness. Mines could be described as potentially profitable, and perhaps they were; roads came in all sizes, shapes, costs, and degrees of usefulness. But a smelter was a specific piece of machinery. Everyone knew what a smelter was; a camp either had a smelter or it didn't have one. There was no middle ground.

Public plans for the first smelter surfaced in the spring of 1881, even while Aspen still lived as a tent camp. The Aspen Mining and Smelting Company, a Philadelphia corporation, began construction in early June. According to published reports, work was "progressing rapidly" on a building, thirty feet by thirty-six feet, an engine room twenty feet by sixteen feet, to house a smelter with a ten-ton capacity. The initial capital mentioned was $5,000, with machinery from Omaha. Throughout the fall, the smelter's firing was imminent—and yet it never fired. The season ended, and recriminations about the smelter failure began. A Leadville paper twitted the young, ambitious camp across the mountains with the comment "There have been a great many Aspen smelters built on paper." Aspenites did not find such comments amusing.[11]

Nor was the season of 1882 more successful. Various attempts to purchase the half-finished smelter building failed, and a new smelter, financed by Leadville investors, capitalized at $100,000 and scheduled for completion in forty days, never got past the publicity stage. The intense disappointment prompted a detailed history in an Aspen newspaper. "It has been the province of the TIMES to give some smelter news in almost every issue since the first copy of this paper was struck off eighty-one weeks ago," the editor wrote. "The long delay in getting any reduction works, the repeated promises that such would come, has had a tendency to discourage everybody, and this fall has witnessed an exodus from the camp that has given the blues to many who remained." Even Ashcroft and Independence had smelters by the end of 1882. Aspen had none.[12]

What became known as the North Texas Smelter was to be the final and most discouraging in this series of smelter failures. On paper, the enterprise was an ideal blending of the expert knowledge of a Denver metallurgist and Texas investment capital. The scientific man was T. P. Airheart, who came to Aspen with a reputation as a professional especially conversant with the ores of Colorado. He had certainly come to the right place. No camp in the nation wanted a smelter as desperately as Aspen. Interested citizens immediately donated a twenty-acre tract on the west side of town as a site. Airheart enlisted as partners a group of investors from north Texas, men who had made substantial fortunes in the range cattle industry. The two parties organized the Texas (later North Texas) Smelting Company in October 1882, with a paid-up capital of $30,000.

What followed was something of a case study in the advantages
and disabilities of the fabled eastern capital that mining camps so
avidly sought. Aspen and its citizens continued to subsidize the enterprise, providing lumber at less than cost and transportation facilities at
a special rate, and the project surged forward through the winter of
1882–83, under the intense gaze of the camp's newspapers. On five
acres of the site, Airheart constructed (with the Texans' money) a
building for the plant, a large ore dump, and a half-mile ditch from
Castle Creek. He transported heavy machinery across the Continental
Divide and reassembled it; he added the necessary tools and supplies
for daily operation, including scale, molds, two hundred cords of
wood, twenty tons of coke, and thirteen thousand bushels of charcoal.
At this point, Airheart had spent the paid-up capital, and the Texans
refused to invest further. They never "blew in" the furnace, apparently
fearful of additional costs. Thus, Aspen now had a smelter owned by
absentee Texans, who declined to put it into operation.[13]

The experience with the Texans was a final blow to the camp's
immediate mining hopes. Concerned about the prosperity of the gold
camp of Independence and about the advances of rival Ashcroft,
Aspen found itself falling behind both. The production of ore remained
almost nonexistent, and what was mined could not be processed except at enormous cost in Leadville smelters. Gradually, the bright optimism of the camp's boosters dimmed in the face of the failure to
construct and fire a smelter. Expanding litigation that involved some of
the best claims and an economic slump in midsummer that affected the
entire camp completed the dismal outlook.

In early June 1882, the great Farwell mines in Independence closed.
Aspen had lost a rival, but Pitkin County had suffered a damaging
blow to its reputation as a mining center. It was, by general admission,
a season of business depression. Many of the camp's most prominent
mines, such as the Smuggler, shut down, ending what had been modest work by small crews. Statistics for the year confirmed the views of
those who saw the camp in trouble. The total output for the year in
Aspen and Ashcroft was $20,000. It was only a slight exaggeration to
say, as one reporter did, "As for the mining statistics, we may say
there are none."[14] In the spring of 1883, Aspen was four years old, and
the occasion prompted no celebration. The camp had not produced a
single bar of silver bullion. Aspen was a mining camp without mining.

II

THE TOWN
Aspen, 1883–1887

6

Jerome B. Wheeler:
The Eastern Capitalist Reshapes
the Camp on the Roaring Fork

Jerome B. Wheeler of New York City arrived in Aspen by stagecoach in the spring of 1883. What he found was an ambitious mining camp still suffering from the depression of the preceding season. Men moved energetically about, acting out the impulse to enterprise that spring characteristically brought to the High Rockies, but Aspen lacked the electric tension that producing camps like Leadville displayed twenty-four hours a day.

Whatever the character of the camp and the exact circumstances under which Wheeler first saw it, his arrival turned out to be the single most important event in the history of the camp. He was the personification of that fabled figure sought by every western mining camp—the eastern capitalist. Wheeler was both an easterner and a capitalist, and over the next decade he proved that, in Aspen's case at least, a single individual might indeed be the answer to a community's prayers. Even those few in the camp who were skeptical of religious figures came to regard Wheeler virtually as God. His economic miracles provided the impetus that transformed Aspen from a struggling camp to a thriving town. He was living evidence that during the transition, in post–Civil War America, from an individualistic to a mass society one person could still make a vital difference on the mining frontier.

Jerome Byron Wheeler was a native of New York State. The local Aspen press always identified him with New York City, perhaps to emphasize his importance and his powerful connections, but he was actually born in 1841 in Troy, New York, a small town outside of Albany. He attended the local public schools in Waterford, a little village at the junction of the Hudson and the Mohawk rivers. Wheeler's quiet, small-town world vanished with the outbreak of the Civil War, the same event that transformed the lives of so many men and women, North and South. He enlisted as a private in the Sixth New York Cavalry, advancing to the rank of captain and then of major, serving as regimental and later brigade quartermaster. For his services, he was brevetted colonel of cavalry. At the close of the war, Colonel Wheeler returned to Troy, where he began a career in business, rising from the post of bookkeeper to a clerkship and eventually to a full partnership in a flour manufacturing firm, Holt and Company.

In 1870, Wheeler married Harriet Macy Valentine. She was the niece (the daughter of the youngest sister) of Randolph H. Macy, founder of what became the largest department store in New York City. This connection brought great changes in Wheeler's career, triggered by a series of deaths. R. H. Macy, the store's founder, died in 1877 at the age of fifty-five, and another partner, Abiel T. LaForge, died the following year, at thirty-five from tuberculosis aggravated by Civil War service. In 1879, Mrs. Wheeler's brother, Robert Macy Valentine, who had long been associated with the firm, also died. This series of unexpected and untimely deaths decimated the ranks of Macy's top management within two years, leaving the largest department store in New York City in the inexperienced hands of Charles B. Webster, a distant cousin of Macy and Valentine. Webster had been a partner in the store only since 1876.

Webster needed help, and in keeping with the tradition established by R. H. Macy himself, he sought it within the family: he invited Jerome B. Wheeler to join the firm as a partner. Wheeler did not have much capital, but neither had the other junior partners when they joined Macy, who liked to keep financial control in his own hands. But the new junior partner from Troy had other useful qualities. He was a respected flour merchant and experienced in business. Observers thought Webster had made a sound decision. For eight years, from 1879 to 1887, Webster and Wheeler were partners in the most prosperous department store in New York City. As managers, both men lacked the dynamic innovation and flair associated with the founder, but so well had R. H. Macy done his work that the store almost ran itself for the decade after his death.

The partnership was not entirely an equal one. Webster owned 55 percent of the stock; Wheeler, the rest. From the beginning, there was a certain tension in the relationship. The two men had sharply contrasting personalities. Webster was one type of those provincial New Yorkers who often went to Europe on business but rarely west of the Hudson. He was a severe, taciturn, humorless model of the nineteenth-century American entrepreneur. He was close with money; some employees said that he was tightfisted.

Wheeler was different. He knew everyone in the store, nodded, smiled, and often paused to speak. The employees liked him. He was also an energetic, driving, ambitious man in his own way. Wheeler soon discovered that Webster did not propose to share his authority. To sit idle was not Wheeler's style. Thus, almost from the beginning of his association with Macy's, he sought outside interests, for Webster's control denied him opportunities for leadership within the store itself. The firm was enormously profitable. Wheeler's partnership earned him at least $125,000 a year, and he quickly began to seek ways of combining his capital and his own considerable entrepreneurial talents. This combination proved ideally suited to the Rocky Mountain mining frontier, where opportunities for investment and leadership lay on every hand. That Wheeler brought his talents and capital to Aspen was a mixture of luck and his own sense of the camp's destiny. Here was a camp four years old, but in mining enterprise still in its infancy. Wheeler could make modest investments and exercise substantial influence over the development of the camp. In the end, his investments would be anything but modest and his influence virtually complete.[1]

Wheeler's immediate introduction to Aspen came through a mining agent named Harvey Young. The mining frontier produced some extraordinary characters, of whom the camp of Aspen had its share—B. Clark Wheeler, David M. Hyman, and Jerome B. Wheeler come to mind—and Harvey Young was certainly one of the more unusual. Young was an aspiring artist and an ambitious mining entrepreneur. A native of Vermont, he mined in California from 1860 to 1866. When the placers proved continuously unrewarding, he took a job in San Francisco as a decorator of carriages. In 1867, he opened a studio without money or training and tried to establish himself as a landscape painter. Finally convinced that he needed formal training, he left for Europe, where he studied in France (1872–73), Munich (1875), and Paris (1877–78). His credentials as an artist firmly established, Young moved to Colorado, settling temporarily in Manitou Springs. His painting attracted much interest in the young resort town, but Young had another ambition: to engage in successful mining ventures.

In 1880, Young came to Aspen. After an apparently unsuccessful year prospecting, he plunged into the speculative world of buying and selling claims. By 1883, he had bought part interest in several Aspen properties and had joined several others in organizing the Castle Rock Mining Company. Because most of these ventures were executed on credit (in good mining-camp tradition), he was chronically short of cash. Hoping to relieve this condition, he persuaded the wealthy Jerome B. Wheeler that Aspen would be a good place to exercise his capital and talents. In November 1882, Wheeler bought controlling interest (actually five-eighths) in the Morning and the Evening Star mines, at the head of Orphir Gulch. The price was $20,000. It was the first of his many important investments in the camp.[2]

Wheeler had thus far committed $20,000 to the camp's future. In consultation with people like Young, he quickly saw what everyone else in Aspen had known for four years—namely, that the camp could not move forward without a smelter. A group of investors from north Texas had begun a smelter in the fall of 1882 with much public fanfare, but the company lacked the capital to finish the plant and put it into operation. Wheeler immediately purchased the half-completed smelter. Although his purchase of the two mining groups had occasioned little comment, news of the acquisition of the smelter hit the camp like a winter snowslide. The *Aspen Times* said it in bold headlines: "THE MOST IMPORTANT SALE EVER TRANSACTED FOR THE MATERIAL INTERESTS OF PITKIN CO." The editor continued, "There have been several transactions in Pitkin county involving more money but none which, under the circumstances of the case is so advantageous to the prosperity and welfare of Aspen and all this portion of Pitkin Co." He concluded, "All thanks to J. B. Wheeler." The *Sun* chose a more literary posture with the same message: "Today capital comes in to widen the avenues opened by brain and muscle, and the four years of toil, perseverance, and patience now find their reward." At last, Aspen had its own eastern capitalist. Overnight, Wheeler had become the most prominent figure in the camp's four-year history.[3]

Wheeler had purchased the smelter and fuel for something between $20,000 and $25,000. In spite of the impatience of the camp, he now spent almost a year putting the smelter into shape, enlarging the boiler capacity, and engaging the best professionals to finish the plant and manage the enterprise. His careful preparations suggested that the North Texas investors had correctly judged the long-term nature of their commitment and that the cost was higher than anyone had thought. He also began to purchase ore from the other Aspen mines to process in his smelter, thus establishing for the first time a local market for silver ores.

Although the delay in firing the smelter proved something of a disappointment to Aspenites, in all other respects Wheeler's activities exceeded the fondest dreams of any camp booster. In addition to mines and smelter, he spread his investment into other areas. Within a year, he purchased large coal mines thirty miles distant in order to provide coke and coal for the smelter. He began construction of a road to his holdings on the outskirts of the camp. Finally, he opened Aspen's first bank, J. B. Wheeler and Company, capitalized at $100,000. To give it suitable quarters, he purchased two lots on the corner of Mill and Cooper streets and constructed an imposing bank building, which opened for business in September 1884.[4]

Wheeler continued to keep mining at the center of his economic interests. In October 1883, he bought one of Aspen's most important mines, the Spar. Negotiations turned out to be long and frustrating. The stumbling block was Abel D. Breed, the Cincinnati casket maker who had originally been hailed for his investment in the young camp. If Wheeler was Aspen's Spirit of Christmas, Breed played the part of Scrooge, and he played it well. For three years, Breed had persistently ignored the pleas of his partner, Henry B. Gillespie, to develop the Spar. He simply sat on his investment and waited for the right offer. He had plenty of capital and could take his time. So the mine stood idle or was heavily involved in litigation. Eventually, outside parties mediated a sale, and Wheeler had enough capital to satisfy Breed's acquisitive instincts. The price was somewhere between $50,000 and $75,000. Gillespie retained his interest and became Wheeler's new partner. The new owners immediately put fifty men to work in the mine. By also purchasing the Galena in the same package, Wheeler and Gillespie ended litigation and developed plans for future mining operations on a large scale.[5]

In the spring of 1884, Wheeler put the corporate seal of approval on his Aspen creation. He brought together his several Aspen invest- ments into the Aspen Mining and Smelting Company, incorporated in New York State for $2,000,000, or 200,000 shares at $10 each. The articles of incorporation named Jerome B. Wheeler as president and Henry B. Gillespie as vice-president. In the fifteen months since he had purchased controlling interest in the Morning and the Evening Star groups, Wheeler had invested $500,000 in Aspen. At least, this was a popular guess, and it was probably not far wrong. The *Aspen Times* delivered a homily on the works of Jerome B. Wheeler that

might have come from the New Testament: "praiseworthy persever-
ance and unstinting generosity have continued to pour a stream of
wealth into our midst, developing mining properties, opening up coal
mines, building toll-roads and purchasing ores, until their outlay at
present in our county approximates $500,000."[6]

Wheeler also brought the first professional metallurgist to Aspen.
Walter B. Devereux, a native of upstate New York, graduated from
Princeton in 1873, and, after travels to Colorado and Tasmania, took a
degree in mining engineering at Columbia University. His career in
mining took him to distant points on the mining compass: to the Upper
Peninsula of Michigan, to Lead (South Dakota), and, in 1881, to Globe
(Arizona Territory) as manager of the Dakoma Copper Company. It
was there that Jerome B. Wheeler persuaded him to come to Aspen as
manager of the smelter. While he trained a group of men to run the
smelter, Devereux also organized transportation to bring in coke from
Crested Butte, thirty-five miles over Pearl Pass, and to transport the
finished product of this industrial process, called matte, to Granite, site
of the nearest railroad, forty-five miles away, for transshipment to
market. Devereux was precisely the kind of professional whom
Wheeler and Aspen required. His arrival and effective management of
the smelter represented another milestone in the growth of the camp.[7]

And what were the other mineowners and the town doing? While
Jerome B. Wheeler poured half a million dollars into the Roaring Fork
Valley, what of Aspen and its citizens? Did they stir themselves or
simply sit on the sidelines and cheer? Throughout the summer and fall
of 1883, Aspen's missing enterprise showed signs of life, but only
sporadically. By the end of September, for example, probably three
hundred miners worked Aspen's claims, yet the numbers at work on
any individual claim remained small. Few if any mining groups had
made a substantial commitment to the removal of ore from their mines.
Indeed, newspaper accounts began to criticize mineowners and managers for hanging back. The appearance of Jerome B. Wheeler and his
purchase of the smelter signified a dramatic movement forward in
Aspen's mining development, but his fellow mineowners responded
slowly to the opportunity. A conservative guess placed Aspen's silver
bullion production for the year at $250,000, vitually all of it produced
since July 1. This figure was cause for some congratulations, doubling
the output of the preceding year. In the same twelve months, though,
the Leadville mines produced silver ore worth $18,700,000. Aspen still
had a long way to go.[8]

Miners and merchants felt tremors of the economic progress associated with Wheeler and his many investments. One professional

group experienced a dramatic rise in business—lawyers. The appearance of Wheeler and the renewal of mining activity revived litigation over claims. The prime objects of the new legal assault were the leading mines, and principally those linked to Wheeler. In early November 1883, owners of the Washington, lying adjacent to the Spar (just purchased by Wheeler), sued, and the court shut down both mines pending the resolution of the legal issues. In late January 1884, Wheeler resolved the problem by buying the Washington and so ending the suit. Perhaps this outcome was precisely what the owners of the Washington had had in mind all along. The presence of an eastern capitalist like Wheeler offered two separate but related opportunities to make money—mining and litigation to prevent mining. Each was profitable in its own way.[9]

Winter came, as it does inevitably and early in the high mountains, but the winter of 1883–84 was different. Buried under the layers of successive snowfalls, Aspen dreamed of the coming season. For the first time in its short life span, the camp seemed to be on the verge of a great leap ahead. This time, it had more than editorials to support expectations; it had physical changes in the form of new mining enterprises and a smelter. More important, it had a single individual whose commitment to the camp had opened up a new future. And so those who wintered in the camp talked, planned, and dreamed.

The mining season of 1884 publicly lived up to these optimistic expectations. By mid-May, production at the Spar was on the order of $20,000 per month, and four mines were producing ore at a combined monthly rate of $60,000. In early July, some three hundred miners were at work, with the Spar, the Washington, and the Vallejo employing thirty men each, and another fifteen at work on the road to those claims. Aspen's mines were now estimated to be producing at the rate of about $1,250,000 per annum. The numbers of miners at work rose steadily, reaching a figure of five hundred in mid-August, with a payroll of $50,000 per month. All of commercial Aspen profited in proportion.[10]

Impressive as these figures looked on paper, they emphasized the unevenness of mining enterprise in Aspen. Most of the more than two hundred mining claims close to the town were idle. Even those that produced did so on a relatively small scale. On Wheeler's most important mining property, the Spar, for example, forty-five men were on the payroll, but only six of these actually mined ore. The others worked in support roles such as timbering, cleaning out the drifts, and constructing buildings on the outside of the mine entrance.[11]

The "blowing in" of the smelter in the summer of 1884 was a milestone in the camp's development. Four years after the first talk of an Aspen smelter and fully twelve months after Jerome B. Wheeler's purchase of the half-completed shell of the north Texans, mining industry became a reality. Because the occasion coincided with the Fourth of July, it could be celebrated by the entire camp. "Aspen and Pitkin county may congratulate themselves, and celebrate the day that J. B. Wheeler became interested in this county," observed one editor. "He, aided by his efficient manager, W. B. Devereux, have produced light from darkness and have dispelled all doubts and uncertainties, and made Aspen a bullion producing camp." Not even the skeptics in Leadville could doubt that Aspen now mined ore and processed it.[12]

The smelter had a capacity of thirty tons a day, and through chemical techniques it reduced these ores to a concentrate worth $600 a ton for shipment by jack train to Granite, and from there by railroad to the Pennsylvania Refining Works in Pittsburgh. Aspen, the little mining camp on the Roaring Fork, had products sufficiently valuable to be transported across half the continent. Through the rest of the summer, the smelter produced about five tons of concentrate a day, or half its capacity. The appetite of the furnaces meant that the smelter needed a regular supply of ores, and the mines of the camp were often hard-pressed to provide them. Producers still numbered only half a dozen among the two hundred claims in the immediate vicinity of the town.

Much of the mining activity undertaken in the less well known mines in the summer of 1884 (and in subsequent seasons, for that matter) went forward under leases. Those miners who wanted to try their luck but lacked capital to purchase mining claims leased them from owners who had no capital or who for some reason did not wish to invest it in developing their claims. Leases had advantages and disadvantages for both parties. For the owners, they provided a kind of continuing development work that was to their long-term advantage. For the lessee, they offered a means of participating with minimum investment in the opportunities associated with mine ownership—a way by which a man could do the labor himself or in partnership (most leases involved more than one person) and, if results were good, employ a work force in proportion to the anticipated results.

The leasing system was part of that distinctive economic pattern under which only a fraction of the mines in even a potentially rich camp like Aspen would ever be developed. Part of the failure to mine had to do with investment. Mines demanded capital, and the more complex the mining at ever deeper levels, the greater the need for capital. But part was also related to the disinclination of some owners to mine. They simply waited for their claims to appreciate in value and then sold out. No law compelled any mineowner to develop a claim beyond the annual minimum requirements set by federal statute at $100 per annum. The appreciation in value of idle mines resembled the pattern of absentee ownership of agricultural lands, under which the speculators benefited through the labor of those around them. The differences in mining were noteworthy. Agricultural land had lower monetary values but a quality of permanence; mining claims might turn out to be worthless and the whole camp disappear within a few months. It was an uncertain route, but for those with little capital to invest, leasing involved few risks.

The most celebrated case of a leased mine in the history of the camp involved the Aspen claim in the season of 1884–85. The story of the Aspen illustrates the extraordinary part played by chance in mining. Three local men—Elmer T. Butler, Louis A. Stone, and Daniel Dunsmore—located the Aspen in 1881. The claim was not considered an especially valuable property; the three men kept up the assessment work but did nothing else. Stone thought so little of his one-third claim that he traded it to D. R. C. Brown to settle a debt of $250. Dunsmore sold his interest to J. B. Wheeler for $5,000. Butler held on to his share, although he had earlier offered to sell it for $100 and found no takers.

At this point, important strikes were made on adjacent claims. When the surrounding properties became more valuable, J. D. Hooper (then the camp's mayor) and two associates secured a lease on the Aspen. In late November 1884, they struck a valuable vein of ore at a depth of two hundred feet. The lease had fewer than sixty days to run. Hooper rushed into the camp, hired all the idle men he could find at the unheard-of wage of $8 a shift, and began to work three shifts around the clock. Setting up a light hoist, the lessees and their crews mined furiously, raising as much as 100 tons a day. Hooper and his men eventually took out silver ore worth $600,000. The smelter could not handle the flood of ore, and there were not enough teams in the camp to transport it over the mountains. So Hooper rented two vacant lots, piled 4,300 tons of ore onto them, and hired guards to patrol the lots twenty-four hours a day. It took several months to process the ore in the smelter, and the task of emptying the ore-filled lots, now covered with snow, kept the smelter running full blast all winter. After the lease expired, the Aspen reverted to its owners. Wheeler profited enormously from the Aspen, but he had extensive mineral holdings elsewhere. For the others, it was a unique opportunity. Brown's casual transaction and Butler's failure to conclude a casual transaction made each man a fortune.[13]

Half a million dollars made a substantial splash in the valley of the Roaring Fork, and Jerome B. Wheeler's investments spread outward in waves to a wide range of economic enterprises, transforming Aspen from a camp to a town. The commercial side of the town shared in the prosperity of the season and the expectations for the next. By fall of 1884, Aspen had an estimated twenty-five hundred people, and business establishments had grown up in like proportion to include four hotels, sixteen boardinghouses, four restaurants, ten places for furnished rooms, and twelve laundries (not a single laundry owned or operated by Chinese, who were barred from the town). The lodging arrangements indicated that Aspen remained home for large numbers of single men or men who had come across the range without their families. Eight stables looked after the horses and carriages that provided the town's transportation. To ward off the hunger of the citizenry, eight grocery stores existed; when they wanted to quench their thirst, Aspenites could choose from among ten saloons. Two newspapers provided the news of the outside world and the gossip of the inside, constantly boosting the camp's prospects, and three churches ministered to the spiritual needs of the residents.[14]

The opportunities for profit in the growing town of Aspen may be spied in the changing circumstances of H. P. ("Grandpap") Cowenhoven and his clerk, D. R. C. Brown. Cowenhoven and Brown had made the hard trip from Buena Vista across the Continental Divide to Aspen with two wagons in the summer of 1880. For the next three years, Cowenhoven outfitted prospectors and miners and contractors alike. Brown married Katy Cowenhoven and became a partner. In the summer of 1883 and through the mining season of 1884, Aspen grew, and the firm of H. P. Cowenhoven and Company grew with it. In July 1884, the town assessor increased the company's assessed value (for tax purposes) from $5,000 to $20,000. Unlike many others in the camp, the officers of the company lodged no complaint with the town fathers about rising taxes. In early October, a large notice in the newspapers announced the organization of the Aspen Mercantile Association, successor to H. P. Cowenhoven and Company. The new company had a paid-up capital of $50,000. Its officers were D. R. C. Brown, president, and H. P. Cowenhoven, vice-president. Brown, who had only recently made the transition to a full partner, had become the senior member of the firm. To these entrepreneurial achievements, he added a one-third interest in the rich Aspen mine. Equally significant, Brown's mining venture in the Aspen allied him with Jerome B. Wheeler, the most important economic figure in the town. The young man from Nova Scotia who had come to the camp as a clerk in the summer of 1880 was on his way to becoming a millionaire by the end of 1885.[15]

A camp growing into a town should offer more services. Aspenites faced these increased demands with their customary reluctance to pay taxes to support the services. The most immediate needs were a water-works, a gasworks, and electric streetlighting. Aspenites generally agreed on the list, but the consensus ended there. Discussions of a waterworks in the city council foundered in the objections of B. Clark Wheeler, who claimed to have a long-standing monopoly in the corpo-rate entity of the Aspen Ice and Water Company. While the council talked, irrigation ditches that formed the camp's water supply ab-sorbed the usual seasonal influx of dust, dirt, debris, garbage, and animal waste.[16]

The county faced a different set of problems. The rising population did not bring new obligations to the county. In a sense, the county's responsibility had been to make arrangements to get the people to Aspen. Now, with its work done and mineowners shouldering a sub-stantial part of the burden for new roads into the mining area, the county found itself saddled with an old debt that it could not manage. As 1884 closed—the most prosperous year in the town's history—Pit-kin County warrants were quoted at twenty cents on the dollar. The county debt remained about $250,000. The issue was an embarrassing one for an ambitious camp-turned-town. A few responsible leaders went so far as to voice the audacious proposal that the town tax the mines, beginning in 1890. That these people were not immediately run out of town suggests the seriousness with which Aspenites noted the county debt, or at least noted the debt without a willingness to do anything about it.[17]

Aspen's newfound prosperity associated with the appearance of Jer-ome B. Wheeler sharpened another old issue—townsite ownership. As more lots had been occupied, the values of those already improved had increased. In short, the stakes were higher, and not surprisingly this most emotional issue for Aspen's citizens had become more volatile than ever. In the panoply of court suits, newspaper editorials, public meet-ings, and frayed tempers, three views emerged. The people in the first group vowed no compromise under any circumstance. For them the issue was as much a moral as an economic one. In their view, the townsite belonged to those who were there—a time-honored frontier principle—and the Townsite Company represented precisely that class of absentee proprietors that should be fought to the last injunction.

A second group endorsed the general outrage expressed by the first, but tempered its views with a sentiment that at some point the future of the town came first and outrage second. These citizens favored pursuing litigation with the company up to a point, and then making whatever compromises might be necessary for the good of the town. A third faction favored an immediate compromise. It represented the large investors in the town, merchants as well as mineowners. In their view, while the prosperity of the town had raised the stakes of the townsite controversy, it also enhanced opportunities for profit in all economic enterprises associated with the town—opportunities that far outweighed abstract questions of "rights." In short, the business of Aspen was business, more specifically the silver-mining business; it was not prolonged agitation over the ownership of the townsite.

The forces interested in compromise began their campaign in the summer of 1883; it coincided with the first of the large investments by Jerome B. Wheeler and with court decisions that seemed to confirm the valid title of the Townsite Company. Some countered these sentiments by noting that the townsite was now worth in excess of $100,000 and that this figure would increase dramatically in the next years. They argued that such increased values belonged to the town and its government, not to absentee proprietors. The issue became the more pressing with Aspen's very considerable physical expansion during the 1884 season. In the spring, the compromise interests restated terms that included the confirming of old-time settlers in possession of their lots at cost; newer residents were to be confirmed for a higher but favorable figure; the remainder of the lots were to become the property of the Townsite Company; and all parties were to drop legal actions. Yet large numbers—perhaps even a majority—objected to such a solution, and no lasting compromise could be effected. In November 1884, the Aspen Town and Land Company began two additional suits designed to confirm its control of the town lots at the expense of the town council. The town replied in court, and the battle was once again joined.[18]

The successes of 1884 seemed only a prelude to the prospects for the next year. The enforced idleness of the winter season provided ample opportunity to let imaginations soar. Silver bullion production for 1884 exceeded $1 million. Many observers thought $5 million in the coming year was not out of the question; in the dark of night or under the influence of a little liquid cheer, a few whispered a number twice as large. Whatever the figures, all agreed that Aspen was a camp reborn, a ghost camp come to life as a town in the most dramatic way. "We can say with confidence that Aspen has a great future," wrote one observer. "None need fear for her prosperity."[19] Indeed, at the close of 1884, Aspen had become in reality everything that the most sanguine supporters had prophesied for it. The camp on the Roaring Fork had turned into a booming town.

To celebrate the camp's triumph and to voice confidence in the future seemed not only appropriate but also necessary. The vehicle was a new organization called the Roaring Fork Club. Founded in April 1884, the club included the fifty most prominent mining and business-men in the town. The celebration took the form of a "reception" in the clubhouse, a richly furnished suite of rooms. The guest of honor was Jerome B. Wheeler. "A most recherche affair," remarked the *Rocky Mountain Sun*, "it was one of those social events which mark the pro-gress of a community." Three long tables were necessary to seat the members of the club, with the honored guest in the center. No expense was spared in the catering, and the meal included "every dish known to the art of cuisine," plus the best in wines and liquors.

This gourmet meal concluded, Aspen's leading figures settled com-fortably in their chairs and prepared to pay homage to the individual who had transformed their economic prospects within twelve months. Charles A. Hallam, president of the club, opened the proceedings by asking that J. B. Wheeler be made an honorary member of the Roaring Fork Club. Fifty eager listeners shouted their approval. Hallam then called on leading members of the community to propose a series of toasts. The toasts and respondents had a dominant theme: the invest-ments of Jerome B. Wheeler in the preceding year that had buried the stagnant past, produced the rosy present, and laid the foundations for a euphoric future. Among the other local resources singled out for praise were the Aspen smelter, the mines of Pitkin County, the Spar mine, and the Roaring Fork Club.

It was J. B. Wheeler's day, and rightly so. He had transformed the camp, and the camp had acknowledged him its "founding father." Yet the toasts and cheers—deserved as they were—dealt with the past. What of the future? Those who came to praise Wheeler also came to hear him. What did he intend to do next? Club members heard news that confirmed their faith in the man from Macy's, for he spoke of the future in glowing terms. And he saved the best news until last: "He had been requested to become a director in a strong company, who proposed to build a railroad to Aspen in the near future, and within sixty days he could more definitely state the details of the project." The magic word "railroad"—so loosely bandied about in newspapers and on street corners—had now been heard from the man of the hour, a figure who had already made fantasy into reality. Few if any who listened that day doubted that J. B. Wheeler would be as good as his word.[20]

After two and a half hours of eating, drinking, and celebrating, the members of the Roaring Fork Club stepped into the bright light of a September afternoon. They had come to cheer the past; they had stayed to celebrate the future.

7

David M. Hyman:
The Eastern Capitalist
without Capital

David M. Hyman, the Cincinnati lawyer who emerged as one of the most important entrepreneurs in Aspen, contrasted in virtually every respect with his counterpart Jerome B. Wheeler. Although their interests occasionally overlapped, the two men were intense rivals throughout their association with Aspen and its mines. Wheeler was the universally known public figure; Hyman, the consummate behind-the-scenes operator. Silver-mining camps had both types. In part it was a contrast of personality; in part, a contrast in business styles. Style is very personal, and each man played the part that was both comfortable and effective. Mining, and especially silver mining, was preeminently the work of few men and few mines. Of the two hundred claims near the town, only eight showed profitable ledger sheets in the years 1883–87. Jerome B. Wheeler was connected with two of these—the Spar and the Aspen; David M. Hyman, with another two—the Smuggler and the Durant. Both men had a decisive influence on the young mining camp and later the town of Aspen, and Hyman's, at least, would last into the twentieth century.

Silver mining—that is to say, the mining and processing of silver ore as opposed to the speculation in mine ownership and mining stocks—demanded large capital investment. The experience of the generation since the development of the Comstock Lode showed that you could raise the necessary capital in two ways: bring it into camp from the outside or generate it within the camp itself. The two principal groups of entrepreneurs in Aspen represented the two techniques. Henry B. Gillespie, Walter B. Devereux, and especially Wheeler followed one route. They were all men who came to Aspen with capital or with solidly established mining credentials that gave them access to capital—or with both.

The second group was composed of men with the same, strong entrepreneurial instincts but inexperienced in mining and without capital of their own. Hyman and Charles A. Hallam typified this kind of Aspen entrepreneur. Hyman sought to generate capital through trading bits and pieces of mine ownership for sufficient cash to meet the immediate and long-range expenses of establishing clear title and of placing the mine in production. He succeeded in almost every respect, but only at the cost of endless negotiations. If Jerome B. Wheeler bought a finished panorama of a mining town, Hyman put together countless little pieces in a never ending search for a workable combination.

David Marks Hyman was born in 1846 into the close Jewish community of a small Bavarian village. His uncles, prosperous merchants in Cincinnati, arranged for his immigration to the United States. They provided for his early education and eventual legal training at the Harvard Law School, from which he graduated in 1869. The young Hyman returned to Cincinnati, married, and began to practice law. He was an extraordinarily capable lawyer, and his practice prospered. Initially, he invested money in Cincinnati lots and buildings. By 1879, he had been in practice for ten years and, by his own account, had carefully invested something on the order of $40,000. His financial prospects were extremely bright, for, in addition to his sound investment instincts, he had a lucrative law practice that provided a steady source of income.[1]

In the course of his professional life at the bar, Hyman met Charles A. Hallam, a Cincinnati accountant. The two men were the same age and at roughly the same point in their professional careers. In spite of differences in temperament and background, the two were immediately attracted to one another and became close friends. In the fall of 1879, Hallam's adventurous spirit led him to make plans for a trip to the West. The two men discussed the trip, of course. Hyman was not inclined to take long trips, especially to the unknown West, and his legal calendar was full. When they parted, however, Hyman asked Hallam to be on the lookout for good investment opportunities, involving perhaps as much as $5,000. He made the offer because he had the capital to invest but, most of all, because he had complete confidence in Hallam's honesty and good sense. The farewells said, Hallam's train pulled out of Cincinnati for the Rocky Mountain West, and Hyman returned to his law office.

Hallam's voyage of discovery initially took him to Denver, where he found a single topic of conversation—the fortunes to be made from mines and mining. Denver was a mass of rumors about mining and everything associated with it: bonanza claims, strikes, stock speculation, railroads, smelters and smelting, and so forth. It was a heady atmosphere for the young Cincinnatian, who could only be impressed with the stately mansions on Larimer Street and the large fortunes so recently made in Leadville. Whether or not Hallam carried with him the open air of the innocent eastern investor, he could not help expressing an interest in mines, and he had come with funds (albeit not his own) to invest in a responsible financial opportunity. His crisscrossings of the financial and investment circles of the city carried him into the arms of B. Clark Wheeler.

Wheeler immediately saw in Hallam the answer to a promoter's prayers: an eastern investor who would provide the capital to match Wheeler's mining knowledge of the West. Denver mining people had heard of the new strikes on the Roaring Fork, a dozen or so claims in one of the most isolated parts of the state, lying adjacent to the lands of the hostile Utes. Whatever the obstacles, Wheeler saw a fortune there, and in Hallam he saw a partner. Hallam would provide the money; Wheeler would contribute his professional knowledge. He promptly assumed the role of investment adviser to the young Cincinnatian.

Professor Wheeler soon introduced the subject of the new claims in the Roaring Fork District. Their value was speculative. The modest investor had the opportunity for large profits not available in established camps like Leadville. At Wheeler's suggestion, the two interviewed mining men about the Roaring Fork District and then took the stage to Leadville, where they talked to some of the original prospectors. Denver may have impressed Hallam with its heady talk, but Leadville revealed the form of the greatest boom camp in the nation: crowds of people jostling for space on the sidewalks and in the hotels for accommodation; continuous noise from the cries of men and horses and the roar of machinery; the combination of opportunity, energy, and vice that kept Leadville running full blast twenty-four hours a day.

Carried along by Wheeler's optimism and his own sense of the extraordinary opportunities associated with mining, Hallam capitulated. He sent a telegram to Hyman. Delivered early on the morning of January 22, 1880, signed by both Hallam and Wheeler, it read, "THERE IS A TIDE IN THE AFFAIRS OF MEN WHICH IF TAKEN AT ITS

FLOOD, LEADS ON TO FORTUNE. WE CONGRATULATE YOU. WE HAVE DRAWN UPON YOU AT SIGHT FOR FIVE THOUSAND DOLLARS." Little did Hyman realize on that cold winter morning that the brief message he held in his hand was a marching order summoning him to a campaign that would last for twenty years and stretch across the continent.[2]

The telegram provided an intriguing introduction to western mining. When Hyman received an explanatory letter from Hallam a few days later, he was less intrigued and more worried. The full account of the transactions that Hallam (with Wheeler) had entered into on behalf of Hyman made it clear that much more than $5,000 was at stake. Hallam had taken a bond on seven and one-half mining locations in the Roaring Fork District, in what was then Gunnison County, Colorado. The total purchase price was $165,000, of which Hallam had paid down (Hyman's) $5,000, the remainder due on June 1, 1880. Hyman now realized that the $5,000 pledged by his friend for investment was only the first payment of a large sum for which he had become obligated. "I never contemplated involving myself in a transaction of that kind and I was horrified when I learned the terms of it," Hyman later wrote. Nevertheless, he determined to explore fully the properties he had unknowingly purchased and to make a judgment about their potential profitability for him and whether this profitability could be used to raise the capital necessary to conclude the transaction.[3]

In February 1880, David Hyman boarded a train for Colorado. It was his first trip west of the Mississippi. While Hyman conferred with Hallam and experienced firsthand the endless talk of fortunes to be made in mining properties, Wheeler skied into the camp on the Roaring Fork and made an on-site inspection. Hyman went back to Cincinnati, leaving Hallam to protect their interests. On his return to Leadville, B. Clark Wheeler telegraphed Hyman that each of the four principal claims—the Smuggler, the Durant, the Monarch, and the Iron—was worth more than the pruchase price agreed to for all the claims. Wheeler did not add, but Hyman probably guessed, that he had "inspected" the claims under five feet of snow. Hyman never really trusted Wheeler, and this incident did nothing to establish his confidence. For Hyman, who dealt in the reality of hard numbers, Wheeler, his arms whirling like a windmill, and his black beard pointed at his listener like a weapon, was a man who talked grandiose schemes involving someone else's money. It was not a style that Hyman liked; Wheeler was not the sort of partner he wanted in his future investment plans.

Still, Hyman was intrigued. He now decided to pursue the acquisition of the claims to the extent of seeing if he could raise the remainder of the purchase price. Hyman later wrote of his reluctance to undertake the mining venture, but he could have backed out at any time. That he determined to go ahead and raise such a large sum speaks more forcefully than his later disclaimers. At the very moment when Hyman contemplated his options, he was called upon by a representative of Abel D. Breed, the former Cincinnatian now resident in New York City, who was already an investor in mines in the Roaring Fork Valley, something Hyman did not know. Hyman knew Breed by reputation as the founder of an enormously profitable casket company, and equally through his sale of the Caribou mines in Boulder County, Colorado, to a Dutch syndicate for $1 million. Breed might be the answer to his problems. So Hyman took the train to New York City in April. Breed was all enthusiasm. According to Hyman's account, his first words were "Young man, I want to congratulate you for you are the first man that I have known who struck a fortune in the very first venture." Hyman could not help being pleased. Here was an optimistic report on his mining properties from a successful mining investor who could provide the capital to purchase and perhaps even develop them.

Breed got right to the point. How much money had Hyman invested in the claims? he wanted to know. Hyman replied that his investment and immediate contractual obligations amounted to $16,000. If he matched that sum, Breed asked, how much of an interest in the enterprise would Hyman offer? Hyman replied one-third. Breed agreed. He immediately sat down and wrote out a check for $16,000, which he handed over with declarations that he would furnish additional funds to help carry the enterprise through. Hyman drew up a document that gave the agreement legal form. He returned to Cincinnati encouraged. For the first time, he had confidence in the value of the mining properties that he had contracted to purchase. If an experienced mining investor like Breed believed in the claims in the Roaring Fork Valley sufficiently to become associated with them, then Hyman felt reassured.[4]

Back in Cincinnati, Hyman discovered that his problems of raising money had vanished, for he found himself surrounded by a crowd of eager investors. Breed spread word of the riches of the mines through his own Cincinnati lawyer. Hyman was transformed virtually overnight into a local sensation. Members of the Cincinnati bar and distinguished judges began to refer to him as "David Millionaire Hyman." Hyman knew full well that the debts of his enterprise far exceeded his small investment, but his experience was instructive in one respect. An Ohio Valley river city a thousand miles from the Rocky Mountains had proved as susceptible to the blandishments of the fortunes to be made in mining as Denver or Leadville had. That hardheaded professional men in Cincinnati believed that David Hyman had become a million-aire in three months by investing a few thousand dollars in Colorado silver mines suggests something of the value system that gripped the entire nation where mining was concerned. The fabled golden cities for which the Spanish conquistadores had searched for three centuries had not disappeared from the imaginations and expectations of nineteenth-century Americans. Now they were silver cities. But no matter, the Americans of David Hyman's Cincinnati believed as devoutly as their Spanish mining ancestors, and they were willing to back their faith with their hard-earned dollars.

Hyman wasted little time pondering the contrast between changes in his fortune and the persistence of human values. He returned imme-diately to Colorado, where he intended to use Breed's funds to change the terms of the original contract. From the arrival of Hallam's letter spelling out the details of the purchase, Hyman knew that he could not realistically hope to make a professional examination of the properties and raise $160,000 by June 1. His only chance for success in meeting the terms of the sale lay in changing the terms. Through small pay-ments and much talk, he persuaded the original claimants to extend the terms and to modify the "bonding" on the properties. Under the new agreement, on June 1 he would pay $55,000, or a third of the purchase price rather than the whole, with the balance due in sixty days. Hyman also engaged the services of John B. Farish, a young mining engineer, to make an on-site inspection of the claims and report his judgments before the date when the first payments came due. The parties now dispersed. Farish went to the Roaring Fork Valley; Hallam, to Leadville to seek a large investor who would become a financial partner; and Hyman, to Cincinnati, where he awaited Farish's report and prepared to raise money from his many friends captivated by the fortunes to be made in mining.

Hyman soon returned to Denver with the necessary funds and, in late May, Farish met him at the Windsor Hotel. The professional opin-ion he offered was not clear-cut: both the value of the mining pro-perties and the condition of the title remained uncertain. Whatever Farish's standing as a mining engineer—and he would later develop a national reputation—he had rightly spied a persistent legal problem that plagued western mining in general and that would confront Hy-man in particular. The issue had to do with the practical circumstances and legal requirements that surrounded the making of an original claim. Under federal law, the claimant located a lode or vein on which he drove a discovery stake with the date of the discovery, the name of the claim, the name of the locator, and a general indication of the direction of the claim. The claimant then had sixty days in which to do the necessary "development work" and then another sixty days in which to mark the boundaries of his claim and file a location certificate with the county recorder of the county in which the claim was located, or of the nearest county thereto (the first Aspen claims of 1879 had been filed in Leadville, county seat of Lake County). The certificate gave the boundaries of the claim. But as the claim had been made by a prospector who was almost certainly not a trained surveyor, the law provided that after the claim had been legally entered, the claimant should have the right to file an "amended certificate," giving the exact legal limits of the claim as described by a professional surveyor.

Many of the mining claims in the valley of the Roaring Fork suffered from the circumstances of their location and subsequent survey. The Leadville party led by Charles E. Bennett that had staked the first claims had employed a surveyor, Jack Christian, to plat their claims in the valley. Christian finished the survey of the Smuggler, but before he could complete the other claims, news of the Ute uprising sent him across the Continental Divide to Leadville. He never returned. Nor did the prospecting parties send someone else. As word of the value of the claims spread—a process in part promoted by the prospectors themselves as a way of increasing the value of their holdings—others reached the Roaring Fork in early spring 1880 and located a number of conflicting claims across the lines of the originals. Farish quite properly pointed out the presence of the competing claims to his employer. Hyman, on the advice of a Colorado lawyer familiar with mining litigation, now demanded a perfect title; when the owners refused to give him one, he declined to close the deal and returned to Cincinnati. There, he gathered up his family for a vacation on Long Island in New York State. His mining "adventure" seemed over.[5]

It was not. Once again, Hyman was awakened by a telegram, this time on a Sunday morning in late June. Hallam reported the discovery of ore in the Smuggler claim so valuable as to constitute a "bonanza." So rich was the strike that Hallam and Farish had carefully covered up their workings for fear the discovery would become known and cause a mining rush to the site. Hallam concluded by quoting Farish's own words: "ADVISE YOU TO RETURN TO COLORADO IMMEDIATELY AND CLOSE UP THE DEAL." On the three-day train ride west, Hyman kept in constant telegraphic communication with Hallam. By the time he reached Denver, the assays had confirmed the importance of the strike (if not a "bonanza"), and the value of the mine seemed beyond question. Hyman immediately communicated his intentions to the owners, and on July 1 the two parties met to consummate the deal. In exchange for the seven and one-half claims under option, Hyman and his associates agreed to pay $55,000 on the spot and the remainder of the purchase price within sixty days.[6]

Hyman returned to his suite of rooms in the Grand Hotel, where he was staying, at three o'clock in the afternoon. There he found waiting for him a telegram from Farish giving decisive reasons against the purchase. In his own words, "It was indeed a disheartening discovery." Hyman, who had returned thinking himself a rich man (or at least a potentially rich man), now had reason to think himself ruined. The two men conferred, and each responded to his characteristic way. "Come let's take a drink," said Charles Hallam. "No," replied Hyman. "This is not the time to drink but to think." Think he did, through the night. Early the next morning, the two men started for Aspen to see for themselves what they had or did not have.[7]

The trip from Buena Vista across the pass on foot in the summer of 1880 with other mining-camp immigrants and the physical experience of the mining camp made an indelible impression on Hyman. He loved the physical beauty of the Roaring Fork Valley, and he responded to the energy and tumult of a new mining camp in its first full summer of life.

At the same time, he found himself confronted with a wide range of things that he knew nothing about. Hyman was a lawyer, a man of extraordinary talents in the fields of law and, if early experience was any guide, of finance and financing. The mining camp was another world. Here, he was the merest novice. By his own admission, he knew little about mining law, nothing about mining, and even less about how to survive in a young mining camp. This education in the world beyond the city limits of Leadville began with the trip over Cottonwood Pass. Hallam and Hyman walked from Buena Vista to Aspen, and Hyman, a man of sedentary habits, did not take kindly to the exercise. The second morning, a prospector offered Hyman a pony for $50, and the Cincinnati lawyer took it. He neglected to remove the saddle, however, and within a short distance discovered that the animal's back had such a severe sore that it could not be ridden. So Hyman walked to Aspen, leading his purchase by the reins.

After he and Hallam had found accommodations, the two men walked up to the Smuggler mine. It lay at the foot of Smuggler Mountain, easily accessible from the camp and distinguished by the enormous outcropping on the side of the hill that marked the site of the tunnel entrance. Hyman peered around, looked at some of the ore, and admired the view. He made several trips up to the mine, perhaps because it was the only one of his properties that was readily accessible. Perhaps he also hoped to gain some insight into his future by studying the rock outcropping up close. What it revealed, if anything, he never said. His account noted only, "I went over to see it many times and wondered to what it would lead."

Hyman and Hallam stayed in Aspen for a week; when they returned, Hyman made some basic decisions. He designated Hallam his general manager in charge of mining operations; in the future, he would confine himself to the financial and legal aspects of the enterprise. Among the properties purchased were two ranches, one of them the site of the camp. Hyman now sold the campsite to a Philadelphia corporation—the Aspen Town and Land Company. He had no time to manage a real estate business along with mining. Henceforth, he would concentrate on the mining properties alone. As he would discover, they were quite complex enough to absorb much of his time and energy for the next twenty years.[8]

Between 1880 and 1882, David Hyman came to terms with the first of his new duties in connection with his new properties—namely, raising the necessary capital and drawing up suitable financial instruments. He now turned his attention to the second—litigation. In many respects, litigation was the key to the development of Aspen. During the early period of struggle to survive as a camp and during the transition to a town in 1884 and 1885 with the arrival of Jerome B. Wheeler, Hyman occupied a central position in litigation over the mines around Aspen. He was plaintiff and defendant. He fought cases in the local courts and in the state supreme court. He became famous for his knowledge of mining law and infamous for enlarging the part law played in a camp's development. As such, he was not a popular figure—indeed, he was sometimes vilified for seeming to hinder the camp's growth—but he was often right in the legal sense. Hyman and his activities lay at the heart of Aspen's growth, because much relating to the development of the camp (and of every mining camp, for that matter) depended on what the law allowed people to do or not do.

David Hyman's experiences in Aspen's first seven years reveal much about the inner workings of a mining camp. What we learn from watching him is that mining was a major industrial enterprise, with overtones of law, high finance, and influence in all sorts of places. The task of carrying a mine from claim to production of silver ore stretched before the owner uncertain, costly, and filled with hidden difficulties. The mines with the richest mineral deposits were not always the most profitable; the ingredients of luck, skill, and timing played significant roles in the mining business. Hyman had the skill to blend with luck and opportunity. He emerged as a consummate financier. He created capital where none existed; he developed new interpretations of mining law and the relationship of this law to the growth of the camp. These were the basic questions about any mining camp and any mining enterprise. Who owned what? Who owed whom? Who was free to mine and under what conditions? These questions dominated Aspen's early mining life. David Hyman not only provided answers to these questions but also helped to shape the questions themselves.

The seven and one-half mining properties that Hyman and Hallam acquired were claims of quite different legal and economic status, as events over the next few years would come to show. The partners concentrated on the Smuggler, where they explored extensively, did development work as required by law, and even selected some lots of ore for shipment to Leadville. The Smuggler was a claim of enormous potential. Exploration work would show that it contained huge deposits of low-grade ore, ranging from fifteen to thirty ounces of silver per ton. Such ore could not be profitably mined and packed over the passes to Leadville for processing. The Smuggler claim needed a railroad. But if Aspen should have a railroad—a condition that all Aspen boosters agreed was inevitable—then the mine would prove immensely valuable. The other quality about the Smuggler was its clear title. It had been carefully surveyed by the professional surveyor sent to the Roaring Fork Valley by the original claimants, and the properly filed amended location put it beyond legal assault. In addition to the Smuggler, Hyman had uncontested claims to other mining properties, principally the 1001 and the Mose, and in due course he applied for and received patents from the federal government for these three mining properties.

The Durant was the other valuable Hyman-Hallam mine. It contrasted with the Smuggler in almost every respect. Flanked on the east side by the Emma and on the west by the Aspen, the Durant lay on Aspen Mountain astride the great mineral belt that gave Aspen its silver riches. The ores of the Durant were extremely rich, giving it an immediate value that put it in a class with the Spar, the Emma, and the Aspen, mines that could be worked profitably with a local smelter (if one existed), and its ores could even be packed by jack train to Granite. Assays of Durant ores ran from one hundred ounces per ton and up. Unfortunately for the owners, an uncompleted survey clouded title to the claim. The Ute uprising had halted surveying activity at a crucial moment. No amended location form had been filed on time, and several counterclaims covered parts of the Durant. As early as 1881, Hyman estimated that he confronted some ten to fifteen of these "adverse suits." By "adverse suit" he meant simply a conflicting claim that encroached somewhere on the Durant's original rectangle.

No sooner had he completed the purchase agreement than David Hyman found himself in court defending the Durant against all manner of interlopers. Under the procedure established by the General Land Office for proving final title to a claim, the claimant was required to advertise the claim for a specified period in a newspaper in the mining district where the property was located. The notice was an official declaration to the public that the claimant had made application for a patent, and under the legal language employed it notified all those who objected to his receiving title to make their objections known. Those who wished to do so had to file an "adverse claim" within thirty days—hence the name of the action. And, within another thirty days, the adverse claimant had to begin suit in an appropriate court, with a view to ascertaining the rightful ownership. After hearing suitable testimony from both sides, the court then became the final arbiter.

The tactics in pursuing an "adverse claim" depended on a variety of factors: the presumed value of the claim, the legal strength of the claim, and the financial strength of the party or parties involved. Litigation was expensive, not only in court but also in tying up the physical resources of the mine. The judge generally began the case by issuing an injunction—if one had been asked for by a party in the dispute—closing down the mine during the course of the litigation. Legal fees might be very high. Delays were common. Almost every substantial claimant liked to compromise "adverse claims" to get on with the business at hand, and many such claims were probably nuisance suits, made with the expectation that the owners of the major claim would buy out the adverse claimants. And it often worked that way. Of course, in this as in so much else in mining, the advantage lay with the stronger parties, who commanded the resources necessary to fight a long legal battle. And all these proceedings focused on a plot of ten acres or less—and some claims were much less—whose mineral value was still a matter of conjecture.

David Hyman later maintained that, on taking over the Durant in 1881, he could have silenced all the "adverse claims" for $25,000. But he did not have the necessary capital, so his only alternative was to fight them in court. While he fought the dozen court cases, the Durant became more valuable, increasing the stakes and escalating the price of compromise. Hyman generally pursued a policy of divesting himself of litigious properties. He made overtures to sell the Durant to David H.

Moffat, board member and later president of the Denver and Rio Grande Railroad Company, and Moffat's partner in many mining enterprises, United States Senator Jerome B. Chaffee of Colorado. Hyman asked $120,000. Moffat had no objection to the price, but at the last minute, after papers had been drawn up, he refused to involve himself in the litigation that obviously continued to surround the mine. Next, Hyman tried to sell the Durant to Jerome B. Wheeler, the New York merchant and financier, who had already invested hundreds of thousands of dollars in Aspen and its vicinity. Wheeler also declined, believing, according to Hyman, that the two Cincinnatians did not have sufficient capital to continue litigation, and he would eventually buy the property for less. Having failed to compromise, Hyman continued his court battles, but they were long and expensive, for as Wheeler developed the Spar and others made great strikes in the Emma and the Aspen, the value of the Durant rose.[9]

By the end of 1884, Hyman had narrowed his interests to the Smuggler and the Durant. He had fought off a dozen "adverse suits" to the Durant, including some that had come to trial. He had comprised where he had thought his interest profited thereby. His legal battles were not ended, however. They had only begun. What had taken place from early 1881 to early 1885 was simply a prelude to the great legal struggle that now loomed on the horizon. The confrontation pitted David Hyman, the Cincinnati lawyer, against the most prominent figure in Aspen's short but active history, Jerome B. Wheeler. The contest matched a man who had created a great mining empire through the investment of $500,000 against one who had created substantial mining holdings from an investment of $5,000. Hyman depended on his knowledge of the law and on his talent for compromise. Wheeler employed the best legal talent in the West and had no intention of compromising. At stake was a fortune for the victor. At stake, too, was the future of the town of Aspen.

8

Hyman v. Wheeler:
The Fight over the Apex

"Having a knowledge of law and litigations I can say truthfully that no litigation equals a mining litigation in its intensity and bitterness." So wrote David M. Hyman.[1] He knew whereof he spoke. Litigation was the handmaiden of mining. The two were inseparable. And in one of those direct relationships that carry their own ironclad logic, the more prosperous the camp, the more litigation. High stakes and the crowds of so-called lawyers raised the level of greed, already well developed in the Rocky Mountain mining camps, where fortunes were made and lost through the possession of a single acre of ground or a single slip of paper. The tendency to subdivide mining claims into ever-smaller fractions increased the numbers of interested parties who might carry their cases to the courts.

At first, camps welcomed litigation. It was a sign of adolescence, a youthful display of energy and an indication that the claims were sufficiently important to fight over, a part of growing up as a mining camp. Yet, like adolescence, it was a stage that mining camps wanted to pass through on the way to adulthood, stability, and producing mines. The camps that prospered and endured were those that carried their claims from speculation and litigation to large-scale production. Such rich producing mines had laid the basis for great silver cities like Virginia City and Leadville.

In Aspen, the fight over the apex—a vein of ore that is exposed on the surface—went beyond any such cycle of growth. Begun in 1884, it lasted four full years. At issue was an aspect of mining law crucial for silver claims throughout Colorado and, indeed, up and down the Rockies. It joined in violent legal combat the town's leading mining entrepreneurs, Jerome B. Wheeler and David M. Hyman, and through them many of the town's other principal figures. This protracted courtroom struggle slowed Aspen's growth, precisely at the moment when the town seemed to be on the edge of prosperity and permanence. Accordingly, the issue engaged the attention of the entire community, for all Aspenites saw themselves vitally interested in the outcome. Litigation in general and the apex in particular brought to the fore a significant aspect of mining—namely, that while mining came to involve a large number of people in urban centers, a few entrepreneurs, technicians, and lawyers made decisions that determined the futures of these men, their families, and their camps. A single mineowner and his lawyer might hold a mining camp hostage almost indefinitely in pursuit of their own interests. Aspen's citizens thus came to think of the fight over the apex as their fight.

Mining camps had been centers of litigation since the first gold discoveries in California in 1848 spurred the development of a body of mining law, lawyers, and courts, all growing in size with the mining experience itself. Heretofore, such litigation in the first generation under American law had taken certain well-recognized (if often deplored) forms. First and foremost was the issue of conflicting claims. The small area at the center of the dispute, the casual ways in which men staked out their claims and then left for long periods, the two stages of the initial claim and the amended location—all of these laid the basis for endless lawsuits about surface ownership.

To these sources of litigation must be added the issue of fraud in transactions. Mining claims constantly changed hands, and most transactions occasioned few remarks and no legal repercussions. The reason for this was simply that most mining claims were unprofitable. When discovery of a particularly rich vein of ore transformed a claim into a "bonanza" for the lucky owners, those connected with the property in the past emerged from saloons and boardinghouses and hastened to cry "fraud." They charged that the new owners had deliberately concealed the value of the mine at the time of the sale and so had acquired the property at a price only a fraction of its real value. Numerous lawyers in search of clients could easily be found who would support such arguments in court. Prospectors, entrepreneurs, and speculators—there were only shades of differences among the three—who had eagerly accepted several hundred dollars for a claim (and had been glad to get it) now demanded several hundreds of thousands.

The appearance of Jerome B. Wheeler in Aspen served as a good case in point. His presence on the Aspen scene rapidly transformed the camp's market in mining claims. Wheeler apparently had unlimited capital and bought extensively in mining properties. Then, through expenditures of considerable additional sums on development, he found several valuable ore bodies. Those who had happily sold to him six months earlier now returned armed with injunctions, writs of various kinds, and companies of lawyers. Lawyers (his own too) and litigation swirled around Wheeler like bees around a honeypot. His presence in Aspen proved a "bonanza" for the legal profession as well as for other enterprises more directly connected with silver.

The fight over the apex did not fit the model of a conflict over surface area or the issue of fraud in sale. Rather, it dealt with the ownership of ore deep underground. To appreciate the importance of the dispute and the part played by Aspen's leading characters demands a brief excursion into mining law. The first great discoveries of gold in California in 1848 and the subsequent rush of hundreds of thousands to participate in this first mining rush took place in a legal and institutional void. California was, initially at least, unorganized. It had no courts, and the nation itself had no body of law for gold and silver that could be readily transferred to the placer-mining experience that engulfed this vast area. So men thrown together in the common enterprise of exploiting these great riches joined in making their own rules. Early California mining law—and later mining law on the other mining frontiers that expanded across the western third of the nation— was a combination of statute law and local custom. Miners' courts enforced these regulations with a kind of crude vigilante justice. What can be said of such arrangements is that they met the needs of new circumstances and had for their sanction the approval of local miners.[2]

In 1866, Congress passed the first comprehensive mining act to cover lode mining. This law accepted the legal status of a vast mining enterprise that had developed with little or no reference to congressional statute. A similar law in 1870 confirmed the same principles for placer mining. In other words, by 1870 Congress had enacted statutes to govern the exploitation of mineral resources, but the laws affirmed the status quo. Thus, the federal government would accept surveys, issue patents, and alienate the claims, and it would serve as a referee in disputes, but the rules were those established by local custom.[3]

The new mining law in 1872 was a considerable step toward a more coherent and consistent policy with respect to mining claims. It noted what kinds of information should be recorded in the local records, specified how the claims were to be marked, and laid out in detail the minimum "development work" necessary for the claim to be retained.

All these changes lent a degree of uniformity to what had been, to this point, inconsistent local sovereignty. At the same time, the new law included a statement on mineral veins that opened up a Pandora's box of troubles that would provide endless employment for lawyers and endless grief for owners. Under the law, the original claimant had to locate the boundaries of his claim in such a way as to cover the top of the exposed vein—or the apex. If he did so, and if the vein was continuous, then he had the right to follow the vein in its course deep underground. Such a right would almost invariably carry him into the underground space of surrounding surface claims.[4]

David M. Hyman, who would become so closely linked with apex litigation, described the law this way: "Under the Statutes of the United States, the discoverer and owner of a claim that has the top or apex of a lode or vein within its side lines, has the right to follow said vein or lode in its descent into the earth to any depth that he can trace the same although said vein or lode so far departs from a perpendicular as to take it outside of its side lines and into the lines of other claims adjoining it and below it; and the claims that are located along the course of this vein but below the side lines of the claims are known as side line claims, in fact they have no vein or lode of their own but simply encroach upon and mine the ore which belongs to the vein or lode the apex of which is in the claim above." Hyman's was the description of an interested observer who had fought over the principle in countless courtrooms. He saw the question as a legal one. A mining engineer, James D. Hague, surveying the wreckage of twenty years of litigation over the apex principle, viewed the issue in economic terms. He had recourse to the Bible to describe its implications, when he wrote, "To him that hath (the apex) shall more be given; but from him that hath not (the apex) shall be taken away even that which he hath." And so it would be, but not without a great struggle.[5]

Initially, the apex principle caused no particular difficulty. The great strikes on the Comstock Lode were more than ten years old in 1872, questions of ownership had long since been fought out or compromised, and the issue on the Comstock was technology and production. The question of the apex first came to prominence with the important discoveries at Leadville in 1878 that produced an abundance of rich claims worth fighting over. But even here the issue was not clear-cut, for Leadville's silver riches appeared in the form of a series of what became known as "blanket contacts," more like huge deposits of coal than continuous veins. Where veins did emerge in the model covered by the law of 1872, legal action followed. The upshot of the several legal cases brought in the Leadville courts was that while the law seemed clear on the point, juries refused to bring in verdicts support-ing the owner of the apex. Public opinion was hostile to the monopolis-tic implications of apex and the unsettling influence of constant litiga-tion, and local hostility overrode the clear intent of the law. Eventually, the several parties settled suits and went about the business of mining. Apex law lay abandoned in Leadville, where through accidents of indi-vidual combinations and widespread compromise the apex principle was never established. One of the unforeseen consequences of this circumstance was that many prominent mining men (and lawyers) as-sumed that the apex principle was dead or, alternatively, unenforce-able, at least in so far as Colorado silver mining was concerned.

It is important to remember that the court fight over the apex in Aspen was not over a matter of principle; it was over money, millions of dollars. The spark that lit the powder train was a flurry of activity on the Aspen claim. The Aspen had never attracted much attention, sur-rounded as it was by other, more publicized claims. In the summer of 1884, two Aspenites, J. D. Hooper (who was also mayor) and Charles Todd, leased the claim. After several months of desultory work, Hooper and Todd struck a rich vein of ore in November 1884. Their lease had only sixty days to run, and the drama of Aspen's first great strike worked against a deadline fascinated the camp. Those who liked to fantasize could walk past the piles of ore on the empty lots, pa-trolled by armed guards, and imagine themselves as owners or, if they were more civic-minded, conceive of the whole camp transformed by a series of such discoveries. Hooper and Todd became local heroes. Their lease was Aspen's first great bonanza. In sixty days, they took $600,000 worth of silver ore out of the ground.[6]

Not everyone was enthusiastic about the fortunes that Hooper and Todd made in the Aspen claim. David M. Hyman knew that the Aspen sidelined his Durant, and he suspected that the strike next door had been made in the vein that had its apex in his claim. The strike in the Aspen confronted him with a stark choice: whether to remain silent or to make a claim to the ore based on the Durant's apex. He himself later wrote of the situation, "I must either raise money enough to assert my apex rights, or dispose of the property to someone else who had the means to fight the case, or abandon my rights altogether."[7]

Hyman decided to fight. He and Hallam had done no work on the Durant. He realized that to permit the ore in the Aspen to go unchal-lenged would cost him a potential fortune, for he lacked the capital to develop the Durant immediately. Furthermore, other strikes on the Durant apex were sure to follow on other sidelining claims. Hyman was also convinced that legally he was right, that the intent of the law of 1872 was clear on this point, and that, barring corruption in the courts, his case was by far the stronger. He filed suit in the District Court of Pitkin County, asking for half the ore taken from the Aspen and for a court-appointed receiver to manage the mine until the court could establish ownership.[8]

Hyman's suit produced a collective consternation in the camp. After four years in the isolated wilderness of the mining world, Aspen was on the verge of the promised land, and at precisely the moment when the endless dreams of prosperity seemed destined to become reality a single man threatened to send the camp back to the Dark Ages. "The people are wild with excitement and indignation," warned B. Clark Wheeler in his *Aspen Daily Times*. The threat came from the reality of Aspen's geologic surroundings. There were by this time some five hundred mining claims in the immediate vicinity of the camp. Yet, only two claims, the Durant and the Spar, covered the apex vein where it surfaced on Aspen Mountain. Thus, the apex doctrine threatened to give these two claims a monopoly on the choicest mining opportunities.[9]

Within twenty-four hours of the filing of the suit, Aspen's citizens had taken sides, and for virtually all of them there was only one side. It was the "sideline" of the Aspen mine and Jerome B. Wheeler. In the popular view of the contest, the "apexers" represented monopoly for a few at the expense of the many, the end to growth and prosperity, and unfair advantage to half a dozen individuals and a corps of lawyers. The "sideline," by contrast, meant scores of prosperous claims and advantage to many entrepreneurs, miners, and merchants alike. The editor Wheeler summed up the issue in (for him) a few words: "No. Aspen is allright. The apex racket must go and the side lines prevail." Hyman could not have been more odious had he canceled the Fourth of July and arrested Santa Claus. Aspenites thought he intended to hold the entire camp hostage in his own self-interest. The camp's newspapers, which disagreed on every other issue of life in the Roaring Fork Valley, united in their denunciations of David Hyman and his apex doctrine.[10]

The preliminary suit *Little Giant* v. *Durant* came to trial in mid-May 1885 before Judge L. M. Goddard in the District Court of Pitkin County. The contest pitted Hyman and his associates against Jerome B. Wheeler, H. P. Cowenhoven, and E. T. Butler, each of whom owned a one-third interest in the Little Giant. The oral arguments—somewhat unusual, for such cases were usually tried by written affidavits from experts—lasted three weeks. Judge Goddard's decision went directly to the basic principles of the case—namely, that the Durant owners claimed a lode or vein such as that identified in the mining law of 1872, that the vein (in this case) dipped into the ground, that it was continuous and went within the surface boundaries of the Aspen mine, that the ore being mined in the Aspen did, in fact, belong to the vein of the Durant, and that the owners of the Durant were entitled to it. In short, the ruling was a complete victory for the apexers. Judge Goddard appointed Tingley S. Wood of Leadville a court receiver for the mine, pending the outcome of the litigation.[11]

Judge Goddard's decision stunned the defendants, the camp, and the legal and mining community of Colorado. On the advice of their counsel, Wheeler, Cowenhoven, and Butler immediately appealed the case to the federal court in Denver. Aside from the natural instincts of any lawyer to reject defeat and to appeal, the circumstances surrounding the case lent credence to their views and the defendants' certainty of their inevitable triumph. For a generation, western mining law had been grounded in local custom, a doctrine recognized and codified in the mining law of 1866. The legal precedents of Leadville only a few years earlier testified to the continuing impact of local influence. Whatever statute law said, Leadville's judges, lawyers, and citizens sitting as a jury had interpreted it in their way, namely, that the doctrine of the sidelines prevailed, and it triumphed for precisely those reasons that had made local mining law so significant. The sideline doctrine represented the greatest good for the greatest number; it stood for stability and the status quo when such conditions supported the continued growth and prosperity of the Leadville camp; and it was a classic case of local juries overruling statute law. The suit in Aspen was another confrontation between the irresistible force of local custom and the immovable object of statute law in the form of the mining law of 1872. This time the outcome was different. Judge Goddard supported the law. The owners of the Aspen claim and their lawyers now carried the case to Denver, confident that the results would be different when they argued the case before a jury of their peers.

In the aftermath of the decision in favor of the apex, the reactions of the camp changed from sly digs against fools on a goose chase to outright denunciations of a conspiracy against a town that had grown to five thousand people. The conflict became personal. It was Jerome B. Wheeler, the personification of virtue and civic-mindedness, against the meddlesome outsider, David M. Hyman. That Hyman had been involved in the affairs of the camp a full three years before Wheeler ever heard of Aspen was insignificant alongside the roles that each now played.

The threat of apex litigation was especially serious because it seemed to endanger the ultimate facility for a mining camp—a railroad. At precisely the same time when Judge Goddard considered the case of the Durant's apex vein, David H. Moffat, Jr., president of the Denver and Rio Grande, and his partner, the former United States senator Jerome B. Chaffee, of the D&RG's board of directors, visited Aspen. The camp greeted their arrival with more public notice than it had since the first appearance of Wheeler. The parallel was an exact one. Wheeler had the capacity to deliver what the camp needed most at the time—a smelter. He had done so. It was assumed that Moffat could deliver the railroad. A single word from him, and a score of mines with low-grade ore could be transformed from holding operations to bonanzas.[12]

The two men stayed five days and left all smiles, impressed with Aspen's beauty and enterprise. Moffat called it "a fine town, full of energy and considerable capital." Yet both men were also concerned about the amount of litigation under way. Chaffee, especially, addressed the problem in terms of the long-range future of the camp: "I have always found that where litigation figured prominently in mining the people suffered, and so it is in this case." He continued with an eloquent paean to the contributions of Wheeler and the duty of the camp to rally around him. "The people of Aspen stand in the same relation to Mr. J. B. Wheeler that the country at large does to the old soldier whose fame ranks with the famous of the earth," he noted, "and they would show an ingratitude unpardonable and a slight appreciation of their interests were they not to render him most efficient aid in the law suits that now envelop him as a fog." Having proceeded to establish Wheeler as the General Ulysses S. Grant of the mining world, Chaffee went on to say why Aspenites should rank themselves under his leadership. "Their own preservation demands it," thundered the ex-senator turned railroad and mining entrepreneur. "With the apex question successful, their little prospects in close proximity to rich mines would be swept away into the vortex of the universal destruction which awaits all interests outside of that little coterie of capitalists."[13]

Aside from the irony of Chaffee and Moffat delivering lectures on the "little coterie of capitalists"—for they were certainly charter members—the message struck a resonant chord in all Aspenites. The apex suit threatened the present prosperity and future prospects of the town, and so affected professional miners, day laborers, and merchants alike; it also blighted the prospects of incipient capitalists who aspired to share in the riches of the surrounding mountainsides. Anger replaced uneasiness. The message seemed to be that the town was fine, that it was the Durant's owners who were out of step with the community.

The apex cases had moved to Denver, but interest remained intense in Aspen. Throughout the fall, Aspenites contented themselves with a mixture of hope and expectation, a sense that the cases would not really come to trial, but that if they did the jury would support the sideliners. Their wild speculations actually had a certain basis in reality. Sideliners as well as apexers had their problems. Wheeler's difficulty was the law in the form of the mining act of 1872; Hyman seemed to have the law on his side, but he, too, had a problem. He was running out of money. The legal costs of the early fight had exhausted his war treasury, and each subsequent legal action forced him to devote a major part of his time and energy to raising additional funds. He began in February, as soon as he brought suit against the Aspen mine. On the advice of his New York friends—Wheeler was not the only principal with contacts in New York City—Hyman approached Albert E. Reynolds, a man experienced in mining affairs and a capitalist of some standing. Reynolds agreed to supply $25,000 of capital in exchange for a quarter share in all the mining properties in which Hyman had an interest. The terms were hard, but Hyman had no choice but to accept. He was confident that victory in the case would increase the value of his holdings more than enough to offset the share now conveyed to Reynolds.[14]

Hyman also tried other strategies to reduce the expense and delay of apex litigation. To begin with, he tried to sell the Durant, and the proposed purchasers were none other than Moffat and Chaffee. The asking price was $120,000. In the end, Moffat declined to become involved in the litigation that would surely result—indeed was already resulting—and, instead, he and Chaffee went to Aspen, where they publicly supported Wheeler and the sideliners. There is a certain irony in their attacks so soon after they themselves nearly became the owners of the Durant.

His first effort failed, Hyman now sought the man who was the logical owner of the Durant, Jerome B. Wheeler. Through intermediaries, he arranged a meeting in New York City between Wheeler and Charles Hallam, at which time Hallam offered the Durant to Wheeler for $70,000. As a principal in R. H. Macy's department store, which held two sales a year, Wheeler would have been pleased to know that the Durant property was now discounted a third from the figure quoted to Moffat and Chaffee. Yet, he, too, after consulting his advisers, declined. Hyman, understandably disappointed, thought that Wheeler had been badly advised. Perhaps he had been.[15]

In hindsight, it was an unfortunate decision, for the costs of the litigation would reach ten times that figure for his side alone. The problem was simply that Wheeler thought he would win. He was so advised by his associates and his lawyers. How could he think differently? Writing on June 10, 1885, just before the case came to trial, James J. Hagerman pressed Wheeler not to purchase. "I forgot to mention that Durant stock. I do not believe I would buy any of it," he advised. "Perhaps we can 'bust' their whole claim. The lawyers seem to think so." For all these reasons, Wheeler decided against compromise or purchase and in favor of a court battle. Perhaps such a course was inevitable. He had dominated the mining world of Aspen since his appearance there, he was accustomed to getting his way, and the Leadville precedent seemed to give him every expectation of victory.[16]

The transfer of the apex case to the federal court in Denver placed it under the jurisdiction of Judge Moses Hallett. Hallett was an outstanding jurist, renowned for his integrity and devotion to the law at a time and in a place where legal skulduggery was all too common. He was also arbitrary and opinionated. He held strong views against receivers. Accordingly, he refused to accept the lower-court order for a receiver to manage the Aspen mine. The Wheeler-Cowenhoven-Butler management remained in control. Perhaps this stance—taken with the usual Hallett vigor—gave the sideliners a false sense of security. Hyman, who came to respect Hallett, always maintained that the failure to appoint a receiver represented a turning point in the failure of the owners of the Aspen to compromise and fixed them in their determination to see the case through to the bitter end. As it turned out, the end was bitter and expensive. The overwhelming expense made it bitter for losers and no better than bittersweet for the victors.

With the case scheduled to come to trial in Denver in late 1885, both sides scrambled to enlist the most-knowledgeable and best-known legal talent possible. In Colorado, the choices were legion. Mining litigation was a huge industry, most of it centered in Denver. Hyman's principal lawyer was Charles J. Hughes, Jr., and he also contracted the professional services of Henry M. Teller, United States senator from the state of Colorado. Wheeler and his associates hired Thomas M. Patterson, Charles S. Thomas, and J. M. Downing, each an experienced and respected mining lawyer. In addition, each side lined up the customary corps of mining engineers to give "expert" testimony in the case. The presence of such a roster of professional people before the case even came to trial suggests why such litigation was so expensive.[17]

There were two cases to be tried in connection with the conflict over the Aspen's ores, one on the question of the existence of the apex within the Durant claim, the second on the apex versus sideline principle. The first case was that of the *Little Giant* v. *Durant*. It came to trial in December 1885, and in late November a mass of mining owners, managers, engineers, and other "experts" journeyed from Aspen to Denver, some to testify, others just to observe, but all determined to be in attendance. The question at issue was not the apex matter but a challenge to the legality of the Durant claim and its boundaries. The plaintiffs argued that the amended location certificate to the Durant had been filed too late to give its present boundaries legal standing. Hyman responded for the Durant that the amended location certificate dated back to and superseded the original location certificate and that the boundary of the mine (even if amended) was continuous and legally sound from its first claim. By agreement of the two sides, the case was tried without jury and before Judge Hallett alone. At the end of three weeks of "expert" testimony and vigorous arguments by counsel, Hallett found for the Durant. The case was an important one, for it established beyond legal doubt the Durant's ironclad claim to the apex of the mineral vein on Aspen Mountain.[18]

The preliminaries concluded, each side settled down to prepare for the main event, the so-called apex principle, under which the owners of an apex vein might leave their sidelines and penetrate into the underground space of the adjacent mines in pursuit of a continuous vein. The loud outcries that accompanied the first rounds in Aspen and Denver were now succeeded by a profound silence, as if the Colorado mining community in general and the silver camp of Aspen in particular held their collective breaths, afraid to exhale lest they disturb some significant mining principle floating in the air before them.

Preparations for the apex trial—*Hyman* v. *Wheeler and others*, as it was known in the courts—consumed the entire year 1886. They involved a frenzy of activity on the part of both sides and of Judge Hallett himself. Hallett was well aware of the stakes involved; the temptations for manipulating the law might be irresistible, especially as the case would be tried before a jury. Judge Hallett brought a man named Wilkie, the head of the United States Secret Service, to Denver in order to prevent attempts to manipulate jurors. Hyman and his associates had what he called "the numerous men employed by us for detective purposes" who circulated through the crowd and tried to ferret out jury tampering. The swirl of the courtroom, with its crowds of counsel, prospective jurors, newspaper reporters, private detectives, expert witnesses, interested parties, and simply observers of all kinds, produced an intense excitement. Rumors abounded—of conspiracy, compromise, perjury, and of the legal decision to come.[19]

In such an atmosphere, Judge Hallett convened the court in November 1886, and the opposing sides began the critical process of selecting prospective jurors. After several challenges and the eventual seating of the jury under the watching eye of Wilkie, Judge Hallett directed that the twelve men chosen be held incommunicado for the duration of the trial and placed them under the charge of the United States marshal, to whom he administered a special oath for this purpose. The marshal kept the jurors secluded at a hotel until the conclusion of the case. The stage was at last set for what the *New York Times* would call "the most important mining case ever tried in Colorado."[20]

In the mining town of Aspen, the trial provoked a frenzy of excitement, a mixture of legal speculation, mining jargon, and emotional appeals. Newspapers set the tone, conjuring up pictures of a deserted camp, empty streets, boarded-up stores, the mining riches of the surrounding mountainsides in the hands of a few monopolists. "The introduction of the apex horror into Aspen was fatal to her best interests, and has blighted, like the plagues of Egypt, her brightest hopes and fairest prospects," commented the *Sun*. As the implications of the extended litigation became manifest on all sides, the *Aspen Times* came out for compromise. Let the two sides reach an honorable agreement that would protect their interests and, by their accord, the interests of the town. "NEVER!" cried the *Sun*. Does one compromise with the devil? Does one compromise with sin? "The chief of the side-line—Mr. J. B. Wheeler, will uphold principle, it is that which makes men; the New Yorker is every inch a man."[21]

On the eve of the trial, the *Sun* attempted to mobilize the forces of public opinion by a series of interviews with a broad cross section of Aspenites to demonstrate the camp's solidarity in support of the side-line principle. Sixty-two opinions appeared in the newspaper, with the respondents identified by name. All were men; all were residents of the town. An examination of their views suggests to us something about the nature of the town and the hopes and fears of the people who lived there together, even beyond the issues of the case, which only a very few of the respondents could have understood in its complexity.[22]

R. C. WILSON: "When Dan Kraft and myself were digging and struggling to find ore on the VALLEJO, there were no apexers to tell us to stop. We found the ore, a hundred thousand dollars was the result. I believe the wealth of the mountains should be distributed among the many; apex means concentration of capital."

JACK ATKINSON: "I have lived in the mining camps of Colorado since 1860; I know nothing but mining. The trouble is Reynolds, Arms, and Hyman capitalists, and men of that ilk, non-residents of Pitkin county say 'you miners have developed a good thing over there; we have got more money than you miners and we will try and take your claims away from you.' I don't believe the laws of this country will permit them to do it."

HOOPES & CO: "If the side line wins not a merchant in Aspen will be able to fill his orders."

J. W. DALTON: "I am praying every night for the side line, and I know the Lord is on our side."

ALDERMAN BURKE: "I am glad to be able to say to you that I am for the side line."

SAM GARRET: "Side line is the people's best friend; it protects the miner, the pioneer and the orphans. The apexers should go to Jerusalem and hunt for the tomb of Christ."

DISTRICT CLERK LONERGAN: "I am neutral, independent, disinterested, and non-commital."

In the midst of the most emotional issue in the camp's history, the men interviewed still managed to sound like themselves: the rugged individual miner who had found success; the equally intense professional who had not yet had luck but still hoped. To these should be added merchants, who cared about business, not about principle. The local politician placed himself carefully on the side of the majority; the public official refused to be drawn into the controversy.

The trial lasted three weeks. As befits a legal issue of such importance, it produced a brilliant display by the most renowned lawyers of the Rocky Mountain West. Crowds of observers competed for seats every day. The parade of witnesses who took the stand gave tangible evidence of what observers already knew—namely, that professional mining engineers disagreed just as strongly as newspaper editors and other amateurs about the applicability of the case of *Hyman* v. *Wheeler and others*.[23]

Judge Moses Hallett's charge to the jury laid out the salient issues of the case. He began by pronouncing the outcropping of mineral on the Durant a "vein or lode" in the language of the mining act of 1872. The vein or lode surfaced within the boundaries of the Durant. The question that the jury had to pass judgment on was the relationship of that vein or lode to the underground mineral deposits of the Emma, some distance down Aspen Mountain. In Hallett's words, "The plaintiffs must show an apex or outcrop within his claim as far south as the Emma claim extends, which is, I believe, about 750 feet." In short, the issue was the continuous nature of the vein. If defining the problem was straightforward—and Judge Hallett believed that it was clear— passing judgment was extraordinarily difficult, for the parties in the case had inundated the jury with all manner of evidence, much of it conflicting. Hallett remarked, "With models and views of the mountain, and maps of all openings in the mine, with ores from the mine and rocks of the different strata, and assays and analyses showing their value and composition, and by the testimony of many witnesses, the parties have done all in their power to enlighten you in respect to the nature of the controversy." He might have added, and did so by implication, that the parties had also done much to confuse as well as enlighten.

Judge Hallett did not permit his toleration of differences of opinion to extend to all circumstances, however, and he singled out the testimony of a witness named Thompson to show such limits. When Thompson had tried to sell the Camp Bird mine two years earlier, he had sworn to the existence of a vein of the kind found in the Spar and the Durant; in his testimony in the present case, he swore under oath that no such vein existed on Aspen Mountain. Upon cross-examination, Thompson admitted that his earlier reports were false and that he had known them to be false when he wrote them. He had issued them with a view to selling the Camp Bird. He continued that he "was not in this country for his health, and that such things had to be done in mining business, although known to be false." Judge Hallett's upright character rebelled at this casual description of mining enterprise. He ordered the testimony stricken from the record, but his righteous anger could not conceal a mining world where Thompson's business principles seemed all too casually accepted.[24]

Even the most dramatic events must come to end. On December 23, the jury filed into the courtroom under the watchful eye of Judge Hallett. "Have you reached a verdict?" intoned the Judge. "We have, Your Honor," replied the foreman in the time-honored language of the Anglo-Saxon court. Amid a profound hush, Judge Hallett polled the jurors one by one. The verdict was unanimous. A jury of twelve peers like those provided for in the Magna Carta had found for the plaintiffs. David Hyman and his colleagues had won. The apex doctrine had been upheld. During the elated celebration of the winners and the stunned silence of the losers came the expected notice of appeal. The triumph was in part personal. Teller, Hughes, and Hyman had emerged with reputations as the greatest legal authorities on mining matters of the day. But the verdict had wider implications. The silver-mining world had changed. Aspen's place in it had become very precarious—at least if we are to believe the dire predictions made at the opening of the trial.[25]

It was better to win than to lose, but David Hyman and his associates knew full well that they had won only a major battle and not the war. The litigation had been enormously expensive, the relationship between the conflicting parties had become progressively embittered over two years of legal struggle, and the mines lay idle. Simultaneously with the announcement that the case would be appealed—which meant that the whole procedure would have to be repeated—the mine-owners in the dispute renewed their search for a common ground. The hunt for a compromise had earlier foundered on the conviction of Wheeler and his lawyers that, on the basis of the Leadville precedent, the sideline principle would be upheld in a jury trial, and on Hyman's equally strong views that his side could convince a jury otherwise. The decision had strengthened Hyman's hand in an absolute sense, but it was not clear that it had brought the two sides closer together. The basic question of how to put the mines into production remained, and, intimately connected to it, the future of the town of Aspen.

The leadership in the search for a compromise fell to James J. Hagerman, president of the Colorado Midland Railroad. Hagerman and his group of investors owned substantial mining interests on Aspen Mountain, including the Forest and the Little Giant mines. Hagerman now proposed a new mining company, and he persuaded Jerome B. Wheeler to put in his holdings and persuaded Hyman and his associates to do the same. The new company would be named the Compromise Mining Company, and it was organized in November 1887, almost a year after the landmark decision in Judge Hallett's court.[26]

In spite of the entreaties of Hagerman and Wheeler, two parties refused to join the new company. Wheeler had only a one-third inter-est in his side of the suit; Margaret Cowenhoven and E. T. Butler also owned thirds. David R. C. Brown, who had married the Cowenho-vens' daughter, managed his mother-in-law's interests. Persuaded by their lawyers, indignant at their defeat, for whatever reasons, Brown and Butler refused to enter into the compromise arrangements. The editor of the *Sun*, in an allusion to the Civil War, compared the contro-versy to the situation that existed at the time of Robert E. Lee's sur-render at Appomattox courthouse. The commanding general had given up, but several wings of his army continued to fight on, either ignorant of the end of the war or simply intransigent. Plans went forward for the new trial, scheduled for May 1888, and David Hyman noted in his account that "there was intense animosity developed on account of the nature of the litigation." Eventually, the two parties ceased communi-cating with one another.[27]

Finally, Hyman approached Senator Teller, one of his lawyers in *Hyman* v. *Wheeler*, to act as an emissary. Teller had known Cowenhoven for many years, and Hyman surmised that, though Cowenhoven would not negotiate with other members of his group, he would listen to Teller. Teller went to Aspen and called upon Cowenhoven in his home. His message got right to the point: it was a shame to spend a fortune on lawyers' fees when the mines were rich enough to satisfy both parties. Teller asked Cowenhoven to think the matter over, and to do so without consulting with his lawyers. Cowenhoven did this and accepted the same terms that had been offered to Wheeler a year earlier. Butler quickly fell into line, and the Compromise Mining Company was in business.[28]

It remained to reckon up the bill and pay it. Hyman calculated that the costs of litigation for his side, including expert witnesses and the intense development work necessary to argue the case in court, exceeded $600,000. For Wheeler, Cowenhoven, and Butler the costs were just as great. Explorations in the Aspen mine after compromise disclosed that it was even more valuable than the parties had guessed. Over the next five years, the Aspen mine produced silver worth $11 million, of which net profits exceeded $6 million. Such numbers suggest that whatever the costs of litigation, the parties had fought over a true "bonanza." They had.[29]

The roles played by Hyman, Wheeler, Cowenhoven, Brown, and Butler scarcely enlarged their reputations as statesmen of the mining industry. Wheeler and his associates pressed the case to a trial in federal district court without regard to expense, but he had the Leadville precedent as a guide. Wheeler had run things in Aspen for some time, and he did not take kindly to being opposed. At the same time, Wheeler and the people of the Aspen had done a lot of work on the mine. The work began with Hooper's lease, but the partners carried it forward vigorously after Hooper's lease expired. Hyman had the stronger legal position (as it turned out), but he had done nothing to develop the Durant. The Durant had produced a few runs for samples in the Leadville assayer's office, nothing more. Hyman had benefited from the actual work done by his competitors, who first demonstrated the actual value of the mining properties surrounding the Durant's contact vein. Only Moses Hallett emerged from the apex fight with his reputation enhanced. As for the principals in the case, they had to be satisfied with money. Hyman made his first fortune; Wheeler simply added to his.

9

"A Second Leadville": Aspen, 1883–1887

"All the world's a stage, / And all the men and women merely players," wrote Shakespeare. Between 1883 and 1887, Aspen was a drama that would have seized Shakespeare's attention: the clash of giant personalities, the conflict over important legal principles, the interplay of conspiracy and counterconspiracy, the drama created by human avarice. It was a large stage, too, with thousands of players, and, though only a few had the largest and best speaking parts, it should still be kept in mind that their speeches and actions represented the dreams, aspirations, and futures of thousands of others who stood silently by but watched the dramatic actions and speeches intently. The courtrooms, corporate boardrooms, and private railroad cars were, after all, the places where the future of Aspen would be decided. During the years 1883–1887, giant corporations and influential lawyers fought over the rules under which the riches of the surrounding mountains would be parceled out, and at the same time thousands of ordinary citizens saw their futures outlined in the most optimistic terms. It was in this period that Aspen emerged in modern form, grew dramatically in size and area, reached a new stage of urban maturity, and began the physical, institutional, and social modifications that invariably accompany such changes.

In the four and one-half years from spring 1883 through autumn 1887, Aspen made the transition from camp to town. This change was marked on one side by the arrival of Jerome B. Wheeler and on the other by the coming of the railroad. These events were only boundary lines.

Between them lay stages of growth through which the camp-turned-town passed. Population and size formed one aspect of this growth; another was the inevitable and necessary by-products of such physical changes. These included a new array of services offered to residents of the town, and aspirations of more in the future. At the same time, problems remained from the past: debt, townsite litigation, conflict over mining claims, the legacy of isolation. They served as constant reminders of the early struggles for legitimacy and permanence.

First came growth. It began with the seasonal surge of people into the valley of the Roaring Fork in the summer of 1883. The larger numbers involved and the physical changes that resulted in the town may be seen in conjunction with the improved mining prospects brought about by the appearance of Jerome B. Wheeler. Wheeler's investments, which would eventually reach half a million dollars, had begun to transform Aspen from a townsite speculation into a mining town where mines were brought into production. People east of the Continental Divide responded to this impulse. The first wave of arrivals caught the town by surprise, coming as it did after the depressed season of 1882. By July 1883, the *Aspen Times* was reporting that the hotels were "crowded" and that late arrivals slept on cots hurriedly set up in the halls. The first extensive mining of ore began in autumn, in response to Wheeler's promises in connection with the smelter and his offer to purchase ore from producing mines. In September, perhaps as many as 150 miners were at work, and Aspen had a housing shortage. Many of the new arrivals apparently intended to stay over the winter. Mining prospects and the employment they offered stimulated other areas of the economy: construction, retail merchandising, transportation, and freighting. The *Sun* estimated the wintering population at 1,200, a remarkable increase.[1]

The population growth and physical expansion in the season of 1884 was even more dramatic. The firing of the smelter in summer and the rising production of the mines seemed to make good the most optimistic predictions of the preceding year. By October, an estimated 500 miners were at work; another 500 wage earners were employed "at other work." The mine payroll of the town was $5,000 a month; that for "different mechanical trades" directly related to mining came to another $1,700 a month. Aspen had roughly 1,000 houses, all of them occupied, and fully 250 of them ("temporary frame structures of the cheap pattern") had been built in the preceding four months. Among the evidences of a thriving construction industry were a brick factory, a planing mill, a shingle machine, a chopping saw, several sawmills, and half a dozen lumberyards. At the industrial center of the town were a smelter, a concentrator, and a sampler. The population was probably about 3,500, or a two-and-a-half-fold increase in a twelve-month period. In the elections of that fall, the voters of the town cast 986 votes, a number (the *Sun* proudly reported) greater than the vote of the entire county of Garfield.[2]

Such growth ushered in a building boom, Aspen's biggest since the summer of 1881. Major business construction included fifteen to twenty business buildings, the Wheeler bank, a "new and elegant hotel," and a large skating rink. In October, more than one hundred houses were under construction. Most of this work took place in the older section of town; developers (if we may call them that) shied away from the newer sites that might be the object of litigation over the question of townsite ownership.[3]

This growth in people, buildings, and facilities demanded an enlarged supply mechanism. The citizens of Aspen—whether new arrivals or old settlers—were like a great army campaigning in the field and constantly increasing in size and demands. The army was separated from its base of supply by a range of mountains fourteen thousand feet high. Most of what Aspenites ate, wore, and worked with had to be imported. Accordingly, the growth of Aspen in 1884 and 1885 signaled a parallel expansion in the transportation and freighting trades. Whereas the movement of people and the transfer of mineral to the East were often seasonal, the town had to be supplied throughout the year, winter and summer, whatever the weather and the conditions of the roads. Freighting conditions were actually better in winter, when the snow gave the heavily used roads a uniform surface, and the damage done by constant use would be quickly and spontaneously repaired by new snowfalls at regular intervals. In spring and fall, the heavy loads had to be transferred to sleighs at the snow lines, then repacked on wagons on the other side, a complicated and expensive business. Freight rates were two to three dollars a hundredweight in winter, slightly lower in other seasons.

The expansion of the freighting enterprise meant prosperity for the supply and transfer towns on the east side of the range, such as Buena Vista, Crested Butte, Leadville, and, especially, Granite (which lay astride the Denver and Rio Grande Railroad line). It also meant growing profits for Aspen freighters and investors. The firm of Stukey and Thode owned a large corral at the east end of Cooper Street, where it had stalls for ninety animals, a blacksmith shop, and a constant stream of fresh water. In March 1885, Henry Thode reorganized and enlarged his operation as the Aspen Forwarding Company, taking in as partners three well-known Aspen capitalists, Walter B. Devereux, J. W. Atkinson, and J. M. Downing. Financed at $20,000, the firm proposed to use some 250 to 300 teams to move forty to fifty tons of freight a day between Aspen and Granite. Another of the major forwarding companies (there were four) moved two hundred tons of freight weekly each way from Granite and Leadville. If we add the business of the small freighters, we find that the total business in Aspen probably reached one thousand tons a week by the summer of 1885.[4]

Amid continued population increase and physical expansion, the Aspen *Sun* could control itself no longer. In April 1885, the editor called Aspen a "Second Leadville," a title originally conferred by a Leadville paper. The editor described Aspen's rebirth in these terms: "From a camp three years ago trying to prove to a smelting company the four hundred tons of ore on its dumps, it is now a camp whose mines fill town lots with their products." Aspen was an example of the interaction of productive mining, population increase, and construction. The *Sun* continued, "The growth in population has necessitated the erection of dwellings which cover the townsite, and this in turn has called for a large addition to our business houses, which latter are occupying three of our broadest avenues." The summer of 1885 brought an important benchmark in the town's life: its first official census as a county. The state's enumerators identified 3,795 people within the limits of the town and another 689 outside, making the official population of Pitkin County 4,484. Editors indignantly charged that the counters had missed another thousand transients with no permanent residence. Still, most Aspenites found ample cause for self-congratulation.[5]

Aspen was not content with its new status as a "Second Leadville." It aspired to surpass the original. Yet the dramatic spurts of 1883, 1884, and 1885 could not be sustained. The census of 1885 marked a high point in the town's second season. The investments of Jerome B. Wheeler had produced a dramatic growth up to a point, but the town had reached the limits imposed by its continued isolation, the nature of its mineral product, and its growing array of problems. So Aspen grew (albeit modestly) over the next two years, to applause and gasps of wonder, but the town's attention was divided. While one eye concentrated on the new business blocks and working-class housing for miners, the other closely watched the progress of the apex litigation through the courts, or the several railroad schemes working their way through boardrooms, bankruptcy courts, up to and around the forbidding terrain of the central Rockies.

The sharp (if uneven) increase in population over four years and the accompanying boom in the construction industry led to a parallel demand for basic urban services. Among the standard services available to American towns in 1885 were those of water, electricity, gas, and fire and police protection. Each demanded a collective effort beyond the capacity of any individual or group of individuals, and each represented a step forward in a town's march to urban maturity. To establish its credibility, Aspen now had to provide such facilities for its growing population.

Water was at the head of the list. Everyone needed it, from the wealthiest mineowners to the poorest squatters. The first pioneers dipped their water out of the crystal clear Roaring Fork River, Castle Creek, Maroon Creek, or Hunter Creek. As Aspen expanded, more tents and wooden cabins appeared and, with them, sawmills and mining operations. More people and businesses needed water, and the water was no longer so pure. Sawmills fouled the water supplies with mountains of sawdust; mining by-products added to the impurities. Two stamp mills in Independence "are pulverizing ore to the consistency of dust," commented the *Sun* as late as 1886, "which, as it passes from the mill into the stream changes the color from an almost perfect translucent and white to a yellow ochre, thick enough and almost of the consistency of a new made cheese. . . ."[6]

The camp-turned-town needed water for drinking and industry; it also needed water for irrigation. Irrigation water would nourish trees, lawns, and gardens. It could be used to put out fires. Drinking water had to be safe, and people liked to have it conveniently available. In response to this demand, water carts appeared. Peddlers sold water for twenty-five cents a barrel, and business was good. Or, Aspenites might pay for water from one of two ditches: the Wheeler Ditch or the Roaring Fork Ditch. The town council examined the question of a municipal waterworks as early as 1883, but it immediately confronted the objections of the enterprising "Professor" B. Clark Wheeler—he had aleady expanded his horizons to mines and a townsite in Garfield County—who claimed to have a long-standing monopoly of the town's water rights through a corporate entity called the Aspen Ice and Water Company. The council challenged his "rights," and two years of bickering followed, in which each side threatened legal action. In the interval, the town doubled in size and then grew by another one thousand, to 3,800 people. While the talk went on, the irrigation ditches that formed the basis of the camp's water supply absorbed the usual daily influx of dust, dirt, debris, garbage, and animal waste from the hundreds of draught animals frequenting the town streets.[7]

The decisive push for the town's waterworks came finally from another direction. It was related, not to the safety of drinking water impregnated with animal waste or cheese-colored mine tailings, but to concern about fire dangers and, indirectly, insurance rates. By 1885, Aspen had a population of 3,800 people and one thousand wooden buildings constructed without reference to any municipal code. It was a gigantic pile of kindling waiting to be lit, and in the infinity of fires associated with cooking, heating, mining, and industrial processes, the opportunities were continuous.

Fire was a universal scourge of mining towns, where so many activities of daily life depended on open fires. Merchants stocked quantities of kerosene and explosives, and the ramshackle wooden structures lay in haphazard patterns. In Aspen's less prosperous early years, numerous empty weed-choked lots had provided unintended but effective fire-breaks, but the renewed immigration and building in the seasons of 1884 and 1885 filled the empty places in the camp-turned-town, and created an urban center whose business district of endless wooden structures looked suspiciously like piles of wood. Insurance rates reflected this condition. A large wooden building and a stock of goods valued at $10,000—a modest figure in the town by 1885—insured at the prevailing rates of 8 or 10 percent per annum meant a premium of $800 to $1,000, a figure that might be the profit for the year.[8]

The council found itself in its customary posture of trying to provide a necessary urban service at little or no cost to the taxpayers. The property valuation for 1883 was $122,000, and the tax rate 2 percent. Yet, of the $2,440 levied in taxes that year, only $200 had been collected by the deadline. The uncollected $2,200 was almost exactly the cost of a good fire engine—as members of the council continued to point out.[9] The service that people demanded in this case could no longer be provided by volunteer labor. This new circumstance helped mark the transition from camp to town.

In February 1884, with taxes still uncollected, the council decided to organize a fire company and purchase a fire engine. It placed an order for a Remington Engine and 1,000 feet of hose at a cost of $2,000. A substantial portion of the price was the charge for transporting the parts over the mountains to Aspen, where the engine would be reassembled. Seventeen prominent businessmen contributed to defray the cost. At the same time, the downtown merchants pledged to pay for cisterns with a total capacity of 10,000 gallons for the central business district. The influence of the important merchants, mineowners, and investors remained strong in Aspen, for their independent wealth enabled them to finance necessary civic improvements that the town could not or would not undertake.[10]

Equipment and citizens were soon tested. In mid-July 1884, Aspen had its first major downtown fire. The blaze broke out in a carpenter's shop. Subsequent investigation established that children playing with matches had ignited a pile of wood shavings. Within minutes, fanned by strong winds, the blaze had consumed half a commercial block. An estimated one thousand men and women formed bucket brigades. "The girls of the camp showed that they are as brave as handsome," eulogized the *Sun*. Volunteers and the organized fire company threw hundreds of buckets of water on adjacent buildings; willing hands tore down others. At last the new engine arrived, "took water from the ditch and threw a feeble stream upon the burning debris." Local observers sensed that the town had narrowly escaped destruction. The loss was about $4,000, none of it covered by insurance. The issue was no longer fire-fighting equipment or fire fighters; it was water.[11]

This concern received further impetus when the Clarendon Hotel—"Aspen's only first class hotel"—burned to the ground. The McLaughlins had started in a tent, prospered, and eventually built a wooden hotel valued at $20,000. It had long been the local headquarters for visitors, celebrated and unknown. The hotel burned down in two hours. The new fire engine performed to the limits of the water supply, which all agreed was inadequate. "Without water the machine is a useless piece of lumber," the *Sun* concluded. The short-run solution was to deepen the ditches. Ditches had carried Aspen's water supply since the first tent camp, but these were inadequate in the face of large fires, and useless in the winter. The solution of what the local press had come to call "the water question" now seemed a question of survival, not one of convenience.[12]

By 1885, the pressing need for fire protection had created the opportunity for profit. As the demand for a water system grew more shrill, the council become amenable to generous terms. The town's attempt to build a municipal waterworks had failed because Denver brokers rejected Aspen's bonds on the grounds that the county debt was already too high. The necessary waterworks would have to be privately financed. The prime movers were two "old-timers" who had arrived with the first settlers and stayed to become wealthy with the town, H. P. ("Grandpap") Cowenhoven and D. R. C. ("Dave") Brown. Brown now organized the Aspen Water Company, with himself as president and Cowenhoven as vice-president. The company acquired the water rights to Hunter Creek, an attractive source north of town, but Brown decided to use Castle Creek. From a small reservoir, Brown piped water two and one-half miles into town. In exchange for the service, the town agreed to pay $3,000 a year for the fireplugs. The

Mill Street, looking south from the Clarendon Hotel. Ca. 1882. This is a view of Aspen as a mining camp, one that might be repeated countless times in the Colorado Rockies every year from 1860 to the turn of the century. Notice the on-lookers in the second-story windows of the building to the left front and the small figure (presumably a child) in the distant center of the street. (*Aspen Historical Society*)

Hyman Avenue from Mill Street, at ground level, looking east. Ca. 1885. The Windsor Hotel (left front with small sign on the top of the building) at 320 E. Hyman marks the location. The several signs testify to the economic diversity of what has become a mining town, but the plain exterior of the buildings and the hard dirt street mark the unfinished quality of the place. (*AHS*)

Mill Street, looking south. Ca. 1890. As a well-dressed woman crosses the street on the left, the man and boy in the center as well as the sense of a street in motion testify to the prosperity of the city of Aspen. The more finished quality of the buildings and the streetlight at the top center give visible evidence of prosperity and permanence. (*AHS*)

Aspen, the mining camp, huddled against the foot of Aspen Mountain, in June 1882. The bulk of the dwellings are in a four square block area, with large vacant areas and few dwellings toward the edge of the settlement. Note the road up the side of the mountain toward the mines. (*Denver Public Library, Western History Collections*)

Aspen ca. 1884, looking south toward Smuggler Mountain. The jumble of wooden buildings and vacant lots must be very much like the scene that Jerome B. Wheeler saw on his arrival. (*AHS*)

Panoramic view of Aspen ca. 1887, looking toward Red Butte. The mixture of wooden shacks, frame buildings, and the imposing three-story Clarendon Hotel (center) marks Aspen on the verge of the arrival of the railroad and transition to the status of city. (*AHS*)

Aspen, the industrial city, of the early 1890s. Utilitarian and unsymmetrical houses in the foreground provide the living quarters for many who work in the mines seen in the background. (*Denver Public Library, Western History Collections*)

Entrance to the Hope mine. The primitive track constructed for the ore car indicates the utilitarian nature of the mining operations in a marginal mine. (*AHS*)

Cowenhoven Tunnel in the late 1880s. A mixture of miners, horses, and machinery posed at the entrance to H. P. Cowenhoven's most ambitious project, a tunnel connecting the major mines on Smuggler Mountain. (*AHS*)

Two girls pose in front of the Mollie Gibson mine ca. 1888. The innocence of the girls in their finery contrasts with the large mining works, railroad tracks, and smokestacks in the background. The mining camp of only a few years before was on its way to becoming a city with the industrial plant necessary to support the employment of 2,500 miners. (*AHS*)

The Smuggler mine works in 1890 or 1891 demonstrate the unkempt but elaborate construction above ground to support the search for ore below ground. Note the railroad line and the city of Aspen dimly visible in the background. (*AHS*)

Not even the stiff formal pose and the flawed print of a studio portrait can dilute the determination and commanding presence of H. P. Cowenhoven. An immigrant from Prussia in 1846, Cowenhoven crossed the continental divide in the summer of 1881 with two wagonloads of goods. He prospered in a wide range of economic enterprises and went on to become one of Aspen's most prominent self-made millionaires. (*AHS*)

Katherine Cowenhoven Brown, in a photograph dating from the late 1880s, radiates the same strength as her father. At this time she was a leader in Aspen's social and cultural life. (*AHS*)

David R. C. Brown and his son, D. R. C. Brown, Jr., born to Brown and his second wife, Ruth McNutt, whom he married in 1907. Aspen's most prominent, faithful, and enduring self-made man would have been about fifty-five years old at the time of this portrait. (*AHS*)

Jerome Byron Wheeler, Aspen's most important "founding father," looked like the Civil War officer that he was. Wheeler's enormous investments after 1883 brought to Aspen prosperity beyond the wildest dreams of its promoters and to Wheeler endless financial confusion and litigation that ended in his declaration of bankruptcy in 1901. (*AHS*)

David Marks Hyman as he appeared in a portrait taken in the late 1880s. Hyman's wide range of entrepreneurial and legal talents enabled him to survive the economic crisis of 1893, but few Aspenites had his continuing good fortune. (*AHS*)

Henry B. Gillespie, whose entrepreneurial career in Aspen began with the Spar mine and ended with the Mollie Gibson, was the first of the "silver kings" to arrive in the Valley of the Roaring Fork and one of the last to leave. (*AHS*)

Mrs. Henry B. Gillespie, who spent the winter of 1880–81 camped on the site of the future city, was one of Aspen's earliest social and cultural leaders. (*AHS*)

B. Clark Wheeler was a self-promoter of grandiose proportions whose occupation was as common in the mining camps of the Rockies as prospectors, miners, assayers, or teamsters. This photograph shows him with his characteristic black beard but not his rough clothing, broad-brimmed black hat, or heavy boots. (*AHS*)

A miner raises a glass of beer in Bowman's Saloon. Saloons were the social clubs of numerous single men who lived in rented rooms in boarding houses. In view of the saloon's importance to the life of the city, temperance movements made little headway in Aspen up to 1893. (*AHS*)

An Aspen miner and a child (probably father and daughter) pose outside the hastily built wooden houses that were home to hundreds of mining families. The pans hanging from the wall in the background suggest that the small quarters were in active use. The building (if it may be called such) demonstrates the cramped and primitive nature of such housing. The picture is the more striking because, unlike the churches, business blocks, and Victorian mansions of bonanza kings, such structures do not survive in modern Aspen. Yet at one time, they (with boarding houses) were the staple housing of a city of 12,000 people. (*AHS*)

Men (12), children (2), and dog (1) pose in front of a large primitive cabin. The men are miners, to judge by their equipment. The presence of children suggests that families lived here or nearby. (*AHS*)

These five men and their log cabin were probably typical of early Aspen prospecting and mining, at a time when mining operations involved only a handful of men in a primitive shaft. The shovels against the wall suggest how these men spent their days. (*AHS*)

A group of Aspen workers, of varying ages, supported by young children and a dog, pose in front of housing that is more attractive than some of the miners' shacks. The stone building in the center has a look of being cared for and permanence about it. The presence of two bottles and at least two glasses shows that in this mining city the consumption of liquid cheer was not limited to saloons. (*AHS*)

An Aspen baseball game is in progress in this photograph dating from ca. 1894. West Aspen Mountain (now Shadow Mountain) and the Holden smokestack provide the backdrop to the scene. The shabby condition of the field was probably typical of the playing fields of the high mountains, but the large numbers of spectators, many with buggies, indicate the high level of interest that surrounded Aspen baseball from the beginning of the camp. (*AHS*)

residents also paid for water service at a rate fixed by the town council. The Aspen Water Company stood to make 35 percent annually on its investment, a tidy sum even in the inflated atmosphere of a mining town.[13]

Construction went forward through the fall and into the winter of 1885. Plans called for a flume 11,725 feet long, running from the reservoirs on Aspen Mountain to the water gates on the outskirts of the town. The flume itself was built of two-inch planks eighteen inches long, furnished by Andy McFarlene's sawmill. McFarlene also had a contract to lay it. Within the town itself ran three-quarters of a mile of four- and six-inch piping made of wrought iron, treated to prevent rust. The piping connected the hydrants that the company had agreed to supply.[14]

The turning on of the long-awaited water system, in March 1886, produced a spontaneous day-long celebration. As the water flowed through the pipes, town officials tested the pressure to confirm that it met the standard set for the fireplugs. It did so with ease. Grown men capered about, taking turns squirting each other with hoses. "It seemed as though Mill Street was a vast fountain of many jets, and the way the crowd had to scamper here and there, was a caution," reported the *Sun*, "while the gutter ran rivers, carrying off hats as well as the rubbish of the streets." Aspen was not yet too stylish to celebrate. Grandpap Cowenhoven had a big smile on his face "and treated the boys handsomely." The superintendent of the company telegraphed the good news to Dave Brown, in Denver for the apex trial. The construction company left the streets a mess, and the council reprimanded Brown, who "promised to have them levelled down immediately." If he delayed a bit, the spring rains and animal traffic would do the job for him.[15]

At about the same time that Cowenhoven and Brown received a water franchise, the council awarded a contract to the Aspen Electric Light and Power Company to furnish electricity to the town. Electricity was as new as water and sanitation were old. Aspen wanted electricity because it signified progress. It also had important technical implications for mining. The single factor that made electric lights possible— for such was the desired end—was an electric dynamo installed in the smelter. Water power generated the electricity, and the promoters of the Aspen Electric Light and Power Company—together with an "electrician" from the Colorado Electric Company—sold the service to individual subscribers. In May 1885, tests began on the "electric lighting apparatus," to the fascination of large numbers in the town. On Tuesday, May 19, the company adjusted the lamps in the stores of the forty subscribers, and in the evening "the electric current was turned on, and the streets presented a varied appearance; wherever there was an arc light it was as light as day, and the intervening spaces were dark and gloomy indeed—the kerosene lamps looking dim and yellow." No one denied that the lighting was "a decided success."[16]

Bolstered by its success, the Electric Light Company decided to build its own power plant at the west end of Cooper Avenue, across the bridge over Castle Creek. The company would construct an aqueduct 1,600 feet long to produce a 49-foot fall of water at the site of the plant. A turbine rated at 150 horsepower would run two dynamos. The power generated would easily meet the needs of the town in 1885. Incandescent lamps would be used in homes and offices, while the arc lamps would be installed on public streets, in part to promote safety. The city council considered lighting cheaper than police patrols. The *Sun* concluded, "Electric lights in the public streets of Aspen will be of more benefit to our people than a city hall building or a chamber of commerce, for these last only will shine for a few and the few shine in them."[17]

In its years of growth, Aspen moved to confront the day-to-day tasks of urban development; those small changes helped to mark the transition from camp to town. For example, the federal census returns reminded officials of what almost everyone in the town already knew—namely, that in a town of thirty-eight hundred people covering an area of one and one-half miles by one-half, people no longer knew each other or all the streets and shops of the town. Considering that the place had doubled in size in two years, many residents were newcomers, and most of those were probably trying to find their way. Accordingly, the city fathers decided to number the houses and put up street signs, dividing the town east and west by Center Street, north and south by Main Street. These two thoroughfares were one hundred feet wide; the other streets, sixty. Lots were generally thirty feet wide. An ordinance of February 1886 made these recommendations law.[18]

The town also had to think about its mail, which was increasingly significant for business transactions. Between 1881 and 1885, the average volume of daily mail had increased from 150 to 2,000 pieces, and by the middle of 1885 the post office served an estimated seven thousand people. The federal government responded slowly and reluctantly to appeals to upgrade the post office, a step that would increase the number of clerks.[19]

The town budget for 1886 reflected the greater costs associated with urbanization. The most significant items by cost were fire department ($9,000), general expenses ($7,000), salaries ($7,000), water and light

($6,000), police ($6,000), and bridges, sidewalks, and streets ($5,000). In general, observers of the press thought that the town services had kept pace with physical growth. The *Sun* summarized this view in mid-1886: "There has been an excellent fire department fostered and encouraged; water works are supplying the necessary fluid in abundance; electric lights are being introduced under a most favorable contract; the city sanitary condition is good; the warrants are selling for 95 cts. on the dollar; sidewalks are stretching out to all quarters. . . ."[20]

To accommodate new growth and new services, the town needed a more elaborate bureaucracy and government. An enlarged corps of public officials reflected Aspen's new size and stature. Physical accommodations, fire protection, and record-keeping functions all grew. The directory of Aspen's officials mirrored these changes. The hitherto modest roster of mayor, council, recorder, marshal, and city attorney added treasurer, city engineer, street commissioner, chief of the fire department, assistant chief of the fire department, and scavenger. Upon the last devolved responsibilities to clean up the town, its empty lots (no longer numerous), streets, and gutters. The town paid $7,000 in salaries to its employees; the days of payment by fees had long since passed. In spring 1886, Aspen made the transition to a "second-class city." This change meant the division of the town into wards (which corresponded to election precincts already established), with two aldermen from each ward elected to the council.[21]

The growth in population, expansion of public facilities, and new construction of the new town of Aspen did not occur without cost. Just as Aspen's civil leaders had struggled for three years to promote growth, so they now labored for three years to cope with and direct it. Violence and crime increased with greater numbers of people. As Aspenites had prospered, so they now had something to lose. When the camp lay huddled in half a hundred log cabins and half a dozen false-front stores, eveyone knew neighbors, houses and stores lay open, and people trusted one another. Now the town had grown to thirty-eight hundred people and teemed with strangers, prosperous merchants had stocks worth tens of thousands of dollars, and luxurious homes (by the standards of the day) were under construction. Aspenites wanted security for their newfound prosperity.

Society had become more unsettled. The magistrate's court continued to handle "drunk and disorderly" cases on Mondays and Tuesdays. Aspen tried to balance the needs of a new working-class and immigrant population against the need to maintain a degree of order. Law enforcement appeared as a prominent item in the town's budget. Public declarations on the issue gave the impression that more order and vigilance were preferable to less. The *Sun* supported this course in its discussion of a public hanging in Leadville. The convicted murderer maintained his innocence to the end and mounted the scaffold before seven thousand onlookers disposed to make the spectacle into some kind of public holiday. The public features of the scene disturbed the editor, but not the hanging itself. "The whole truth may never be known," he observed. "But the dignity of the law is vindicated by a sacrifice, and should be satisfied with one life for a life, though the real culprit may be at large among men."[22]

What Aspenites recognized or perhaps only vaguely sensed was the changing nature of the population. With the opening of some important mines to production, a development closely associated with the blowing in of the smelter in summer 1884, Aspen became a "mining" town in a new sense of the word. The emphasis was increasingly on production of ore, not on prospecting for claims. Jerome B. Wheeler had raised the stakes for everyone in Aspen. It cost a lot more to buy into the mining game that had begun in Aspen when the first prospectors returned to Leadville in fall 1879. The days of penniless but voluble and optimistic promoters like B. Clark Wheeler had passed; these men had been replaced by financiers like Reynolds and technicians like Devereux. Lone prospectors, wild-cat promoters, marginal mine-owners, and merchants with a wagonload of goods on credit had all disappeared or found themselves confined to the fringes. They had been succeeded by investors with capital, technicians with high levels of training in the industrial processes associated with mining and ore processing, and an enlarging work force of professional miners.

Among the maturing institutions of the new town were political parties. In this period of growth and prosperity, the Republican and Democratic political organizations increased in size, prominence, and influence. Summaries of the activities at the meetings, public declarations, and manifestos all made their way into print. Yet the differences between the two parties in Aspen remained largely cosmetic. Allegiance to a party seemed based on cultural heritage rather than on the issues of the day. Party identification was something that pioneers carried across the passes with them into the new camp-turned-town. The events of the past and the issues of the present did not seem to divide the parties in Aspen as they did nationally. The Civil War—the great national experience of the nineteenth century—was scarcely mentioned except in connection with the presence and activities of a vigorous chapter of the Grand Army of the Republic. An active branch of the GAR included aspiring political figures, but its attitude was one of sorrow rather than of hostility. The early southern element in Aspen had largely faded in the face of heavy immigration from the Midwest and the Plains.

Nor did the parties in Aspen debate the great national questions of the tariff, civil service reform, railroad regulation, or the monetary standard. Aspenites did not care about the tariff; they remained unaffected by federal civil servants except when they asked for more of them in the post office; they desperately wanted railroads, for they could not regulate railroads without having them in the first place. And, of course, on the silver question, all Aspen spoke with a single voice, and each party assumed that it had the most progressive stance in protecting the silver standard. So the vigorous campaigns at election time centered on the traditional frontier issues of economy in government, the candidates' personalities, and the best way to promote the town. Prominent mining figures remained uninvolved in politics as office seekers, but every declared candidate promised to do whatever was necessary to promote Aspen's mining enterprise.

There was something attractively old-fashioned about Aspen's political tradition wherein gentlemen candidates (the only acceptable kind) did not actively seek office and, when nominated, did not campaign, but rather found themselves reluctantly swept into the political arena and later into office by a spontaneous ground swell of public opinion. As late as the election of 1886, the *Sun* expressed genuine outrage that a candidate had actively sought office to the extent of printing election tickets in his name and paying newsboys to distribute them. Although the candidate in question was a good Republican and the *Sun* a strong Republican paper, it led the fight against him with appeals to the "Churches of Aspen" and "To the Heads of Families," presumably the fountains of moral influence. "In hotel, lodge and church the edict has gone forth that the nomination must be downed, that principles must be honored." The candidate lost, and the paper rejoiced in his defeat.[23]

The impression persists that Aspenites wanted to be progressive as a town, but they narrowly defined progress as economic development. They were very traditional, and indeed conservative, in their attitudes toward politics and social values. Accordingly, Aspen politics was old-fashioned and comforting. No sharp class or economic distinctions found political expression. The town still lived in the age of consensus that characterized early mining camps, when pioneers banded together against the slurs and slanders from the outside, praised the camp's prospects, damned the Chinese and the Indians, and prophesied ultimate triumph. In the aftermath of the election of 1886, for example, the newspaper editors characteristically found comfort in the reflection that the successful candidates for the town council were "old timers," as if residence in the camp in 1881 somehow provided insights into the needs of the town in 1886. The *Sun* concluded, "Aspen now, as ever, needs a government which men shall respect for its moral worth as well as public spirit."[24]

In the final analysis, perhaps Aspen's political life was another and ultimate tribute to Jerome B. Wheeler. His financial gifts to the town far exceeded anything that a nineteenth-century town government could have raised through taxes. In that sense, he was the government, or often acted in place of the government. All elected officials had to do was manage a consensus of the town's affairs, keep violence and scandal to a minimum, and act as arbiters rather than as initiators. In short, with Wheeler on the scene to provide the means to "public spirit," Aspen's government could afford to be "moral."

In a world where technology was synonymous with progress, Aspenites loved new inventions and their application to the town in the valley of the Roaring Fork. Technology affected mining enterprise in the most direct way; it also began to influence aspects of life in the town. In 1885, the Spar Consolidated mine installed Aspen's first telephone. It ran from the mine to the home of the company's physician, Dr. B. J. Perry, and an extension connected to Crosby and Reese's Drug Store "at all times of the night." The New Clarendon Hotel, rebuilt after the disastrous fire of November 1884, also reflected the technology that had entered into American life. The new structure was "piped for gas" and had three electric lights and an electric alarm and call apparatus to reach guests in their rooms.[25] The New Clarendon might have symbolized the New Aspen, a town rather than a camp, where success was taken for granted and where quality of life drew on the newest conveniences found in urban centers east of the mountains.

Surrounded by the physical advances of four heady years, Aspen's civic leaders eagerly looked forward to the future and more physical improvements. At the top of the list was a brick hotel. Jerome B. Wheeler had already expressed an interest in financing such a structure himself. The community also wanted a larger, more elaborate opera house. After all, someone noted, "the spring rush to the camp must be properly amused." Plans, already well advanced by spring 1885, called for an opera house built by public subscription. The enlarged bureaucracy needed an enlarged courthouse. The town fully expected to build one, befitting the county seat of the largest and most prosperous town on the Western Slope. Finally, plans were already in the works for a "street railway." Aspen was developing its own suburbs. People who lived at a distance from the center of town needed public transportation—to work, to shop, to socialize.[26]

In examining the growth and prosperity of the town between 1883 and 1887, Aspenites considered the past as simply prologue. These substantial achievements were only the groundwork for a future in which the rapidly advancing technology of the nation would be brought to bear to open up the enormously rich mines that lay on every hand. By 1887, Aspen was about to take a great leap forward that would place it alongside (and some thought in advance of) Virginia City and Leadville, the nation's most important silver-mining cities. The opportunity to share in this experience should not be missed. Aspen now issued an invitation to a broad range of Americans to share in this opportunity for a new and richer life, "from the orphan boy to the old maid school teacher; from the blushing bride to the toothless grandmother."[27]

Aside from the usual hyperbole of editors promoting their own, what was necessary was the resolution of the apex litigation and the construction of a railroad. In the summer of 1887, both problems seemed on the way to solutions. Even as mineowners and lawyers resolved the legal issues of apex/sideline in the interests of profits for all, railroads began to build up the valley of the Roaring Fork. The editor continued, "With two broad gauge roads in Aspen this fall, traversing a country and a trail heretofore known only to the burro, who can limit its possibilities and narrow the avenues of commerce awaiting the youthful energy of this land! Come from the fervid tide of the capital city; come where there is room and opportunities suited to your abilities and your purse. Come and make yourself a home, and mingle in common fellowship with the mineral kings and the independent miners of these mountains."[28]

10

"The Frontier Atmosphere Has Long Since Departed"

In the spring of 1887, the Aspen *Rocky Mountain Sun* addressed the character of the large numbers of people who had transformed the ambitious town in the Roaring Fork Valley into a crossroads of the mining world: "The steady growth of Aspen, its wealth, society, the architectural beauty of many of its buildings and handsome residences, make this city in advance of many mountain towns. The frontier atmosphere has long since departed, and Aspen presents the cultivation and order of older settled communities."[1] For an editor who had spent earlier years trying to rid the public streets of hogs running at large and to shame merchants into building sidewalks, the new focus on architecture and the character of its citizens signaled a change fully as striking as those associated with population growth and mineral production.

This transition from a frontier condition to a more stable and permanent world was a stage of development reached by many agricultural towns but relatively few mining camps. Agricultural communities grew in the same slow and sure way as the economic enterprise of agriculture itself, with both crops and villages eventually reaching a condition of stability and permanence. In contrast to those of market towns, the risks of mining camps were great, and the opportunities for wealth were enormous. The transition from the first to the second stage in a mining setting, symbolized by the change from camp to town, meant the shift from a transient to a permanent population, physical changes in construction from false wooden fronts to brick business buildings, from reliance on water barrels to the existence of a wide variety of urban services such as water and electricity. This physical growth and institutional maturity led Aspen to compare itself to Leadville and Denver, not to Granite and Buena Vista. Social and cultural life also matured, parallel to the growth of wealth and leisure. Such changes were less obvious than statistics of people, construction, or ore production, but they were no less significant for the people who lived in Aspen, and they marked the emergence of a new kind of community.

The obvious physical changes in the new and expanding town serve as an introduction to a more complex society. Aspen always had a group more concerned with the Literary Society, masquerade balls, and the Sunday school than with baseball and boxing. After 1884, this group enlarged its social displays. Rising prosperity widened the gap between those at the top of the economic scale and those on the bottom. At the top of the scale was a group of wealthy families who lived in luxurious houses (by the standards of the day) and traveled extensively; at the other end were day laborers, unemployed vagrants, and drifters. In the middle was an enlarging corps of professional miners, many with families, who labored in the increasingly active mines for daily wages. This group formed its own, separate community, subdivided by ethnic, religious, or regional differences. In the period 1883–87, Aspen had become a more diversified place than it had been in its years as a camp.

To describe the different societies that emerged in Aspen between 1883 and 1887 is an exercise that demands caution. The socioeconomic elite—if we may use the term—were the most visible of those, because of the public coverage of their activities, so it is easy to overemphasize their presence. Nonetheless, they were important, for they occupied positions of leadership, and they had wealth and authority to influence the nature of the community beyond their numbers. Among the special variables of their world were their economic status, place of residence within the town, opportunities for travel, and choices of recreation and entertainment. On one thing most observers agreed: the social and cultural elite were also the economic elite. One observer made the connection clear when he reported that a concert in the spring of 1887 was "filled with the fashion and wealth of Aspen."[2]

Aspen wealth had a wide range. A useful distinction was origin, the difference between those who brought money into Aspen and those who made money in the town. One group was composed of those who came in from the outside as wealthy investors, people of established social and economic standing elsewhere, bringing their credentials to Aspen with them. It included, first and foremost, Jerome B.

Wheeler, but Wheeler spent little time in the town other than on business trips and the Wheeler family no time at all. There is no record that Wheeler's wife, Harriet Macy Valentine Wheeler, ever visited the town of Aspen. Influential figures in the first waves of settlers with more physical presence in the town included Charles A. Hallam and Henry B. Gillespie. The Hallam family spent summers in Aspen; the Gillespies were year-round residents from the fall of 1880 on. Mrs. Gillespie organized the Literary Society and a Sunday school in the winter of 1880–81, when the permanent population of the camp was no more than thirty-five. David M. Hyman belonged to this group economically, but his social roots remained elsewhere. To these should be added new arrivals of 1884 and 1885, financiers, entrepreneurs, and technicians, sometimes with their families and sometimes without. They included the Walter B. Devereux family and the Albert E. Reynolds family (brought in by David Hyman in his search for liquid assets during the apex suit), to mention only two.[3]

Alongside these capitalists should be set another group, those who had come to Aspen in modest circumstances and made fortunes. The most important of these families were those of H. P. Cowenhoven, D. R. C. Brown, and J. D. Hooper. They were the core of Aspen's first indigenous social and economic elite. Their large fortunes had been made through mining enterprises. Others who provided goods and services had also done well. They included McFarlene with his sawmill, McLaughlin and his Clarendon Hotel (the great fire notwithstanding), Thode in freighting, and others in construction, merchandising, and law. All had prospered with the growth of the town; they represented the wide range of opportunities associated with a prospering mining town.[4]

From its beginnings as a camp, Aspen's social and cultural leaders had always mounted a certain public display of their position. This social coverage expanded in 1884 and 1885. The usual occasions for such notices were weddings, balls, and concerts. A wedding in January 1884 was characterized as "of some importance in society circles," because of the bride's connection to the family of William T. Root, the county clerk. A highlight of the fall social season was the "Grande Masquerade Ball" sponsored by the Aspen Dancing Club and given at the skating rink. The costumes were put "on exhibit" for viewers, and tickets were sold to spectators, who might observe from the balcony. Only those with costumes—and by implication, only those who could afford costumes—were permitted on the dance floor. Firemen's balls continued to be popular annual events, combining social display with benefit for the entire community. Such balls also highlight the early

connection between volunteer fire-fighting units and the acknowledged social standing of their wealthy sponsors.[5]

With the close of the "social season" in the spring, social emphasis
shifted to the reception. Such an affair in honor of Mr. and Mrs. J. M.
Downing ("prominent lawyer") drew "many of Aspen's most favored
society ladies and gentlemen" to an evening of dancing with an "elegant repast" at ten o'clock. On another occasion, the parents and
friends gave a "reception" in honor of Miss Aggie Hedges on her
departure for Denver to attend St. Mary's Academy. By the summer of
1885, Aspen's two newspapers had weekly "Social Gossip" columns to
cover the activities of organizations and individuals prominent on the
Aspen social scene.[6]

The infusion of new wealth occasioned by physical expansion, the
greater production of the mines, and the arrival of outside capitalists
intensified the social activities of the town. These reached something of
a climax in a grand reception in the spring of 1886, an event that
seemed to mark Aspen's passage to a new social level. The occasion
was the reception given by Mr. and Mrs. E. T. Butler at their new
residence on Hallam Street. The *Sun* described it in these terms: "The
company was large and brilliant, the gentlemen appeared in the regulation swallow tail, and the costumes of the ladies were both rich and
elegant. Dancing, cards, and an elegant supper were the order of exercises. It was the most brilliant society event that ever occurred in
Aspen."[7] Aspen had come a long way in the six years since thirty-five
wintering residents sat down to a homemade Christmas dinner. A
reception in swallow-tailed coats and evening dresses marked the
transformation from camp to town as surely as did the production
figures from the mines.

Receptions took place at private residences, and the celebrated Butler affair indicated the parallel between rising social consciousness and
public display and a new set of private residences rising on Aspen's
streets. The Aspen construction boom was private as well as public.
Elegant homes provided tangible physical evidence of the prosperity
and permanence of the town. Perhaps the most impressive of the new
homes was that of D. R. C. Brown. A description emphasized its gran-
deur as a tribute to the man and the town: "The new mansion residence of D. R. C. Brown on Hallam street is 34 × 72 feet on the ground
floor, two stories and tower in height, has 12 rooms besides a commodious apartment in the tower. It will contain all the modern improvements, such as heating furnaces, hot and cold water pipes, bath room,
etc. The outside of the building is ornate and handsome, of the mansion style of architecture, with red sand stone foundation, broad and

sweeping roofs and wide porticos. The cost of this structure, when completed, will be about $6,000."[8] Brown and his father-in-law, H. P. Cowenhoven, had spent their first summer in Aspen in tents. His change of status was a symbol of the change in the camp on the Roaring Fork. Not all had risen so remarkably, of course, but that such individuals and physical structures had emerged was symbolic of the transformation of Aspen itself.

New mansions needed things in them, furnishings that would be equal to the structures themselves. Aspen had these too. Its commercial establishments advertised the latest interior designs, brought directly from Denver. In the summer of 1885, the first pianos arrived in Aspen. They had been ordered for the residences of Henry B. Gillespie and Henry Webber, and each cost $1,000. The instruments were shipped by train from Denver to Leadville, where they were disassembled and packed onto a jack train for the passage over the mountains to Aspen and reassembly. Transportation fees accounted for much of the expense. Aspen was not exactly on the direct route for the importing of cultural objects, but where sufficient wealth existed, ways could be found. Some Aspen families had the wealth, and by 1885 they wanted pianos.[9]

The interest of the social elite in cultural affairs remained a symbol of their ambitions for the town and for their own exclusive ways of expressing them. The changes were matters of degree. This four-year period opened with continued amateur dramas, sponsored and performed by local talent. With willing hands and friendly audiences, they staged A Bachelor of Arts, Sweethearts, and Under the Gas Lights for their friends. Thanks to the completion of a new theater, seating eight hundred, the setting became large-scale and the performers were imported professionals. In the winter season of 1886, within a month of one another, occurred Aspen's first performances of opera and of Shakespeare. A visiting troupe staged a comic opera, The Mascotte, before a large and appreciative audience at the skating rink. (The transformation was not yet complete, however, for between acts the audience was entertained with miscellaneous "charming songs and dances," and it stared "agape with wonder" at a woman with an iron jaw and the form of John L. Sullivan.) The Shakespeare consisted of several selections from Macbeth, recited by a lady elocutionist. The audience enthusiastically welcomed the first speeches of the great English bard in the Roaring Fork Valley, incomplete as the presentation might have been. The lady received $50.[10]

Aspen's greater prosperity seemed to generate a greater emphasis on women and their affairs. If men had their clubs and public affairs, women had a focus of interest too. It was art. A wave of fascination for art and artists ran through the town in the summer of 1885. "A visit among our ladies of taste and culture is a rare treat to lovers of art," reported the *Sun*, "and a decided surprise to anyone not familiar with the high standard of refinement our ladies of Aspen have attained."[11]

A proliferation of clubs accompanied the rise of wealth. The Roaring Fork Club, Aspen's most prestigious, continued to prosper. Joining it was the Alpine Club, whose monthly receptions during the social season from September through May served as a barometer of the town's social life. These receptions featured dancing, a supper at Garrison's about 11:30 P.M., followed by more socializing until early in the morning. The Alpine gained a happy reputation of "making Aspen a pleasant place in which to spend the long and often dreary winter months." Unlike the Alpine, which organized monthly balls during the social season, the Gladiators, a bachelors' club founded to protect its members "against the wiles and smiles of the fair female sex," met the year round. The fifty charter members had clubrooms "elegantly furnished with fine Turkish carpet on the floor and aromatic Turkish tobacco on the veneered, marble top mahogany tables, elegantly upholstered chairs and perfect divans where the weary can repose at their leisure. . . ." The founders immediately sponsored a lecture entitled "The Delights of Celibacy," but the constant activities of the club and its members suggested that its purpose was to attract rather than to discourage the attention of Aspen's eligible ladies.[12]

Receptions, clubrooms, and balls designed to save Aspenites from the dreary winter months served those who stayed. Others left. The news of departures customarily began in late autumn, generally in November. The irony was that the celebrated social season of the winter months went forward without some of the most prominent members of Aspen's economic and social order, who disappeared over the Continental Divide by Thanksgiving, to await the late spring before returning. Leading capitalists, men like Jerome B. Wheeler and David Hyman, maintained permanent residences elsewhere. Ease and range of travel was one hallmark of social class in Aspen.

The successful among the original pioneers now joined the absentee investors in absenting themselves. The social and economic leaders of this small group were David R. C. Brown and Katy Cowenhoven Brown. In May 1884, after Brown's good fortune with the Aspen mine, the family traveled to Black Hawk and concluded its tour with a week in Denver. The return to Black Hawk must have been a triumph for Dave Brown, who had left there in the spring of 1880 as Cowenhoven's clerk. In the intervening four years, he had laid the foundation of a substantial personal fortune in a new town, and the camp he left had steadily declined.[13]

Amid Aspen's many changes of these four years—the lawsuits and the talk of railroads, clubs for women and clubs for men to avoid women, new mansions and pianos—two themes emerged. The first declared that the former camp on the Roaring Fork had overcome isolation and economic uncertainty to create a society as conspicuous in its physical displays and as adept in its public forms as any in the West—or in the nation, for that matter. "As the City of Aspen grows in wealth, society and its refining influences keep pace with material prosperity," argued the *Sun*. "It has thrown off its provincialism, until now, as on the evening of this reception, . . . the toilets of the ladies equal the richness of material and splendor of design those of the charmed circle in the metropolis."[14]

Another persistent theme was that such social distinctions were perfectly natural and not at all incompatible with the democratic ideal to which the town and its citizens paid homage. Even as the *Sun* praised the opportunities for all people in Aspen, it noted the "division of the people into sets, with distinctive ideas and purposes." These differences were natural ones, parallel to "the varied temperaments, tastes, and degrees of education, both acquired and hereditary, of the human family." The outgrowth of these differences was that "we at once see the justice and fitness of society taking on as many phases as there are colors in the rainbow."[15] Within the context of late-nineteenth-century America, where agricultural laborers made one dollar for a workday that extended from dawn to dusk and where the new industrial laboring worker made slightly more at much greater risk of death and injury, social classes were as accepted as differences of wealth and poverty. The rapidity with which the fortunate few might ascend the scale—especially in the lottery that was mining on the Rocky Mountain frontier—did not lessen the distinctions of class.

For all their clubs, balls, travel, and prominence in the local society columns, the members of the elite social and economic class (the two were synonymous in Aspen) constituted only a small portion of the population. Perhaps fifty families and individuals made up the group, generously including those who spent much of their time outside the town. With Aspen's population in 1885 numbering 3,800, the proportion was tiny. Who were these other people? What roles did they play? What was their lot in life? And why were they so relatively invisible?

These larger numbers of Aspenites worked, bore children, raised families, managed the home, and pursued recreation in their own way. It was a middle class in the sense that it fell between the top and the bottom, but the term is too general. We may generalize about these people, however, using the census of 1885 to examine the diversity of the growing mining town on the Roaring Fork. In sitting for its census portrait at the age of five years—the town was incorporated in 1880—Aspen outwardly displayed many of the demographic characteristics associated with mining camps. Almost three out of four residents (72.4 percent) were male. Aspenites were overwhelmingly white (99 percent), with a handful of blacks, mulattos, and American Indians. The town contained no Asians. In identifying their places of birth, the residents of the valley of the Roaring Fork suggested that mining towns were a gathering place for citizens from the length and breadth of the entire nation and several European countries. The most common birthplace was New York, followed closely by Colorado, Pennsylvania, Illinois, and Ohio. From the foreign nations, the Germans and the Irish were most heavily represented. If we include the English, Scots, and Welsh, the representation of the United Kingdom was strong; if the Canadians are added, English-speaking immigrants dominated Aspen.

Occupations of Aspen residents generally followed the economic profile of a mining town. Among the men the largest categories were "miner" (450) and "silver miner" (360, for a total of 810), to which might be added "prospector" (115). (Note that the census taker and the men themselves distinguished between miner and prospector.) Others associated with mining included assayer (12), mine engineer (8), and mine superintendent (8). Also numerous were the support groups directly related to the mining enterprise, of which the most numerous were smelter workers (39), charcoal burners (6), and sawmill workers (26). The larger economy of the town also appeared in outline, with the construction industry well represented by carpenters (157) and, to a lesser extent, by contractors (3), painters (9), brickmasons (9), and plasterers (2). Among those in the retail trade were grocers (20), butchers (20), "fruit dealers" (4), and "shoe dealers" (4). The freighting occupations profiled a busy and growing mining town before the arrival of the railroad, with a sizable number of teamsters (55), freighters (60), and blacksmiths (35) to keep the draft animals on the roads.

Aspen also had a good range of professionals. Doctors (8), lawyers (31), schoolteachers (4), druggists (11), printers (12), and accountants (1) constituted the professional side of the town. Real estate brokers (12) were also plentiful. Others, with lower status but equally necessary in running a town with a high proportion (63.7 percent) of single people, were hotelkeepers (22), lodging house proprietors (9), barbers (16), cooks (22), and waiters (17). The substantial number of laundresses (48) identified another important service.

A mining town also needed an entertainment industry. Aspen had a good representation, with saloonkeepers (41), bartenders (31), prostitutes (4), gamblers (8), and "actresses" (5). The occupational terms were imprecise, of course, for some men and women surely worked at more than one job. Others may have been at pains to disguise their occupations—there may, for example, have been more than 4 prostitutes or more than 8 gamblers. To these professionals (in their own way) should be added a sampling of less obvious ways of making a living in the mining town of Aspen. Could a "dancing professor" make a living in Aspen? At least one thought so. The "scavenger" cleaned the city streets. Aspen in 1885 also supported one "water wagon proprietor," one "jockey rider," and one "candy maker."

Although the town was predominantly male, almost 1,200 women lived in Aspen. Their presence is also documented by their occupations. Aside from those already noted in the service and entertainment areas, the most prominent by numbers were the categories of "housewife" (212) and "keeps house" (208), whose combined total (420) almost equaled the number of miners. To this should be added smaller groups, offering a range of services, such as dressmakers (16), seamstresses (12), servants (24), and a governess (1). When we add to these several varied occupations those who were "at school" (102) and "students" (168), who totaled 270, Aspen emerges as a multidimensional town. The days of miners, merchants, and saloonkeepers (if they ever existed) had disappeared, to be followed by a town with a wide range of occupations, and an equally broad representation from different sections of the nation and European states.[16]

In the years 1883–87, Aspen witnessed the emergence of a new distinct group: a working class associated with the mines and mining. It was not made up of prospectors or those who inhabited mining camps in their formative years, hoping to invest little or nothing in what would turn out to be a valuable property. These were professional miners, men who went to work when mines began to produce silver ore. They arrived in substantial numbers when speculators had departed and when a second generation of entrepreneurs inaugurated systematic mining for silver ore. This condition began in Aspen in the summer and fall of 1883, coinciding with Jerome B. Wheeler's investments. By September of that year, some 150 men worked in mines on the surrounding hillsides. Considering the number of claims in the Roaring Fork Mining District, this was not a large number, but it created a group of men with similar skills and needs and, above all, with a common identity. Some of these men had come with families; others had arrived without; a third group was composed of single men.

Single men exercised an important economic and social influence in the town. They used the saloon as their social club. The Bank Saloon was fully as significant in their lives as the Roaring Fork Club was to Aspen's leading capitalists—perhaps more so, because the wealthy had attractive homes to retreat to, while the miners had lodging houses. The outlines of other parts of the entertainment industry are visible only dimly. Four women identified themselves as "prostitutes" in the census of 1885. Perhaps there were others, less open about their profession. Miners also had more public recreations. Wrestling and boxing were two of the favorites. The first big wrestling match took place in the summer of 1884, when Morice Tracey and J. M. Williamson met for a $100 side bet. Matches were held regularly thereafter. Boxing appeared the next year. "Aspen's glory is complete—we have had a prize fight," noted the *Sun* with some sarcasm. Whatever the *Sun* thought, working Aspen liked wrestling and boxing. These two spectator sports, which could be presented indoors in the winter, supplemented the continuing interest in baseball as the principal summer sport.[17]

Aspen's new immigrants of 1884 and 1885 needed accommodations. Those with families required houses. In the summer of 1886, Mr. J. C. Connor, who owned a tract 300 by 600 feet at the foot of Deane Street stretching to the foot of Aspen Mountain, subdivided his holding. In so doing, he established Aspen's first working-class suburb. Connor divided his land into lots 25 by 100 feet and laid out a great boulevard down the center: "This street will be macadamized and have asphalt sidewalks on each side, and four rows of cottonwood trees on either side of the walks." The Aspen Water Company laid down a water main under the main street before paving. The *Sun* commented, "These lots will be very desirable homesteads for miners working on the mountains, as they will be so convenient to the roads and trails leading to the mines."[18]

The emergence of a distinctive working class associated with mining produced other economic and social changes. Miners needed to purchase special clothing and equipment, and merchants began to stock and advertise such goods in the press. Much of the rhythm of life in the town was set by the cycle of shifts in the mines, and this quality became more significant as the numbers of miners increased steadily up to 1892. When shifts changed, workers with proper clothing and equipment, carrying lunch pails and wearing lights, emerged from their residences and began the walk to the mines. Gradually, their isolated meanderings merged into streams, as scores of men snaked their way up the trails toward the mine entrances. Aspen had taken its first steps in a transition from mining camp to industrial city. The change would be completed after 1887, but the outlines appeared in 1885 and 1886.

The growth of 1885 and 1886 brought immigrant groups to increased prominence, both as workers and as members of the community. The late nineteenth century was a period of massive European immigration to America—numbering some twenty million in the twenty years from 1880 to 1900. These people created ethnic enclaves in the great cities of the East, where they did the hard manual labor associated with the industrial world that emerged, where they handled the duties as domestics in thousands of middle-class homes, and where their children grew up in confused worlds that demanded allegiance to the old ways while offering opportunities to those who would try the new. A proportion of these new arrivals—supplemented by the children of an earlier generation of immigrants—made their way to the mining West. Some of them came to Aspen, attracted to the economic opportunities associated with a booming town, which offered employment in the unskilled tasks that were often their lot.

The most prominent ethnic group in Aspen were the Germans. The census of 1885, in which 179 Aspenites declared Germany as their place of birth, reflected their presence. The Deutsche Verein held an organizational meeting in April 1885. February of the next year brought the first "German Dance," where "all of the latest and most fashionable and fascinating figures were given. . . ." The German Social Club gave annual dances, drawing the fashion leaders of the camp to watch the exhibitions, where dancers in native costumes contrasted with gentlemen in black dress suits.[19]

The Germans were among the most obvious of a wide range of immigrant groups. The Irish (defined as those born in Ireland) were actually more numerous (with a count of 193 natives) but less distinctive, because they blended in with the dominant Anglo-American culture of Aspen. In addition, a dozen major European nations were represented, as well as the different sections of the American nation. The *Sun* liked to boast of the range of regional characteristics brought together in the town on the Roaring Fork: "We are a people with traits characteristic of every state in the Union; the meditativeness of the middle states and the imagination of the south, combined with the western frankness."[20]

One immigrant group was not welcome in Aspen. The Chinese had been part of western mining as early as the 1850s. They first came to America in large numbers a decade later to work on the Central Pacific Railroad. Of the immigrants, the Chinese were the most clannish, most ethnically separate, most visible, and most discriminated-against group in the mining camps. Aspen offered no exception to this general attitude, except that hostility toward the Chinese kept them out of the town altogether, not even permitting them the poor claims and the laundries that had been their lot in so many Rocky Mountain mining camps. Because of the camp's remote location, few Chinese came in the early years. Those who did, did not stay long. Town officials and newspapers offered no apologies. Indeed, the press reported with approval many anti-Chinese incidents of violence elsewhere in Colorado. The official policy—if one existed—emerged in an incident in February 1886, when a young Chinese rode into town. Confronted immediately by the mayor and other officials, he told the hostile committee in fluent English that he was a Christian. The committee was unimpressed and put him forcibly on the next stage leaving town. The editor of the *Sun* commented, "He is objected to on general principle—he is a Chinaman."[21]

In 1885, women made up about one-quarter of the population of Aspen. The newspaper columns emphasized their prominence in society and the importance of their traditional duties as wives and mothers. Some women participated in the life of the town beyond hearth and schoolroom. When Aspen had its first major fire, in the summer of 1884, women as well as men manned the bucket brigade, leading the *Sun* to comment, "Their conduct should give them the right of suffrage." It was a theme that the editor did not take up again when the ashes of the fire had cooled. The interest in public office assumed a reality in the fall of 1887, however, when a woman ran for the position of superintendent of schools. Pauline S. Miller received the support of the *Sun*, who called her candidacy "a good pure and simple idea of reform." Apparently, the candidacy of a woman automatically conferred on her the concept of purity, simplicity, and reform, all qualities associated with a woman. She lost. No other woman tried to gain public office in the next six years.[22]

The question of what young women could do in Aspen engaged the attention of all groups. "What to do with our daughters is an ever recurring question to every father and thoughtful mother," commented the *Sun*. "True it is that the avenues of business are yearly widening to admit our female population, but when we consider the small pay and long hours our sisters must submit to, the question arises how long can they endure it?"[23] Those in the working class gravitated to domestic service. Women from more affluent families might attend school and become teachers. In a school system with only nine teachers, however, opportunities were limited. The expectations of society were that they would soon marry and become proprietresses of families, where they would provide the moral, spiritual, and cultural influence that was woman's contribution to a proper society. Yet the issue was not quite so simple. Presumably, some did not wish to stand idle in the wings waiting to be called to domestic service as servants or as wives and mothers. Perhaps some of their parents even shared this concern.

Children were also prominent in Aspen. They were present in greater numbers, as might be expected in a town with more families. Taxpayers, who had to provide schooling, churches, which established Sabbath schools, and merchants, who stocked clothing and toys, all noted their presence. Newspaper advertisements appealed to them and to their parents. At Christmastime, for example, ads for toys appeared alongside those for guns, ammunition, blasting powder, and drills. "TOYS. The Most Complete Line Ever Brought to this Side of the Range. TOYS." An enterprising reporter inspected the toy selection at Beard's Art and Toy Emporium and issued this report: "On the tables, around about the store are bell toys of every description, and tin toys of every variety. Mechanical toys that are a wonder, that amuse and instruct the young, and afford hearty laughter to the children of larger growth. Wooden toys representing everything in nature and the realms of art. Rubber toys that squeak and grin and jump to the delight of children."[24]

Aspen's varied societies, including women and children in greater numbers, a distinct class of professional miners and their families, and identifiable ethnic groups, pulled the town in different directions. For those who laid down regulations regarding public and private conduct, compromises were probably inevitable. The town needed professional miners and others less skilled to do manual labor as much as it needed capitalists. Such workers meant commercial opportunities in the form of construction, boardinghouses, saloons, gambling, and even prostitution. Still, it was not surprising that at some point a group of citizens emerged to express concern about standards of morality.

In August 1884, the city council took up the question of vice in Aspen. Debate centered on a motion to tax gambling, and on the question whether the tax should be imposed by saloon or by individual table. When one minister issued an impassioned plea that gambling simply be abolished, he was interrupted by the town attorney, who declared "that sentiment was good in sermon, but in a town government human nature must be handled differently; gambling cannot be suppressed, and consequently it should be made to bear some of the burdens of society. . . ." The council voted a tax of $25 per month ("in cash") on each saloon where gambling took place, plus $10 for the first and $5 for each additional table.[25]

The same ordinance imposed a tax of $5 a month against "sporting women." The term "sporting women" was not further defined in the ordinance, and presumably those who made the law, those who enforced it, and those against whom it was directed knew what it meant. The councilman who introduced the resolution used the word "prostitute." The death of a "sporting woman," Fanny Chambers, in the fall of 1884 led to an elaborate funeral, "attended by some dozen of the sporting women and the sporting fraternity generally." The funeral sermon had as its text "Let him who is without sin cast the first stone. . . ." The rich casket was "the gift of her sisters in life." The *Sun*'s portrayal was a combination of sympathy and horror.[26]

The question of alcohol was another emotional reform issue. The nation was in the midst of a vigorous debate over prohibition, a half-century crusade that would achieve success with the Eighteenth Amendment in 1919. Aspen's residents, new and old, had probably already heard the liquor question canvassed, and it is not surprising that many carried strong convictions into the valley of the Roaring Fork. Liquor was a concern in mining camps generally, because of the large numbers of single working men and the inevitable saloons that catered to their needs. In the absence of homes, many men made saloons the center of their social activities, spending long hours over a glass of beer with their friends. It was a situation calculated to attract the reform instincts of those already aroused by the liquor issue. The enormous growth of the town in 1884 and 1885 brought this concern into focus. The *Sun* remarked on the significance of the prohibition question for the first time in November 1884, noting that it was "bound to cut no inconsiderable figure in politics in the future." Although prohibition never became an issue in elections for the city council, it did attract considerable attention in council sessions. In spring 1885, the council passed a new liquor control law that prohibited sales to "habitual drunkards" and minors. The legislation reflected both the rising interest in the liquor question and the determination of the council to deal with it by means of mild strictures that propitiated the reform element and hardly interfered with the customary patterns of alcohol consumption.[27]

Part of the concern may have flowed from Aspen's increased use of spirits. As the town grew, so did its consumption of alcoholic beverages. By the end of 1885, the town's consumption of beer was estimated at thirty barrels a day in winter and forty to forty-five barrels a day in the summer. The beer came from Kansas City, St. Louis, Milwaukee, and Denver, packed over the range with other supplies. So substantial was the business that an Aspen brewery opened. Aspen's newest industry apparently did well.[28]

Such expanded consumption produced a hostile reaction. In the summer of 1887, a Mrs. Beach opened a branch of the Women's Christian Temperance Union. The union turned out to be an energetic one, quickly undertaking a variety of reform activities throughout the community. Concerts raised funds; a night school offered adult education with a moral message. The *Sun* called the school venture "a real progressive movement in our city." By 1887, Aspen was showing a range of issues and reform institutions that had much in common with other American industrial towns.[29]

Churches were the center of Aspen's expressions of morality and respectability. The *Sun*'s comment "The attendance at church and school is generally accepted by modern thinkers as a fair index of material, moral, and intellectual standing" reflected national values. "Church Notes" became a weekly column in the newspapers, featuring sermons, prayer and Bible study meetings, funerals, weddings, and social functions, which were often associated with fund-raising. By 1886, Aspen had achieved the prosperity necessary to build permanent church buildings, maintain ordained ministers, and underwrite a panoply of supporting institutions. Its Sabbath schools instructed the young people in the standards of the community; its prayer meetings and church suppers provided spiritual and social outlets for adults. Aspen celebrated its churches, noting at the opening of 1886, "[T]he spiritual and moral well being of the community is looked after, at present and in the field, by four representatives of as many different denominations."[30]

The most important denominations were the Congregationalists, Methodists, Episcopalians, and Roman Catholics. Characteristic of the Protestant denominations were the rapid turnover in ministers, the prominent town figures on the boards, and the relatively small numbers of members. Ministers rarely stayed in an Aspen Protestant pulpit for more than one year, and some stayed for a shorter period. Among those on the first board of trustees of the Congregational Church was H. P. Cowenhoven. Founded in 1881 (Aspen's oldest), the Congregational Church declined in direct proportion to the growth of the town after 1883, and in July 1886 the Congregationalists merged with the Presbyterians, where D. R. C. Brown was on the board, along with D. M. Van Hoevenberg (Wheeler's bank president) and J. M. Downing. The Aspen Grace Episcopal Church was established in the fall of 1884 (perhaps taking some members from the Congregationalists), but the congregation was so small that it built a chapel, not a church. The Methodists organized slowly, holding their first service in March 1885, at the skating rink. In April 1885, the church had only twelve members. Within a year, they had constructed a large Gothic-style church, with a sixty-five-foot tower and thirty-two electric lights. Membership had increased to sixty, with some sixty-five young people attending regular Sunday schools. The impression persisted that Aspen's Protestant churches, at least, served a small, select socioeconomic group, and this group and their churches did not enjoy a growth parallel to that of the town between 1883 and 1887.[31]

The Roman Catholics were among the earliest to organize, and their congregation had a continuity and sense of community that seemed far beyond the reach of their Protestant counterparts. Established in June 1881, Aspen's Catholics were first served by itinerant priests from Leadville, who came over the range to hold masses, confessions, baptisms, and funerals. The first resident priest, Edward Downey, came from Central City in 1883. Father Downey knew life in mining camps well, and his ministry was the most successful of any of Aspen's churchmen, in part because of Downey's continuous service to his parishioners. Until the church was completed, in the fall of 1884, he held services in a private home. His plans included an addition to the church, a rectory, a schoolhouse, and a residence for the Sisters of Charity, who taught in the school. Father Downey also purchased four lots at the corner of Galena and Aspen streets as the site of a future hospital. His departure for Fort Collins, in January 1891, was the occasion for a great public outpouring of appreciation. He had come to Aspen when it was a camp, and he had stayed to minister to the town and the city.[32]

Schools offered another evidence of the transition from camp to town. In Aspen, they reflected the growth of the town and the changing population profile, which showed more families and children. At the same time, schools also demanded resources. A town had to be willing to allocate tax dollars to serve its school-age population. Aspen's professed concern for education received a stern test with its dramatic growth in 1884 and 1885, when rising enrollments necessitated new facilities. By the close of the school year in May 1885, Aspen's single schoolhouse had 175 pupils in a place adequate for 150. A census of the town found an estimated 320 children of school age. Furthermore, the town had expanded physically to the point that students living in the area east of Galena Street had a long walk to and from school.[33]

Over the summer, school officials, civic leaders, and the newspapers canvassed these questions. All agreed that the present facilities were inadequate and would become more so with the anticipated growth of Aspen in the next year. Accordingly, the school board decided to establish another school district, to build a second school, and to call a special election on a bond issue. The voters overwhelmingly supported the $10,000 bond issue. Construction of the new East Aspen School began in late August 1885, and it opened in late October. The completed building had two rooms, with a capacity of one hundred students in the elementary grades. The larger Central School had eight rooms for four hundred pupils. The new school attracted praise for the excellent facilities now available to Aspen's school-age children. It was just as well. Within the year, by August 1886, Aspen's schools had more than four hundred students. Schools in Aspen were no longer an auxiliary. They were part of the services that an ambitious and progressive town had to offer to its residents.[34]

In educational philosophy and curriculum, Aspen's schools were orthodox. They thought of themselves as preparing young people for the world around them, with proper proportions of patriotism, discipline, and public display. The curriculum in the grammar school consisted of arithmetic, reading, grammar, and composition, plus geography, orthography, etymology, elocution, music, and drawing. Officials designed the high school course of study "to prepare the pupil for life work, or, if he chooses to enter the State University." Those in positions of authority assumed that those matriculating at the State University of Colorado would be men.[35]

Schools appeared in the public eye twice each year: at opening, when the numbers of pupils and their facilities raised questions about cost, and at closing, when a public performance before officials and parents mixed music, drama, recitation, and awards. In June 1886, for example, students presented a "cantata" representing the Queen of School and her subjects. The latter turned out to be "good girls and bad boys." Published accounts suggest that many attended grammar schools in Aspen but that few took the high school course. This may have reflected the fact that most of the children in town were of grammar school age, but at the closing exercises in 1886, from the three hundred–odd pupils attending Aspen's schools, only twelve grammar school graduates received certificates entitling them to enter the high school.[36]

The emergence of socioeconomic distinctions in Aspen, the several identifiable ethnic groups, the competing religious denominations, and the growing differences in wealth tended to divide and fragment the community. At the same time, several influences continued to unite it.

The most important of these was boosterism, the defense of the town against outsiders, a unity in the cause of growth and prosperity, in which all individuals and all groups presumably had a common interest. Another unifying feature was the residual frontier instinct to come together in the face of disaster. Fires, blizzards, avalanches, mining accidents, and any other natural catastrophes produced an outpouring of common assistance and genuine concern that transcended group identification. Helping to cement this fragile common bond were the great public celebrations that brought together the entire community in remembrance of past triumphs. At these times, the public ceremonies reminded the many participants of their common heritage. The two largest such occasions were Decoration Day and the Fourth of July.

Decoration Day marked the sacrifices of the nation for the preservation of the Union. Every year, the mayor declared May 30 a town holiday. The ceremonies were highly organized, with an emphasis on widespread participation. Winfield Scott Post No. 49, Grand Army of the Republic, led the memorial rites. On a typical holiday, Post No. 49, Sons of Veterans, and other old soldiers would assemble at nine o'clock ("sharp") for the parade. Behind them would be arrayed the Fife and Drum Corps (providing the prescribed "martial music"), City Council, "Judiciary," Hose Company No. 1, Cowenhoven Hose Company No. 2, Red Star Hose Company No. 3, J. D. Hooper Hook and Ladder Company, Juvenile Hose Company, Schoolchildren, Women's Relief Corps, and Citizens. It is a wonder that others could be found to watch, and yet in 1885 an estimated one thousand Aspenites lined the streets to observe the parade. The marchers wound their way through the streets of the town to the Evergreen Cemetery. Ceremonies there included the invocation by the Chaplain of the Day, a hymn, a "song by public schools," decorating the cenotaph and graves, presentation of the colors and a salute by the "firing squad," public singing of "My Country 'tis of Thee," a benediction, and a return in formation to the center of town. Afternoon services at the skating rink included two major orations.[37]

The center of the evening's entertainment was a "Grand Ball" under the sponsorship of one of the fire companies. It was preceded by a dinner served by the Women's Relief Corps. The ball in 1886 took place at Hallam Lakes, with "feasting and dancing and boatriding and strolling and having a general good time." The following year, it was held in the Grand Army Hall. In both places, the organizing committee hired an orchestra and arranged for a large dance floor and booths for refreshments. While many went to the "Grand Ball," others celebrated with a glass of beer at the Bank Saloon.[38]

Independence Day had fewer ceremonies and more recreation. Tradition had the houses and businesses of the town decorated with evergreen boughs and American flags. After the parade, which involved no elaborate public ceremonies or speeches, the day was given over to contests and entertainments. In the morning, the fire engine companies competed for cash prizes ($35 to the winners) and blue ribbons, which the members of the victorious companies wore in their hats for the remainder of the day. These contests took place on the main streets of the town, generally Hyman Avenue, and featured the liberal distribution of water to contestants and spectators alike.

In the afternoon, contests of skill took place at the racetrack. The organizing committee erected a grandstand to seat five hundred, and charged admission, fifty cents for adults, twenty-five for children. The first contest was a drilling match among teams and individuals. Next, a group of mounted riders in knightly costume competed in a tournament of tilts and riding to spear rings. The afternoon concluded with serious "horse and jockey races." Visitors from other, smaller camps came for entertainment or to compete with locals for the cash prizes.[39]

The accelerated pace of Aspen's growth, its new construction of brick business blocks and luxury homes, its churches and schools, its energetic public celebrations—all carried the town forward on a rush of progress and prosperity. A sense of how the little camp on the Roaring Fork had grown up emerged in September 1886 with a call for the organization of a "Pioneer Association." It would include those who had come to the camp before the fall of 1881. According to the organizers, the purpose of the association was "to perpetuate the bonds of union made memorable by the struggles, trials and hopes of the early days of Aspen, to rehearse and preserve the history of the infant camp, and to cultivate a spirit of sociability among those who tramped over the Indian trails across the great divide to plant the foundations of a new empire in the then wilderness of the Roaring Fork valley."[40]

It was a remarkable invitation. Seven years after the first mining claims had been staked out and five years after incorporation, the camp-turned-town now wished to celebrate the past, the struggles against nature, the sarcastic barbs of competing camps, the bitter disappointments of failed smelter projects, and the unresolved townsite ownership. The move to resurrect and enshrine the past marked a new phase in the town's history, for the past is preserved by those who possess the luxury of confidence in the future. Aspen now had time for both. With the future assured, it could afford to look back.

III

THE CITY
Aspen, 1887–1893

11

"This Hour of Triumph and Joy": The Railroad Comes to Aspen

"Aspen needs a railroad!"[1] In its New Year's edition for 1886, the Aspen *Rocky Mountain Sun* stated in print what Aspen's citizens already knew. Everyone connected with the town, from Jerome B. Wheeler to the lowliest mucker at the bottom of the mine shaft, would have agreed. Aspen was not the first town to think in these terms. Such sentiments had become universal in ambitious towns everywhere; indeed, the mating of railroads with mining enterprises offered great advantages to both. Mining towns, often located in the most inaccessible places in the high mountains, needed the advantages of speed and carrying capacity offered by railroads. In transporting large shipments of ore to the outside world, railroads stood to reap large fortunes.

When mining began in the valley of the Roaring Fork, railroads had already been a feature on the American economic landscape for half a century. The ancestor of the modern railroad appeared in England about 1825, and the railroad—like other technology—rapidly immigrated to the United States. By 1830, several American railroad companies had been chartered and a few actually built; ten years later, the railroad mileage in the United States was twice that in Europe.

Such growth was only a prelude to the next decade, for it was in the 1840s that the railroad became a dominant economic force in this country. The railroad was ideally suited to the introduction of the factory system and the greater distances imposed by national expansion. This was the decade when the American nation annexed Texas (1845), acquired the Oregon Country by treaty (1846), and seized California, Arizona, and New Mexico by war (1846–48). The new continental American nation needed continentwide communications, and the railroad and the telegraph emerged as the sinews to hold together the diverse and distant parts of a single nation. The decade of the 1840s witnessed not only America's greatest physical growth since the Louisiana Purchase but also the first great boom in railroad construction. At the opening of the decade, water transportation by river and canal was the basis of American commerce and communication; by its end, railroads were in the ascendancy. Five thousand miles of railroad track were built during the 1840s, and by the time this initial burst of construction had spent itself, in 1854, the basic rail network east of the Mississippi was in place.

With their enormous influence already established, railroads became the subject of political controversy. The debate was partly about the support necessary for their construction (who should benefit and on what terms) and who should choose the routes where railroads would be constructed. Expansion out onto the plains and eventually over the Rocky Mountains intensified these political aspects. The new Republican party had made the construction of a transcontinental railroad line part of its political platform. Now in office and preoccupied by a great Civil War, it still pressed forward on its promise to promote a railroad to the Pacific. While men fought and died in the eastern half of the continent to see whether one nation would become two, railroad lines began to spread west of the Mississippi River. Congress provided federal support in the form of land grants and financial subsidies for the Union Pacific and Central Pacific companies in 1862, and later to other transcontinental lines. The federal government had made a decision to bind the nation east and west as well as north and south. It succeeded. The Union Pacific and Central Pacific lines linked up at Promontory Point, Utah Territory, in 1869. By the time a severe economic depression halted railroad construction in 1873, the major transcontinental lines had been laid down.

The close of the first generation of railroad construction also marked the end—if any mark was needed—of any reservations about the railroad's importance or influence. In the movement of goods and passengers, the railroad was such an improvement over what preceded it that there was no basis of comparison. In speed, regularity, and carrying capacity, it represented a remarkable advance in all areas. It cut the time of movement from New York to Chicago from three weeks to three days, to cite only one obvious example; it ran on a fixed schedule throughout the year, largely impervious to ice, snow, and mud; it moved goods and people in such quantities that it remade traditional economic patterns. The development of a railroad transportation network paralleled the appearance of the modern factory system and, with it, of a national rather than a local or regional economy.

None of these enormous advantages should suggest that railroads were without their own problems, either for themselves or for the people they served. To begin with, they were expensive to build and complex to run (by 1900 the number of railroad employees would exceed one million, to cite only one striking example). Because of the difficulties associated with financing them, they established new financial patterns and, not surprisingly, were often in financial trouble. These troubles came not only from honest overextension of construction but also from machinations, chicanery, and dishonesty on the part of officials. From the beginning, railroads were built on credit, supported by subsidies from the federal government and from states and communities that they would serve. Even under the most effective and honest management, they suffered from the fluctuations of national business cycles, not to mention the uncertainties of an infinity of local economies. And the management was not always honest or sensible. Bankruptcy, receivership, and the courts came to have an important impact on western railroads. The town of Aspen would encounter all these influences in its struggle to attract a railroad.

Railroads turned out to be ideally suited to mining enterprises. In one of those fortuitous intersections of time and place, the first great period of railroad expansion coincided with the discovery of gold in California and the great transcontinental migrations of the forty-niners and their successors. The spread of the mining frontier over the West in the next generation paralleled the expansion of the railroad network over the western half of the continent. Railroads performed functions ideally suited to the second wave of mining enterprise—that is to say, mining as corporate industry, in which large investment, reduction plants, and a work force of professional miners replaced the individual enterprise of single prospectors and their patient burros.

Railroads carried the heavy machinery necessary for the reduction of low-grade ores; or they carried the ore itself by the carload from the site of the mine to a distant industrial complex for smelting. These services were especially useful in silver mining, where large deposits of low-grade ore demanded treatment by industrial processes. For all its lovely mountain scenery and the exotic lore of lone prospectors, silver mining was, after all, another one of the industrial enterprises becoming part of the American landscape in the generation after the close of the Civil War. Furthermore, the arrival of a railroad in a mining camp led to a dramatic fall in the price of food, clothing, and other basic supplies, making the camp a more attractive and cheaper place to live. The arrival of three railroad lines in 1870 changed Denver from a sleepy village into the financial and industrial center of Rocky Mountain mining; a decade later, railroads transformed Leadville from an isolated mining town into a mining city.

The financial crisis of 1873, which struck especially hard at railroads, was a demarcation line in the direction of railroad construction. Up to this point, roads had built trunk lines into new areas of the nation in order to preserve their rights of way and to lay claim to a share of the support provided by the federal government, state governments, and individual communities. From then on, emphasis shifted from trunk lines to feeder lines that could be constructed to especially prosperous economic centers for freight and passenger traffic. Mining camps in the Rockies were among the most attractive opportunities. The difficulties lay in the high costs of construction into some of the most forbidding mountain terrains in the world. The risks were increased by the shaky condition of many companies emerging from financial crises of the 1870s and by the instability of silver-mining enterprises that produced silver cities one year and ghost towns the next.

Still, it remained a cardinal principle of railroad building in that age, at least in the Rockies, that no company could afford to give up an attractive route to a vital market, whatever the financial risks of construction. The result was that numerous communities languished without railroad service, while others had duplicated facilities. Major silver strikes occurred in Leadville in 1878, for example, and by the summer of 1880 this most remote of the nation's mining camps, at 10,500 feet, had two competing rail lines. Mineowners were delighted at the competition; railroad executives were worried about the low rates; stockholders were appalled at the additional debt involved in constructing lines side by side.[2]

These qualities of railroad construction—daring expansion, financial manipulation, confusion, and changing directions, in short, entrepreneurial statesmanship of a high order mixed with base cupidity—were nicely illustrated in the story of Colorado's own railroad. The Denver and Rio Grande Railroad line came to life as the vision of one man. William Jackson Palmer, born in 1836, had served his apprenticeship as private secretary to the president of the Pennsylvania Railroad (1858–61). During the Civil War, Palmer recruited and commanded the Fifteenth Pennsylvania Cavalry in campaigns at Antietam, Gettysburg, Chickamauga, and Atlanta. He was mustered out a brigadier general in 1865. The same year, he came west as treasurer of the Kansas Pacific Railroad, later a division of the Union Pacific. Palmer fell in love with the West, its plains and its mountains. Most of all, he loved its economic opportunity. Even as he helped to complete the Kansas Pacific into Denver in 1870, he dreamed of his own railroad that would run north and south down the front range of the Rockies, connecting Denver to new towns at the foot of the mountains, and eventually across Raton Pass to Albuquerque, on the Rio Grande.

Palmer's vision was simple and direct, but the task of making it a reality turned out to be fraught with all sorts of unanticipated twists and turns—a condition characteristic of so much railroad building in the 1870s. His pleasing personality, well-connected marriage, and many influential eastern friends gained him financial backing. Palmer began to construct the Denver and Rio Grande from Denver in the summer of 1871, and that autumn the first train streamed into Colorado Springs, seventy-six miles to the south of the capital city. From these auspicious beginnings, the line moved steadily forward. Palmer and his road reached Pueblo the next year, only to be halted by the economic collapse of 1873, which stopped railroad expansion everywhere in the nation.

Beyond these economic constraints that affected virtually all lines, Palmer discovered that what had started out as a relatively simple exercise in railroad construction had become complicated by various issues over which he had little or no control, but all of which seemed to threaten his enterprise. To begin with, he soon found himself hedged in by other, larger lines coming at him from the east and south. The Kansas Pacific (Palmer's old employer) eyed his little line from the east with predatory interest; the Atchison, Topeka, and Santa Fe challenged his route from the south, eventually denying him access to Albuquerque. Other small lines, such as the Denver and South Park, appeared to complicate his plans further.

A new economic focus now appeared in the form of a series of mining camps in the remote reaches of the Rockies. Four railroad lines jostling for routes and markets in Colorado found their attention diverted from the front range of the Rockies to the inaccessible interior valleys. Lines could not stand idle while competitors absorbed the best of the new silver camps, so Palmer and the D&RG were forced into expensive and litigious construction toward silver camps, new rail lines that the company could ill afford and whose economic returns were uncertain. The business of silver mining was, after all, extraordinarily

147

volatile, as any mineowner could have told Palmer. Palmer already knew. But in the style of railroad leaders of the period, he believed in expansion first and sorting out the lines and providing for the cost later. Unhappily, this policy had already severely strained the financial resources of his company. By the winter of 1877–78, the "Baby Road"—as it was affectionately known in Colorado because of its small corporate size and narrow gauge—had defaulted on its bonds and failed to pay dividends to its impatient stockholders. In the wings hovered the hungry Kansas Pacific, eager to pick up attractive routes to Colorado markets or, should the malaise prove fatal, the entire railroad line.

At this especially difficult moment for the D&RG road, another target appeared on the horizon in the form of the new silver El Dorado of Leadville. The great strikes of 1878 had made Leadville the most talked-about mining camp in the Rockies. A railroad line into the new camp would be expensive and risky; it might also mean a fortune. Palmer now tried to shift his expansion, from south toward Albuquerque to the west and Salt Lake City. The change was in part his decision, in part necessitated by the aggressive work of the Kansas Pacific, which had gained control of Raton Pass and so blocked him to the south. A line toward the City of the Saints and the Mormon trade would carry him across the Rockies and let him shoot a branch line into Leadville. After a vigorous fight in the courts about rights-of-way and a noisy but bloodless confrontation between rival construction crews, Palmer's personal appeals to bondholders to keep the faith, and endless behind-the-scenes manipulations, Colorado's "Baby Road" reached Leadville in August 1880. The battle over the Leadville route had lasted two full years and cost Palmer almost as much in litigation as the construction itself. Nothing daunted, he pressed on aggressively toward the west and Salt Lake City, pausing in flight to run branch lines to likely silver camps. In 1881, a branch of his D&RG reached Crested Butte, the southern gateway to Aspen. The young camp on the Roaring Fork could almost hear the whistle of the iron horse, a scant thirty-five miles away.[3]

"Within a year Aspen will no doubt be reached by the Denver & Rio Grande railroad," announced the *Aspen Times* in its first issue of 1882.[4] After all, the D&RG had reached Crested Butte. It was just a short step to Aspen. Railroad rumors swept the camp with the same regularity as plans for a projected smelter. There were at least two feasible routes: from Buena Vista by way of Taylor Pass or from Leadville via Hunter Creek. Parallels between the smelter and the railroad were noteworthy: the camp needed both, each represented a substantial investment and involved the latest technology, and stories about each plagued the camp and invariably led to disappointment and frustration. Perhaps most significant, a railroad or a smelter could be constructed only by a substantial investment of outside capital. Neither was an improvement that the camp could finance on its own.

A railroad into Aspen would be difficult and expensive to build. The shape of the land posed problems for construction of simple roads; a railroad promised to be many times more difficult. A railroad could not be built with the casual labor of the camp and paid for in depreciated warrants. The line would be very expensive, and even the most optimistic builder, like Palmer of the D&RG, could build only if his line was in good financial shape and if he had prospects of a good return. In 1882 neither condition existed. The "Baby Road" was in a state of financial exhaustion, and Palmer's leadership was under attack from rival roads and dissatisfied stockholders. Furthermore, the collection of tents and wooden buildings on the Roaring Fork was a mining camp without mining. Railroad talk gradually died out. The camp turned to the question of a smelter.

The season of 1883 brought Jerome B. Wheeler and his money to Aspen. Within a year, the camp on the Roaring Fork had grown into a town and, in the style of mining towns everywhere, a very ambitious one. Present growth and future prospects loosed a burst of enthusiasm once again for a railroad. This time, expectations seemed realistic. The town had a smelter, symbol of its transition to producing mines. Real estate and construction were booming; new people were flooding in. Aspen was in the summer of its rebirth. The great reason for optimism was Jerome B. Wheeler himself. The man from Macy's had brought new roads, producing mines, and a working smelter. Surely his power could produce a railroad. In September 1884, Wheeler gave the response to this query at the Roaring Fork Club on the occasion of a celebration in his honor. Fifty invited guests hung on his every word as he told them how he had become a director "in a strong company, who propose to build a railroad to Aspen in the near future." He would supply further details within sixty days, he told his delighted audience. In view of Wheeler's achievement of the past twelve months, no one doubted that he could deliver a railroad, by himself if necessary.[5]

The company to which Wheeler referred was the Colorado Midland. The Midland was new; whether it was "strong" remained to be seen. Like the town of Aspen and its new benefactor, Jerome B. Wheeler, the Midland emerged from the panoply of economic opportunities offered by Rocky Mountain silver mining. Silver camps needed railroads, and, where the larger lines would or could not provide them, smaller companies could be found or would be formed that would. Railroads became another important investment opportunity associated with mining camps. A small spur line could make a camp's future; it could also breathe life into the surrounding mines. Not surprisingly, railroad builders and railroad investors often bought heavily into the mines of the camps they proposed to serve. Jerome B. Wheeler was a good case in point.

A group of Colorado Springs businessmen organized the Colorado Midland Railroad Company in 1883. Wheeler owned a home in Colorado Springs, and he also owned mines in Aspen, a mining town that needed a railroad. It was natural for him to become associated with the enterprise. Among the initial proposals for construction was a line from Colorado Springs to Aspen. It was this prospect to which Wheeler referred in his remarks to the Roaring Fork Club. Unhappily for the town on the Roaring Fork, these original investors could not raise the estimated $2.5 million necessary to begin construction.

Soon Aspen's great expectations intersected with the large-scale ambitions of another entrepreneur. James J. Hagerman, who had made a fortune in the iron business as head of the Milwaukee Iron Company, came west for reasons of health—he suffered from tuberculosis—in the autumn of 1884. He bought a mansion in Colorado Springs, and his restless energy immediately propelled him into business ventures linked with the mountain West, mines and railroads. His interests eventually came to rest on the Colorado Midland. Hagerman seemed to have the access to capital that the original organizers of the company had lacked. The board of directors elected him president (and Jerome B. Wheeler vice-president) of the line in June 1885, and he now moved forward aggressively to raise the money necessary to construct a railroad line into the promising mining camps of the Rockies.[6]

To put these plans in operation, Hagerman chartered a Pullman car ("$35 per day including service"), and in January 1886 he went to New York. Although he failed to convince Andrew Carnegie of the prospects of the Midland, in two months he lined up subscribers who pledged $1,300,000 to the new railroad company. Jerome B. Wheeler put up another $100,000 to build a line to Aspen, and Hagerman solicited $25,000 each from David R. C. Brown and E. T. Butler, two of Aspen's best-known mining entrepreneurs. The capital now available, Hagerman and the Midland began a standard-gauge line into Leadville. Aspen seemed to be the next likely target.[7]

The town certainly thought so, as did the Denver and Rio Grande. The D&RG was in an awkward position, deeply in debt, unable to raise capital for future construction, threatened by the appearance of the rival Midland. Financial crisis had forced the road into receivership in 1884, and it was under the control of Judge Moses Hallett, the federal judge who would soon preside over the apex/sideline case. In July 1884, Hallett appointed as receiver William S. Jackson, a Colorado Springs banker and former treasurer of the road. In a reorganization two years later, Jackson became president. He tried to buy off the Midland with various agreements and compromises. Hagerman rejected all such blandishments.[8]

Jackson now appealed to the D&RG's reorganization committee to support one last gamble; the "Baby Road" must build into Aspen—preferably ahead of or, at least, alongside the Midland. Jackson emphasized the importance of Aspen in his annual report for 1886 to stockholders: "Aspen is recognized as second only to Leadville as a mining camp, but its development had been seriously retarded on account of its practical remoteness . . . as the wealth of the camp is largely in low grade ores, it is not surprising that work in most of the mines has been almost suspended, except for the purpose of development, until the advent of the railroad."[9]

Rebuffed for years in its search for a railroad and the object of pleasantries from well-endowed cities like Leadville and Denver—"there is a vast amount of paper railroad building to Aspen," commented one paper—Aspen now luxuriated in the attention of two rival lines. In the spring of 1885, the prosperous town on the Roaring Fork prepared to listen to the proposals of railroad entrepreneurs. The first to arrive were the representatives of the Denver and Rio Grande. Jackson had been forced to share authority with David H. Moffat, elected to the board of directors in April 1884. Moffat was a mining and banking entrepreneur of grand proportions. He had opened a stationery store in Denver in 1860 but soon went into banking as cashier of the First National Bank. Through the bank, Moffat met Jerome B. Chaffee, who would become one of Colorado's first United States senators. The two men began a partnership in mining investments that eventually included interests in more than one hundred Colorado mines. Political connections and mining interests led Moffat and Chaffee to railroading, with the former actively involved in management and the latter utilizing his many political connections as a former senator to look after their interests. They were a formidable combination.[10]

Moffat and Chaffee came to Aspen in June 1885. For the town, it was a time of jubilation and anxiety. The "railroad magnates"—as the local papers called them—were at last in town, but the apex suit loomed on the horizon. The two visitors, subjected to the maximum hospitality that the town could muster, stayed for a week and departed with guarded smiles. Moffat gave an interview at which he declared himself impressed by the energy and vitality of the camp and by the attractive mining properties in the surrounding mountains. "Aspen is not like Paris," the senator declared, "but it is similar to several of the mountain villages in Switzerland." He explained, "This camp is the hardest place to get to of any place I know of."[11] This was not news to Aspenites, who had wrestled with the problem for years. Equally discouraging to the prospects of the town, Moffat had also been struck by the amount of litigation under way that involved the most important mines, especially the impending apex case. It did not seem an auspicious moment to persuade a railroad company to make the large investments necessary to build into an inaccessible and litigious mining camp.

Aspenites need not have worried. The pressure of two rival lines, combined with the growing attractions of the town, dictated the decision to build. Aspen had a population of thirty-eight hundred people; its mineral production was probably on the order of $900,000 annually. In the style of Colorado railroad construction, Aspen, as a prospering silver-mining town, was a target that no road could afford to ignore. And as things sometimes worked out in the world of mining, Aspen would move almost instantaneously from being a town without a railroad to being a town with two railroads. Such continued duplication of resources—whether in smelters or concentrators or railroads—had become a trademark of the silver-mining world. It was now Aspen's turn to enjoy the spotlight. It was a "star" status that would last for seven years.

In the race to build into Aspen, the Midland took the lead. Already in Leadville, it struck out toward the west through the Hagerman Tunnel (modestly named for the road's president), which would bring it by way of the Frying Pan River into the valley of the Roaring Fork. The Midland had the shorter route, but the more difficult construction challenge. In July 1886, the road applied to the city council for a right-of-way into the center of the town. The line would run down Deane Street, the depot to be located between Hunter and Spring streets. Jerome B. Wheeler, a large investor and vice-president of the line, was among the interested spectators at the meeting when the council granted the request. His presence assured much publicity and community support for the project—not that Aspenites needed to be persuaded of the value of a railroad. But Wheeler was, after all, the leading public benefactor of the town, and if the railroad construction were to be a race, his presence on one side might persuade much of the town of the justice of the Midland's cause.[12]

After a slow start, the D&RG responded to the challenge. In April 1886, Judge Moses Hallett gave his consent for Jackson to make surveys from Leadville (actually Red Cliff) to Glenwood Springs. Like a good railroad executive, Judge Hallett had come to believe that the only way to protect the interests of the D&RG stockholders was to press forward with construction. Jackson responded forcefully, handicapped by an empty treasury. In the late autumn, he persuaded a reluctant board of directors to throw the full resources of the shaky company into the race for Aspen on the Roaring Fork. The figure mentioned was $5 million dollars. Aspen would not come cheap.

The year 1887 was the time when the competition to reach Aspen moved from the corporate boardroom and behind-the-scenes maneuvering to the construction of track. The business of constructing a railroad in the high mountains was an enormously complicated logistical task, made the more difficult by the forbidding nature of the land and the remoteness of the mining camps. Aspen qualified on both counts. The work was generally seasonal, because the high altitude of the camps meant a restricted period between frosts. Large crews (generally Italians at this time) graded the roadbed, and immediately behind them came the track-laying crews. The effective superintendent of construction must bring together rails, ties, track fastenings, water tanks, switches, coal, wood, and men in the right proportions. And with men must come food, tools, and animals.[13]

The D&RG had a new commanding general, David Moffat, elected to replace the tiring Jackson. Beginning at Red Cliff, a Leadville extension, crews graded toward Glenwood Springs. The sense of competition grew over the summer, as the two lines reenacted in miniature the great race of the transcontinental lines toward Promontory Point, Utah Territory, in 1869. In reckless disregard of the road's shaky financial condition, Moffat laid on extra crews. By early spring, more than one thousand men and a large number of teams were at work. In early August, D&RG tracks had stretched to within sixteen miles of Glenwood Springs. On October 5, the first engine emerged from the just-finished 1,300-foot tunnel and steamed into town, establishing Glenwood as the newest resort community in the Rockies.

But the prize was not yet won. Even before the sounds of celebration had died away, construction crews turned toward Aspen, forty-two miles away, up the valley of the Roaring Fork. Rio Grande contractors raised wages and offered bonuses for especially difficult construction problems. With characteristic business "push," the D&RG also began to run resort trains to Glenwood and sometimes shunted to sidings important construction materials in favor of all-day excursion trains from Denver. Construction engineers were furious, but the crews pressed forward and the track inched up the valley behind them, amid reports of the Midland's frantic progress down the Frying Pan. By November 1, eager Aspenites who climbed up the side of Red Mountain could spy the construction crews at work down the valley. The track drew closer day by day, reaching Snowmass on October 21, Woody Creek on October 24, the concentrator on October 26, and the site of the Aspen passenger depot the next day. The line from Glenwood Springs to Aspen opened for business on November 2, 1887.

The Midland matched every economic incentive and strained its corporate resources in the race to be first into Aspen. The road's financial condition was actually better than the D&RG's, and it had begun construction some months earlier. The factor it could not control was the landscape through which it had to build. Its construction course forced it to tunnel through the Continental Divide (the celebrated Hagerman Tunnel was 2,164 feet in length), emerging near the middle fork of the Frying Pan, where the road turned toward Aspen. The Midland built the tunnel in good time. What it could not manage was the last section of line into Aspen, where it had to bridge both Castle Creek (280 feet long) and Maroon Creek (650 feet in length). In mid-August, as the Rio Grande had reached Glenwood Springs, the Midland had already completed grading to the corporate limits of the town, but construction came to a halt to await bridging materials. Thus, by the middle of September, the Midland had come to the threshold but now had to stand aside and let its rival claim the prize.[14]

Aspen watched the approach of the railroads with a combination of high excitement and deep satisfaction. The prospects of the town justified such attentions, of course, but at the same time Aspenites could recall the recent slights and slurs of the outside world as it struggled for recognition. Now at last the moment was at hand, and the importance of the railroad was not diminished by the long wait. "Today the iron horse stands on the banks of the Roaring Fork, within the limits of our city, snorting with a noise louder than our mighty and roaring stream," the editor of the *Sun* wrote. "He will haul over our baby road the first carloads of minerals to the outer-world and return laden with the coin of the realm and the products of our brothers on the eastern slope." He predicted that the completion of the two lines would double overnight the number of miners at work, from 650 to 1,400. And as for the railroad itself, he concluded, "The D & RG is a benefactor not only to the citizens of this state, but to all the world."[15] Aspen's citizens would surely have concurred. Stockholders of the Rio Grande might have preferred some long-deferred dividends.

The celebration promised to dwarf anything in the town's short history. A committee of Aspen's most prominent citizens, including D. R. C. Brown and J. M. Downing, spent a month planning the affair. It would last a week and cost $5,000. Events began on the evening of November 1 with the anticipated arrival of the first official train, carrying President Moffat and his entourage of railroad officials, Colorado's Governor Alva Adams, and Senator Henry M. Teller to a barrage of bonfires, explosions, and speeches.

Aspen officials came to the station at seven in a large parade of carriages and mounted horsemen. There, they and an estimated four thousand of their fellow citizens gathered for the long-anticipated event. The train was an hour and a half late; for a town that had waited seven years for a railroad, the extra time was nothing. The crowd passed the time watching roman candles and rockets explode against the background of the mountains. Eight giant bonfires had been built high on the mountainsides. These were lit at the appointed hour and awed the crowd but burned out before the train appeared.

The editor of the *Sun* was there. Let him take up the story: "At half past eight o'clock the sound of locomotive whistles was heard, and, at a signal from a rocket, additional fires were lighted on the mountains, steam whistles blew, and giant powder reverberated from hill to hill. Three long trains twenty-five cars in all, came into the depot and were received by committees and citizens with a fervor which surprised even the Rio Grande officials."[16] President Moffat stepped down from his private coach to the tumultuous welcome. Aspen was deliriously happy.

Mayor Harding made a flowery speech of welcome, to which railroad officials offered appropriate responses. Then, leaders of state, railroad, and town mounted carriages, and a great parade crisscrossed a mile-long route to cover the three blocks from the D&RG station to the Clarendon Hotel. Marchers passed through every major downtown intersection to give Aspen's citizens ample opportunity to hail the local officials and distant celebrities who had made this dramatic occasion possible. The town itself had been scrubbed clean and was decked out in its finest. At the top of Mill Street, the parade route passed under an arch, where letters of red, white, and blue glass lit by electricity spelled out the message "WELCOME D & RG." Immediately thereafter came a stretch of a quarter mile lit with Chinese lanterns. "The effect was magical on officials and on excursionists. Here was a sight in the Rocky mountains which Denver could not surpass, even if she might equal." Leadville was no longer the basis of comparison.

The transparencies dwelt on the themes of the old contrasted with the new. Among those carried along the parade route, "One bore the picture of a stage coach on one side and a train of cars on the other side—'Coming to Aspen in '81' and 'Coming to Aspen in '87'; one other represented a snow shoer coming to Aspen in '79." James William Tanfield led a burro "packed with a prospector's outfit—it was the freight train of '86." All served to remind Aspenites that as recently as the year before, burros and horses were the only means of moving people and supplies across the mountains and to and from the mines. It was a fitting symbol of the revolution wrought by the arrival of the railroad.

After the honored guests had checked into the Clarendon and refreshed themselves, all adjourned to the opera house. There a banquet had been laid for 280 guests. Not a chair was empty. The feast began with oysters, "green turtle soup," and "buffalo tongue"; it concluded two hours later with "Coffee, Cognac, and Cigars." The toasts that followed extolled the virtues of railroad pluck and enterprise, mining, free silver, and the town of Aspen. No superlative was left unsaid; no glass, left half full. The range of speeches covered the history of the state, railroad, mining, and the town. The last toast, "Aspen," brought the crowd once again to its feet, where it had spent much of the evening and early morning. J. M. Downing rose to reply. His response served as a benediction to the close of the day:

> Then here's to our Aspen, her youth and her age,
> We welcome the railroad, say farewell to the stage;
> And whatever our lot and wherever we be,
> Here's God bless forever the D. & R. G.

The banquet guests emerged from the opera house to mingle with the ordinary citizens of the town, for no one had gone to bed. While invited guests had dined and toasted in the opera house, another group in the town had thrown a giant barbecue for six hundred railroad construction workers. A committee had also found beds for four hundred excursionists. Only visitors went to bed on the night of the most important day in Aspen's short, eight-year life.[17]

The arrival of the railroad—and within sixty days, two railroads—assured the future of the town. Headlines in the *Sun* proclaimed, "THE MORNING LIGHT IS BREAKING," and the editor went on to note "[T]he words of the old hymn are most applicable to the events of the last week." Everything had now fallen into place. The divisive apex issue seemed on the way to compromise; the question of the townsite and individual lots also appeared resolved. The railroad would make Aspen a producing camp.[18]

The coming of the railroad and the economic transformation that followed revealed again a salient quality that dominated mining camps in Colorado and up and down the Rockies, from the Canadian border to Mexico. No matter how rich the claims, the huge investment necessary to make producing mines ensured that only a few camps would make the transition to towns and that fewer still would make the leap to the status of city. Outside influences became paramount, especially the requirements of "eastern capital" and influence in high places. Nowhere did these qualities emerge in clearer highlight than in Aspen. Jerome B. Wheeler stepped down from a stagecoach in the spring of 1883 to lay the foundation for the transition from camp to town; on November 5, 1887, President David H. Moffat of the Denver and Rio Grande Railroad stepped down from his private car to the station platform, and in so doing he ensured that the town on the Roaring Fork would become a city.

12

"The Finest Mining City in the World": Aspen, 1887–1893

"Aspen to-day is the most prosperous city in Colorado." No one in the valley of the Roaring Fork would have disagreed with the *Sun*'s judgment in December 1887. It simultaneously conferred the new urban designation "city" and noted the prosperity triggered by the railroad. The arrival of the railroad in November transformed the town on the Roaring Fork into a city. The change, like the coming of the iron horse, took place virtually overnight. Reality now squared with fantasy as, in the words of the *Sun*'s editor, "the most brilliant visions of the past the present has fulfilled."[1] All the dreams of the young mining camp seemed to be realized. It only remained to bask in the light and warmth of long-anticipated success and to claim the rewards.

As the railroad had influenced every world it touched, whether England at the opening of the nineteenth century, the eastern seaboard a generation later, or the Middle West at the close of the Civil War, so it affected every aspect of Aspen life. The most immediate and obvious beneficiaries were the mines and mineowners. At sunrise the day after the great ceremonies of welcome, while large numbers of celebrants slept late, ore cars of the Denver and Rio Grande began to carry the silver ore of the town-turned-city down the valley. During the first forty-five days, ore shipments averaged twenty carloads (each car with a capacity of about twenty tons) a day. In the first month, Aspen shipped ore worth more than $1,000,000. Although the shipments dropped slightly thereafter, as the ore dumps built up over so many years were gradually emptied, the production of Aspen's mines increased steadily over the next five years, turning the new city into one of the half-dozen leading mining centers in the nation. Within thirty days, Aspen's mineral product rose from $900,000 a year to $6,000,000.[2]

At the other end of the transportation cycle, freight trains rolled into the Aspen yards loaded with machinery, mining supplies, and merchandise. The revenues of the railroads were almost evenly balanced between shipments in and out of the city. Thus, the railroad had an enormous impact on commercial relationships within the city and between the city merchants and the outside world. The railroad also affected Aspen's young industries. Access to smelting plants in Denver, Pueblo, and even distant Kansas City produced overwhelming competition for local smelting operations. Within six weeks of the arrival of the D&RG, the Aspen Mining and Smelting Company smelter had suspended operations.[3] This early gift to the town of Jerome B. Wheeler had served its purpose; the arrival of the railroad and a connection with larger and more-efficient industries east of the Continental Divide rendered local smelting operations obsolete. From this point on, the railroad replaced Wheeler as the most powerful single influence within the city.

A railroad connection to the industrial complexes and commercial centers in Denver, Pueblo, and even Kansas City refashioned the economic relationships of the city. Consider transportation. Heretofore, jack trains had supplied the town, laboriously moving across the range everything from canned goods to blasting powder and petticoats. Such an arrangement had established a strong commercial connection with railheads at Buena Vista and Crested Butte; it had fostered a large-scale freighting enterprise, involving hundreds of teams, with supporting teamsters, feedlots, and corrals near the center of the town, and a continuous demand for the hay cut by nearby ranches. This transportation pattern shaped mining and merchandising, for the cost and pace of mule transportation across the range dictated the pattern of business practices. The arrival of the D&RG, and within sixty days, of the Colorado Midland, changed these patterns. Railroad cars now carried from three to four thousand tons of ore each week to industrial processing plants; the returning cars brought quantities of goods for stores, basic commodities (foodstuffs, clothing), and luxury items (toys, interior decorations for the home). The traffic worked both ways, of course. Aspenites now found it easy to travel to Denver, and the competition between the two rail lines made for low fares. By the spring of 1893, several Aspen merchants complained that low railroad rates encouraged people to shop in Denver, and their businesses had suffered accordingly.[4]

More people, a new prosperity, and an air of permanence and stability gave Aspen a greater diversity of retail stores and a new emphasis on consuming. Aspen was a city with families. Specialty stores appeared for ladies' wear, home furnishings, and children's toys. This specialization also pointed to a community involved in a commercial economy, where people worked for wages and spent their wages at the stores. The days of barter, makeshift, and homemade had long passed.

Through all these variations in the commercial face of the city, Aspen prospered and grew. Growth was still something to be celebrated—a measuring device to show how far the little camp on the Roaring Fork had come and a basis of comparison with other Colorado cities. In the five years after the arrival of the railroads in late 1887 and early 1888, the population expanded at the rate of about 1,000 a year. The official federal census of 1890 enumerated 5,108 people in Aspen City (as it was known in the census tables) and 8,929 in Pitkin County. Editors fumed at the low count, and probably with some justification. Urban areas in general and mining centers in particular had large transient populations that did not appear in the enumerations. The growth was not entirely symmetrical. Periods of stagnation alternated with boom times, but the overall direction was always up. By the end of 1891, more than two thousand miners worked in the mines around the city. Local observers estimated that the population of the city itself probably exceeded 10,000 by the end of that year.[5] A table with some of the major variables reflects this steady growth:

	Mineral Product	Miners	Ore Shipments
1887	$2,360,000		
1888	$5,300,000		2,700 tons/week
1889	$9,000,000		
1890	$7,100,000		3,100 tons/week
1891	$9,300,000	1,767	
1892	$9,200,000	2,500	4,000 tons/week

Like industrial America everywhere in the late nineteenth century, Aspen was also increasingly a city of large corporations with large investments to meet the demands of a silver-mining business. To put silver mines into production cost large sums; to adopt the newest technology as it became available cost more. The corporations that invested these sums had their headquarters in Denver, Kansas City, and New York. Jerome B. Wheeler's Aspen Mining and Smelting Company was a case in point. In May 1888, the company shipped an average of nine hundred tons a week, one-third the city's total product. Its payroll averaged $30,000 a month. The Aspen Mining and Smelting Company was a private company and, accordingly, issued no report of its annual operations. Yet its profitability may be surmised. In November 1888, President Wheeler gave an interview to a New York mining journal in which he said that the company, capitalized at $2,000,000, had returned a net profit of $480,000 (after expenses and debt retirement) for the year just ended. Company officials reinvested these profits or returned them to the fortunate stockholders in the form of dividends.[6]

The annual meeting of the stockholders for 1888 took place on December 11 in the company headquarters at 54 Wall Street, New York City. At this time, President Wheeler presumably made the good news official. The small coterie of stockholders—the stock was listed on the New York Exchange in April 1889, but none was owned by the public or available for public sale at any price—elected (reelected) the directors for the next year. Those chosen included seven New Yorkers, among them Jerome B. Wheeler, who gave his address as New York City (it was one of his many addresses); Theodore M. Davis of Newport, Rhode Island; Thomas Edsall of Glenwood Springs; and two Aspenites, Walter B. Devereux and Fred G. Bulkley. Devereux was Wheeler's financial and technical adviser; Bulkley, the general manager of company operations. The officers included Wheeler as president and four New Yorkers.[7]

Thus, the single most powerful economic force in Aspen in 1888 was a corporation with its headquarters on Wall Street in New York City. The nature of large-scale silver mining made this condition almost inevitable. Aspenites, to the extent they noticed, probably accepted it happily in view of the benefits accruing from their city's relationship with Wheeler. Yet the impersonality of the business reflected the change from town to city, from small-scale development work in the mines to large-scale production and shipment, from the sense of intimacy of the small town to the impersonal and intense competition of the city. As Aspen assumed its new status of city, mining enterprise was increasingly a cold business, with large labor forces, and huge investments by absentee corporations. Aspen had become simply another part of industrial America. The new industrial landscape that had transformed New England, Pennsylvania, and the Ohio Valley had reached the valley of the Roaring Fork.

The prosperity and growth that characterized Aspen after the ar-

rival of the railroad(s) led to renewed prospecting and heavy investment. In the year 1888, new investment in the city and its surrounding
mines exceeded $1,000,000. In 1889, only the three miles around the
city of the thirty miles in the so-called Aspen Mineral Belt had been
developed. By 1892, the belt had been prospected for a distance of
fourteen miles, many mines developed (or "proved up," to use the
local phrase), and a handful had actually produced ore for shipment to
smelters. The largest claims began to buy out their smaller neighbors,
establishing a few large "consolidated" mining companies. The extensive investment involved in these activities supported Aspen's continued prosperity over these four years. Yet, despite the public tribute to
the energy and achievements of "thriving small mines," Aspen's production of silver ore was the work of eight major mining operations.
The increase in the ore shipments from the first use of the railroad, in
the fall of 1887, to the great year of prosperity, in 1892—from fifteen
hundred to four thousand tons per week—did not reflect more large
producers. It simply meant that the same few mines produced more.[8]

At the climax of its silver-mining enterprise, in 1892, the Roaring
Fork Mining District had some seven thousand recorded claims. Of this
number, perhaps as many as two hundred had been "developed" in
the sense that work had been done on them beyond the annual improvements specified in the law to retain title. Producing mines probably numbered no more than thirty in any year. Of this select number,
no more than ten ever paid a dividend to eager shareholders. These
figures suggest that the usual long odds of making money in silver
mining were as true in Aspen as in any other silver-mining district.
The large profits of a few mines served as a continuing inspiration to
the many claim owners and stockholders.[9]

In the six years from late 1887 to late 1892, eight mines dominated
the Aspen mining scene: the Aspen, the Compromise, the Smuggler,
the Argentum-Juanita, the Park-Regent, the consolidated Aspen Mining and Smelting Company, and beginning in 1891, the Mollie Gibson.
The press referred to them in respectful tones as "the big bonanzas."
And so they were. For their employees, production, profits, and (in the
case of public companies) dividends dominated the city. In August
1891, for example, of 1,767 miners at work in the district, 664 worked
for six companies, which employed about 100 miners each. None of the
remainder of the fifty or so smaller mines employed more than 20 men.
By 1892, the Aspen mine alone employed 400 miners, and probably as
many as 2,000 people in the city depended on this single mine for their
livelihood.[10]

The Aspen was a good example of the movement toward economic concentration. The Aspen Consolidated included the original claims to the Durant, the Emma, and the Aspen. After the legal agreement of 1887 that compromised the apex issue, the Aspen became one of the great producers of the district, and within a year dividends ranged from $70,000 to $84,000 a month, rising to $130,000 a month in 1889 and to $175,000 the next year. These numbers reflected the extraordinary production figures of this consolidated mining enterprise and the careful, creative work of Dr. Henry Paul, the acknowledged leader of mine superintendents. At the close of 1891, the mine had produced $7,500,000 since its discovery, $5,834,000 in the preceding three years. A work force of four hundred men shipped an average of 150 tons each day, seven days a week. Such figures made good reading in Aspen and across the nation wherever investors discussed silver mines and profits.[11]

The Smuggler was one of Aspen's oldest producing mines, for it dated from the first voyages of discovery in July 1879. It was also distinguished by continuity of ownership. David M. Hyman and Charles A. Hallam purchased the claim in the spring of 1880, and they retained control of it throughout the endless mining transactions and litigation of the succeeding ten years. After years of leasing the mine out to others, the Smuggler regained prominence in 1890, with discoveries of rich ore bodies on the surface. The production of the mine shot up with the opening and development of these great surface deposits. Hallam took over as superintendent. The Smuggler paid its first dividend in February 1892, and by the summer of that year, new strikes had made it Aspen's largest shipper of ore. The Smuggler had joined the short list of Aspen's great "bonanzas."[12]

These mines and half a dozen others made enormous profits from silver ore in the great Aspen contact vein—ore that they located by extensive exploration, mined, raised to the surface, processed, or shipped for smelting east of the mountains, all at great expense and some risk. But mining silver ore was only one way to make money from mines. An attractive and increasingly common alternative (or supplement) was through stocks and stock speculation. "Stocking" a mine, as it was known, increased potential profits for the company and for the small investors. It also spread the risks of failure. "Stocking," the issue of stock for purchase by the public, had come to widespread notice with the great fortunes made in mines associated with the Comstock Lode. Many of these fortunes had been made in stock. Shares in the Consolidated Virginia, which could be purchased for $1 in July 1870, reached $700 a share in early 1875. These were numbers to catch the eye of the most conservative investor. Nearer and more recently, stock speculation had been closely tied to the Leadville bonanzas. This route to profit became an important part of Aspen's mining story after 1887.[13]

In a sense, Aspen had shares of mines from the first claim. In the early years of few owners, ownership or part ownership of a mine was generally expressed in fractions, such as a half interest or a one-third interest. These interests might also be converted to shares of stock, but the stock was held by a few large investors like David M. Hyman, Abel D. Breed, Jerome B. Wheeler, or James J. Hagerman and not available to the public. Hyman and Charles A. Hallam, for example, owned all the stock in the Smuggler; Wheeler and a few associates owned the stock of the Aspen Mining and Smelting Company. In closely held companies, the stockholders were liable for additional payments, under which they might be "assessed" so much for each share in order to generate funds for the mining operation. Stock ownership, in short, was for the wealthy few who not only invested large sums in mines but also were expected to contribute additional money to retain their stock rights. Yet the continual publicity surrounding the profits of a few of these closely held mines whetted the public's appetite for a share of the profits associated with mining.

At a propitious time, the proprietors might sell stock to the public. The decision had many advantages for the mineowners. To begin with, it enabled them to raise funds for use in exploration, or development, or simply to meet the ongoing expenses of the mining operation, thereby freeing them from "assessments." It also established a specific value for their own stock, giving a specific number to their paper holdings. Of course, there were risks. If the stock could not be sold, the reputation of the mine suffered. The owners could also sell some stock and reserve the rest for a time when the value had grown. They had complete authority in their selling or withholding strategies.

In theory, the sale of the stock to the public also benefited the small purchaser. It gave a "democratic" tinge to the successful mining venture that had earlier seemed to be the exclusive property of the wealthy. Under the new public sale, the small investor might participate in the great profits that the newspapers celebrated, and the new purchaser had two chances to benefit: the stock might go up in value, and the investor might sell at a profit; or the company might pay dividends to the shareholders.

In fact, the chances of making money in mining stocks were about the same as those of profiting through mining operations themselves. The two were closely related, for the most profitable mines were generally the best stocks. But there were differences. Mining operations were usually the business (or plaything) of wealthy entrepreneurs who had made fortunes elsewhere and who had money to invest, some of it at long odds. The small investors on the stock market could sometimes ill afford the losses. Still, the low price of most mining stocks—many of them started at twenty-five cents a share—and the dramatic rise of a few made the lure almost irresistible. In short, most mining stocks for the small purchaser were not an investment; they were pure speculation.

Public stock in Aspen mines became a prominent part of the mining scene after the arrival of the railroad and the beginning of Aspen's mining boom. It was a period of intense interest in the mines of the Aspen mineral belt, with strikes reported weekly in the local press, accompanied by rumors of great investments and greater profits. Through the sale of stock, the high cost of development and exploration might be spread to the public. Aspen's emergence as a city and a mining center of national reputation coincided with the organization of the Denver Mining Stock Exchange. New York and San Francisco had exchanges, and a stock exchange in Denver to deal in mining stocks was a logical step in Denver's growth and in the maturity of the Rocky Mountain mining industry. For the public, the establishment of the Denver Mining Stock Exchange not only offered easy access to stocks but also endowed stock purchase with a degree of respectability and, presumably, safety. The bylaws of the exchange provided for the examination of the prospective stock, with careful perusal of financial reports, and testimony from supposedly reliable and disinterested persons. The new Denver exchange began trading in September 1889.[14] The timing was perfect for Aspen, where rising mining receipts were sure to attract the attention of a public eager to share in the profits to be made through mining.

The Denver Mining Stock Exchange handled only a few of the best-known Aspen mines, perhaps six or so in the period of greatest activity. A far larger market developed through local Aspen stockbrokers who sold shares in a wide range of Aspen mines that could not or did not want to be listed in Denver. B. Clark Wheeler, who stood second to none in business enterprise, bought and stocked the Bushwacker and the Little Annie. He sold shares of the Bushwacker to Aspen's working women and miners at twenty-five cents a share. In the Little Annie, Wheeler developed a scheme under which miners worked for the customary $3.00 a day, $1.50 paid in cash, the remainder in eight shares of stock valued at twenty-five cents each.[15] That he succeeded in selling his stock to workers above and below ground was a tribute to his resourcefulness and to the spell cast by the rumors of great wealth. Wheeler had an additional advantage: he owned a newspaper, which he used to promote his own stocks. Yet he was the rule rather than the exception. At the height of Aspen's mining boom, in 1892, numerous respectable brokers in Aspen handled stocks in as many as thirty local mines.

Aspenites lived in an atmosphere charged with news of strikes and profits. On the streets of the city they might meet H. P. Cowenhoven, who had come to the mining camp with two wagons filled with food and clothing and become a millionaire. Or they might see David R. C. Brown, once a clerk in Cowenhoven's store, who now had an income of $66,000 a month from investments in a single mine. All Aspen knew these stories of wealth and a dozen others like them.

Aspen's great economic prosperity and accompanying physical expansion after 1888 came to include industrial capacity above ground as well as mining below. The Aspen mineral belt and the two hundred developed mines tapping it laid the foundation of fortunes based on natural resources, but the processing of these resources was a complicated and expensive business. Transportation and smelting costs ate into the profits. From the Aspen mine's three-year (1889–91) production of $5,834,000, for example, the mine paid $628,000 in smelting fees and another $806,000 to the railroads.[16]

Newspapers, civic leaders, politicians, and even mineowners raised a cry to establish local processing industries and to keep these monies within the city. The development of an industrial complex in Aspen was a logical extension of the mines in the nearby hillsides and also a deliberate attempt on the part of boosters to make Aspen more self-sufficient. Aspen needed its own smelting facilities, but to establish them in the risky, competitive, and highly technical world of metals processing demanded extensive capital investment. And such a step would fly in the face of the interest of the railroads, which profited immensely from moving the thousands of tons of bulky silver ore to distant processing plants.

The industrial processes associated with silver mining came in several forms: sampling works, to give prompt analysis of ore samples; concentrators, to reduce several tons of low-grade ores to a concentrate; smelting plants, the final sites in the transformation of ores to metals. Each of these processes demanded the latest in technology, and they demanded skilled professionals to run them. By 1890, five samplers served the Aspen mines, although in slack times there was insufficient business to keep all working at capacity. Samplers depended for their business on exploration; concentrators reduced several tons of low-grade ore—say, ten tons of forty-ounce ore—to a single ton at three hundred ounces. The economic advantages of such industries were enormous. The processing steps would remain in Aspen, providing jobs and adding to the wages spent within the city. The product would be shipped by rail to a smelting facility, but in this case the mine would pay freight charges on a single ton of concentrated ore rather than on ten tons of low-grade ore. The Mollie Gibson mine built a concentrator in 1889, where it processed its own ore and the product of several other mines, principally that of the adjacent Smuggler.[17]

Aspen's plans to establish industrial facilities west of the Continental Divide achieved success with the construction of the Holden Lixiviation Works. Observers declared that "the sweet day dreams of those who have longed to see Aspen a great city [were] about to be realized" by the construction of the reduction works. The facility would employ one hundred men, and the city's population would double within a year because of it. The plant lay on the west side of Castle Creek, and the city built a bridge at the foot of Hallam Avenue to connect the works to the city. Incorporated in 1890 with a value of $500,000, or 5,000 shares at $100 each, the Holden Works (as it was called) was the city's largest and most expensive industrial plant. Among the principal stockholders was a wealthy Englishman. It was good that all stockholders were wealthy, for the facility cost $250,000, a figure that suggested the level of investment necessary to enter the smelting business.[18]

The Holden Works began operations in November 1891. By the opening of 1892, the works treated one hundred tons a day, including some ore shipped across the mountains from Leadville, a circumstance that gave Aspenites enormous psychic satisfaction after so many years as a poor relation. Some users objected that the charges of $12 a ton were too high, and Holden felt himself unjustly treated. After two years in the role of the industrial savior of the city and after great expenditures, he now found himself cast as the villain.[19] Amid the struggle of Holden to make a profit on his investment and the interest of the city in running the works as a civic resource, the presence of this large industrial plant remained a symbol of Aspen's growth and its emergence as an industrial city.

As the railroad stimulated mining enterprise and commerce to new levels and as Aspen developed an industrial complex, the construction industry boomed. A growing city needed varieties of new buildings, some utilitarian, others for civic pride. Among the most prominent features of new physical growth were business buildings, especially so-called business blocks. It was the custom of the day for a successful businessman to build a city block in a unified architectural style, using the best location for his own business and renting out the others. The business block was a symbol of the prosperity of the town, the affluence of the figures who financed them (and for whom they were named), and a growing emphasis on the physical appearance of the city, and the solid brick-and-stone facades bespoke permanence. Aspen's business blocks celebrated all these aspects, and the year 1888 marked their beginnings. Among those who laid plans for construction of their own business blocks that year were H. P. Cowenhoven, David R. C. Brown, David M. Hyman, and Jerome B. Wheeler. These business blocks are among the few vestiges of the mining city to have survived into the late twentieth century.[20]

The most important construction in the physical completion of the city involved two buildings that were significant beyond the potential return on investment. Jerome B. Wheeler was appropriately associated with both. The Wheeler Opera House and the Hotel Jerome were projects involving great civic satisfaction as well as utility. Every successful mining city could boast of a brick hotel and an opera house. The leading figure in the development of the city often built the opera house as a token of appreciation for his good fortune. Horace A. W. Tabor had done so in Leadville and Denver.

Wheeler now undertook such a project for the city of Aspen. It was entirely fitting, for no individual had been more influential in raising the mining camp on the Roaring Fork to its present, exalted status. By December 1888, workmen had covered the new opera house against winter and begun the final finishing work. Outside, they laid stone sidewalks instead of the usual wooden slats. The completion of the Wheeler Opera House in the spring of 1889 offered an opportunity to use this architectural wonder as a symbol of the progress of the city: "This building, built of red sandstone, is one of architectural beauty, and in cost and appointments equals many of the best buildings in the city of Denver." The banking house of J. B. Wheeler and Company occupied the corner of the three-story building. It was a fitting focus to a business district that now covered twenty city blocks.[21]

Wheeler had not yet finished with the city of Aspen. The large brick hotel that he financed and that carried his name remained a final and crowning achievement for his adopted city. Three stories high, 85 by 100 feet on the ground floor, brick with red sandstone trimmings, the building was situated at the corner of Main and Mill streets, which gave it the most commanding location in Aspen. Wheeler also intended it to be the most commanding building. Prejudiced Aspenites pronounced that its style, appointments, and decorations made it the finest hotel between Denver and San Francisco. The grand opening in November 1889, the social and civic event of the season, indicated that Wheeler had succeeded. Let us approach the front door in the footsteps of the two hundred Aspenites who gathered on that Thanksgiving Eve to marvel at Jerome B. Wheeler's newest civic masterpiece:

> Entering by this door the visitor is in a tiled rotunda, in which is located the office beneath a skylight of many-colored glass. To the right of the entrance is the reading and smoking room, and to the right of the office is the bar, back of which is the billiard room. . . . A broad stairway on either side of the rotunda leads to the upper regions. In the centre front of the second floor, entered by a wide portier, are the parlors, handsomely furnished. . . . The top floor is arranged much the same as the second. The building is thoroughly heated with steam and lighted by electricity. There are to be, when finished, over 300 electric lights in the building.[22]

Accompanying this private construction was a major new public building. At a special election in November 1888, Aspen voters approved a bond issue to build a new courthouse. The gathering of dignitaries in the fall of 1890 to lay the cornerstone at the corner of Main and Galena streets nicely symbolized the mixture of ceremony and practicality that dominated life in the city. City officials and representatives of various civic organizations in Aspen met at the site and offered appropriate speeches on the spirit of progress that propelled the city ever onward and upward. Their words mixed with the continuous chorus of sounds associated with a large mining enterprise. The *Sun* noted, "Owing to the constant passing of trains on the Rio Grande much of the exercises could not be heard."[23] It was a nice commentary on the changing nature of the new city on the Roaring Fork.

The completion of the railroad to the Aspen city limits did not mark the end of the drive for transportation facilities. The Denver and Rio Grande, and within two months, the Midland, began the construction of railroad spur lines to the most accessible producing mines. Throughout 1888, these new feeder lines snaked out in several directions—to the concentrator, to the Aspen-Smuggler Tunnel, to the Smuggler Tunnel ore chutes. Owners of means whose mines lay in more remote reaches of the valley provided their own facilities. J. B. Wheeler, H. P. Cowenhoven, and David R. C. Brown—an Aspen paper referred to them as "men of means and well known push and executive ability"— built a tramway up Aspen Mountain to their Aspen mine. The "tram," with eighty-six buckets, each with a carrying capacity of 150 pounds, ran from the head of Ute Avenue more than a mile up the side of the mountain. It had the capacity to move two thousand tons of ore each twenty-four hours to the large, commodious ore building erected at the base of the tram. The tram went into operation in December 1888, and after initial problems with the machinery it became a prominent part of Aspen's mining scene and a feature of one of Aspen's most profitable mines.[24]

The presence of the railroad at the ceremony at the courthouse and the continuing improvements by individual entrepreneurs symbolized the mixture of public and private in Aspen. The public celebrated the achievements and values of the new city; the private laid the foundations of these achievements by continued business investment. Both groups benefited from innovations in technology that assisted mining enterprise and the transformation of town into a city. In perhaps no other American industry—including railroads, steel, or petroleum, all late-nineteenth-century giants—did invention play as great a role as in mining. The *Sun* described the relationship in these terms: "The successful mining region often enjoys the latest strides in science far in advance of older communities, and the engineering skill finds in it a most inviting and profitable field." Examples lay on every hand. "The most approved and costly appliances for the extraction of precious minerals from the hills" had replaced the miner with pick and shovel; broad-gauge railroads had replaced "the patient jackass of scripture days."[25] Aspen swept along on this heady tide, rejoicing in the speed of progress, while mindful of the dangers in falling behind in such an intensely competitive race.

Perhaps the single most significant technical innovation for mining was the increased use of electricity. Indeed, Aspen was something of a pioneer in the use of electric power in deep mining. Wheeler's Aspen Mining and Smelting Company early installed electric motors for pumping out water, hoisting ore, and hauling. So successful had the experiment been that by the fall of 1888 the company had made plans to build a large central power station to generate electricity from waterpower for its own use and for sale to the other mines. Electricity became more significant in its application and more necessary to mining enterprise as water began to seep into the mines. With the arrival of the railroad, mines drove shafts deeper into contact veins in search of paying ore, and the deeper shafts began to fill with water, sometimes at the rate of several hundred gallons a minute. Coping with the inrush of water was one of the most significant technical problems in Aspen mining, and electricity became the most common solution. Huge electric motors powered elaborate drainage systems that made productive mining possible at depths down to one thousand feet below the surface.[26]

The advantages of technology fell unevenly on the mines, favoring those with the attractive locations and strong capital backing. The mines with entrances low on the sides of Aspen and Smuggler mountains had the best access to the railheads, and railroads built feeder lines to the largest producing mines. The growth of the city and the fabulous wealth generated by a few mines after the arrival of the railroad led to the expansion of Aspen mining to ever more remote areas—to Tourtelotte Park, to Maroon Park, and up Hunter Creek. These small mining operations—those with half a dozen workmen and an owner or owners who worked alongside them—pursued development work and production in ways that recalled the camp and town of ten years earlier. Jack trains moved up the primitive tracks cut into the sides of mountains to carry supplies and return with a few tons of ore, a remainder of Aspen's past still actively involved with its present. In the spring of 1889, for example, from sixty to seventy-five jack teams hauled supplies and ore to and from Tourtelotte Park. The mixture of past and present kept Aspen—and other mining cities—a place of variety, where the bonanza producing mine continued to share space with a hundred ambitious but less well developed enterprises.[27]

As Aspen grew from six thousand to twelve thousand people, between 1887 and 1893, the city had to offer housing and services to the new arrivals, especially to the professional miners and mining families that formed such an important part of the population. Fewer people could be accommodated within the old city limits, and the city had to reach out to them in more distant places. In September 1889, the city council chartered a company to build a municipal streetcar line. The first horse-drawn cars appeared on the tracks in early December. Within three weeks, two cars had begun regular runs. The early rides on the Aspen Street Car Company lines were adventurous affairs as cars jumped the tracks, but drivers soon mastered the necessary skills and fractious horses gradually settled into their routine rounds of the city. The completed streetcar system eventually stretched more than two miles, crisscrossing the city and extending its limits. Thereafter, descriptions of Aspen referred with pride to the "street railway" that enlarged the numbers and area of those served by the city. Promoters of the real estate developments took note. Charles Hallam advertised his new subdivision (cut out of the ranch that he and David Hyman had purchased in the spring of 1880) with the slogan "Regular Street Car Service Guaranteed."[28]

Streetcars changed the character of Aspen—as they changed the faces of cities everywhere in the nation in the late nineteenth century—for they enlarged the city beyond the limits of pedestrians to the limits of horse-drawn conveyances available at a price within reach of all. In Aspen, the fare was five cents to anywhere on the line. In this way, miners might be brought close to work, their wives might come to the center of the city to patronize the wide range of stores there, and their children might find easy access to public schools. In short, Aspen was in the process of creating its first suburbs.

Another modern device that knit together the dispersing population of the city was the telephone. Its application was still limited. In the fall of 1889, the Aspen Telephone Company had 137 subscribers, with 150 expected by the end of the year. Many professional people— doctors, lawyers, and mining brokers—had telephones. By 1890, most stores included a telephone number in their advertisements. Already talk had begun of a telephone connection with Leadville, on the other side of the range.[29]

On the tide of mining prosperity, civic improvements, business construction, and the arrival of industry, the central feature of life in Aspen as a city from 1888 to 1893 was the continuing growth and rising prosperity of "the finest mining city in the world." The *Sun* used the phrase in its first issue of 1892. For the year past, Aspen had produced silver worth $9,299,300, or an estimated one-sixth of the silver mined in the United States. Furthermore, the city lay astride a great belt of mineral thirty miles long—the "Aspen belt" was a common term—and there was no reason to assume that such growth and prosperity would not continue and indeed expand. Predictions for silver output in 1893 were $12,000,000, a figure many considered conservative. Mining had reached the 1,000-foot level, and although there were continuing problems with flooding at that depth, technology had solved Aspen's mining problems before, and there was no reason to assume that it would not do so in this case. "In mining machinery, pumping plants, and the use of scientific mining appliances Aspen stands at the head of all mining camps." Several mines had already installed large electric pumps, which gave promise of a successful and efficient solution.[30]

Construction had kept pace. Physical improvements in 1891 alone included the Holden Works, a new concentrator, four brick business blocks (including David Hyman's), three stone churches, an armory, a schoolhouse addition, and a city jail. The construction of private houses was equally impressive, with 320 new houses completed. Construction in that single year exceeded $1,000,000. At the close of 1891, the value of improvements exceeded $7,500,000, and there was "not a vacant house in the city." Such numbers provided an index of the city's growth.[31]

Yet Aspen was more than a growing collection of public buildings, business blocks, and private houses. Mining had laid the basis of an attractive and progressive city: "Its streets are broad and level; water works were built early in the day, so that the old fashioned evil was never known in the corporate limits; electric lights were introduced so early in the city's development, that gas works have never been built." In short, concluded the *Sun*, "all things are new in Aspen, and of the latest and most approved kind." Part of the appeal of the city, in retrospect, lay in its initial slow growth: the gradual evolution of Aspen stood in vivid contrast to the helter-skelter and uncontrolled development of Leadville. Now, at last, Aspen had both economic prosperity and an appealing place to live.[32]

The year 1892 seemed to provide confirmation of such expectations. A steady rise in mineral production had made Aspen the most important mining city in Colorado, surpassing Creede and even Leadville. It now ranked third in population, behind Leadville and Denver. Talk of paving the streets began. The mud and ruts did not impress visitors in the spring, and, given Aspen's new dimension as a tourist attraction, its appearance was doubly important. The city's manner and outlook had changed. This was no longer just another mining camp; it was a city that shared a sophisticated urban outlook with other cities across the continent. As one observer said, "the tastes, wishes and pride of our people also are taking a metropolitan turn."[33]

The crescendo of prosperity and optimism reached a climax in early 1893. About the dramatic physical achievements of the city, there could be no question. In an age of boosterism and brag, one could say, "Aspen is the greatest producing camp in the world." Pitkin County had 227 "developed mines," and 2,500 professional miners worked in them for three dollars a day. The concentration and reduction works associated with the city employed another 250. By a conservative estimate, the capital invested in mining exceeded $15 million. The population was estimated at 12,000, with probably another 5,000 transients.[34]

The city itself had kept pace and formed an appropriate setting for such magnificient achievements. A roll call of its public buildings, private residences, business blocks, public services, and social and cultural facilities made it the equal of any city its size in the nation and certainly the urban marvel of the age in the Rockies. Two major banking houses served the city, the Aspen National Bank under J. J. Hagerman and the J. B. Wheeler Bank under Jerome B. Wheeler. Two broad-gauge railroads—the D&RG had changed over to standard gauge in 1888—reached the city with regular service, ten passenger and four freight trains daily. The city was home to the third-largest opera house in the state; in the Hotel Jerome, it could lay claim to the finest luxury hotel on the Western Slope. A waterworks, electric lights, a hospital, and a streetcar system provided a full array of urban services to its population. Half a dozen newspapers, including two dailies, spread news, rumor, and gossip in the usual proportions. A large-scale and efficiently run public school system served the needs of a growing community, and stone churches housed the Catholic and major Protestant congregations. Finally, in the Mollie Gibson, Aspen had the largest producing silver mine in the nation, an acknowledged wonder of enterprise, technology, and profitability, in a state and nation of such wonders. With absolute confidence could the *Sun* declare in February 1893, "Aspen is the greatest silver mining camp in the world to-day if indeed, it is not the most wonderful in history."[35]

13

The Mollie Gibson: "The Richest and Most Wonderful Silver Mine Ever Discovered"

The Mollie Gibson mine began life as one of many claims on the west side of Smuggler Mountain. Its ordinary beginnings and its unprepossessing outer appearance of rock outcroppings and scrub bushes disguised the enormous riches underground that would make the "Mollie," as it was affectionately and enviously known, the most celebrated of the Roaring Fork District's seven thousand mining claims. In the days of its heady prosperity, most especially in 1891 and 1892, the Mollie Gibson achieved a reputation for riches of ore and profits for its owners that ranked it (in the eyes of its followers) alongside the famous Consolidated Virginia, the great producer of the Comstock Lode; the Homestake mine of Lead, South Dakota, the largest gold producer in the nation and the foundation of the Hearst fortune; and the Little Pittsburg of Leadville, the first bonanza producer of Horace Tabor. Had the fates of the international economy and domestic politics been kinder to the price of silver, the Mollie might well have produced a similar volume of riches. That it failed to do so does not diminish its sparkling albeit brief achievements. In the space of a few years, the Mollie Gibson became the darling of Aspen's present and the symbol of its future.

In the rush to stake out claims in the valley of the Roaring Fork in the spring of 1880, John Adair located what would become the Mollie Gibson on the then largely deserted side of Smuggler Mountain. He named the claim for his sister, Mollie, the wife of Judge C. M. Gibson of Pueblo. Early development work disclosed the contact vein, but the mineral was of such low grade that it was not worth mining commercially. Adair soon traded a half interest in the Mollie Gibson for a part ownership in the Josephine Mining and Prospecting Company. He sold some of the remaining stock to his sister and brother-in-law. The assets and stock of the Josephine Mining and Prospecting Company eventually passed to the Era Mining Company and from the Era to the Mollie Gibson Company. It was a story typical of the endless trading of claims of unknown value by early prospectors in the first years of a new mining district.[1]

The Mollie Gibson soon became embroiled in litigation over conflicting boundary lines with its neighbor, the Lone Pine, which had been more fully worked, with the same indifferent result. Two trials gave one verdict for each side, and in April 1885 the competing parties finally consolidated their properties with the Sequoit, a claim on the west side. At the time of the compromise, the Lone Pine received most of the attention, for it was regarded as the most promising of the three marginal claims. The Mollie Gibson was one of hundreds and eventually thousands of claims in the Roaring Fork District distinguished by its proximity to the camp and its location next to the Smuggler claim of David M. Hyman and Charles A. Hallam. Mines tended to be known by the neighbors they kept; rich and prosperous neighbors increased the value of every surrounding claim, whatever the level of work done or the mineral actually showing. So the Mollie drew casual mention as one of those claims associated with the more promising Smuggler, the J C Johnson, and the Lone Pine.[2]

The Mollie's early neglect had to do both with the nature of silver mining and with the special circumstances of the camp at Aspen. Silver mining had already shown, and the Aspen experience reinforced, the need for capital to transform promising claims into producing mines. The Mollie Gibson did not seem sufficiently promising to warrant such investment. Indeed, the most important early claims lay on Aspen Mountain, where the Emma, the Aspen, and the Durant dominated the mining efforts of the first few years. Their prospects received further confirmation from the litigation that soon surrounded them. Added to the absence of investment capital before 1884 was the isolation of the camp. When the cost of transportation across the mountains to the Leadville smelters was four cents a pound, or eighty dollars a ton,

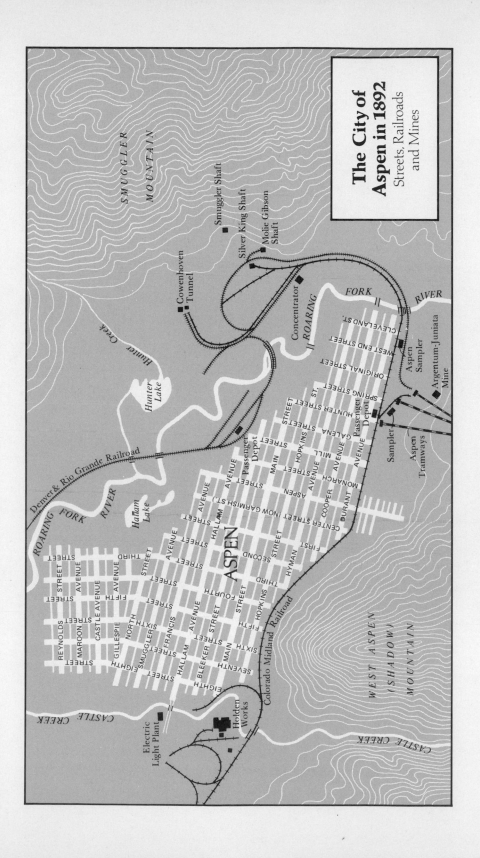

The City of Aspen in 1892
Streets, Railroads and Mines

SMUGGLER MOUNTAIN

Smuggler Shaft

Silver King Shaft

Molie Gibson Shaft

Cowenhoven Tunnel

Concentrator

ROARING FORK RIVER

Hunter Creek

CLEVELAND ST.

WEST END STREET

Aspen Sampler

ORIGINAL STREET

Argentum-Juniata Mine

Hunter Lake

SPRING STREET

HUNTER STREET

Passenger Depot

Sampler

Aspen Tramways

GALENA STREET

STREET

Denver & Rio Grande Railroad

Passenger Depot

MILL STREET

AVENUE

MONARCH AVENUE

DURANT AVENUE

ROARING FORK RIVER

Hallam Lake

AVENUE

STREET

MAIN STREET

ASPEN STREET

COOPER AVENUE

AVENUE

HOPKINS AVENUE

CENTER STREET (NOW GARMISH ST.)

FIRST STREET

HYMAN STREET

THIRD STREET

AVENUE

AVENUE

STREET

STREET

STREET

STREET

SECOND STREET

HOPKINS STREET

FIFTH STREET

THIRD AVENUE

FOURTH AVENUE

FIFTH AVENUE

SIXTH AVENUE

REYNOLDS STREET

MAROON STREET

CASTLE AVENUE

GILLESPIE STREET

NORTH STREET

SMUGGLER STREET

FRANCIS STREET

HALLAM STREET

BLEEKER STREET

MAIN STREET

HOPKINS STREET

SIXTH STREET

SEVENTH STREET

EIGHTH STREET

EIGHTH STREET

Colorado Midland Railroad

WEST ASPEN (SHADOW) MOUNTAIN

CASTLE CREEK

Electric Light Plant

Holden Works

CASTLE CREEK

only the richest ores justified the expense. The mines on Smuggler Mountain had a reputation for large bodies of low-grade ore, hardly assaying at levels that justified their transportation across the mountains by jack train. These claims would become the bases of later fortunes when the railroad arrived. Such was the argument of the camp's boosters. The experience of the first few years seemed to prove them right.

The arrival of Jerome B. Wheeler and his subsequent investments changed the level of production and speculation in Aspen mining. A few mines became producers, namely, the Aspen and the Emma. The latter soon became the subject of the famous apex litigation. But Wheeler's appearance led to renewed prospecting, a smelter, and talk of a railroad, and his investments increased the value of every mine in the district. Mining activity, at least in the form of exploration and development, increased on Smuggler Mountain, but producers remained few. In January 1886, of scores of claims on the Smuggler, only the J C Johnson could be described as a "pay mine."

Over the next three years, Aspen grew dramatically—in numbers, in physical size, in the range of services provided its citizens. It was a heady atmosphere of a booming present and an unlimited future triggered by the arrival of the railroad in November 1887. The production of the town-turned-city increased six times almost overnight. And around everything swirled the litigation brought on by immediate profits and the rumors of further strikes and fortunes. In the midst of this boom, bustle, headlines, and courtroom drama, the Mollie Gibson remained ignored. It was simply another claim on Smuggler Mountain, one that might, with sufficient investment, become a producer of low-grade ores. In the buying, selling, and consolidating of mining properties, it was just another card of uncertain value in the endless poker games of silver mining, in a world in which a dozen claims and fractional claims changed hands every day.

Henry B. Gillespie was a veteran of such games. His arrival on the site of the future camp in the fall of 1879 gave him the reputation of an "old-timer," a status that he shared with his wife. Both were long-established social and cultural leaders in Aspen. In the early history of Aspen mining, theirs emerged as a classic success story that later arrivals aspired to emulate. Gillespie, or the "Colonel," as he liked to be called, represented Abel D. Breed of Cincinnati in the acquisition of the Spar, one of the most prominent of the Aspen mines in the early years. For his services, he received a share in the mine. In partnership with Byron Shear, Gillespie managed the mine and Breed's absentee interests, and when Jerome B. Wheeler bought the Spar as a part of his widespread investments in the camp, Gillespie and his wife found themselves wealthy.

Whatever the exact numbers, the Gillespies enjoyed themselves. They were what the local papers referred to as "high rollers." They entertained lavishly. Playing the role of successful "bonanza king and queen," the Gillespies went to San Francisco and from there visited Honolulu. Their tidy fortune disappeared into several speculative ventures. The Colonel invested in Chicago wheat futures and came up a big loser. He also went into politics, promoting himself as a Democratic candidate for lieutenant governor in 1884. He lost, although he ran a strong race in a Republican state. Politics was another expensive hobby, involving investments in newspapers to boost his candidacy. By late 1885, most of the money was gone, and the Gillespies returned to Aspen, the scene of their earlier financial and social triumphs, where they resumed their roles as civic, social, cultural, and entrepreneurial leaders.

Aspen had undergone a remarkable transformation in their absence. Jerome B. Wheeler's presence had created a town in place of a camp. Casting around for opportunities to repeat his earlier successes, Gillespie sought work as a consultant. Early in 1888, the district court, noting his credentials as a former general manager of one of Aspen's leading mines, employed him to establish the value of some Smuggler Mountain mining properties then in litigation. Among the mines that he inspected was the Mollie Gibson. Gillespie noted that, while the value of the mine was minimal for litigation purposes, it lay adjacent to the most-celebrated mining properties on Smuggler Mountain. His responsibilities to the court concluded, he borrowed some money and in collaboration with his old partner, Byron Shear, acquired options on several of the properties in litigation. Foremost among the claims in his package was the Mollie Gibson.[3]

Gillespie now had cards to play in the game of Aspen mining. As with a poker hand, his options were numerous, and his possible courses of action closely paralleled those open to the first prospectors in the autumn of 1879. He could develop the mine into a producer. This was a task greatly simplified by the recent arrival of the railroad, but he would need to buy and install machinery, pursue development work, meet regular payrolls, and finance the technology necessary to process the low-grade ores that presumably characterized the Mollie Gibson. Each of these steps would involve large capital investment, the whole probably adding up to several hundred thousand dollars. It was capital that Gillespie lacked. Or he could promote the claim and sell it at a substantial profit to investors, preferably innocents from the East or from Europe, both on the Aspen scene by this time. With the arrival of the railroad to supplement the investment of Wheeler, Aspen was attracting capital from all over the nation. Gillespie also had a third prospect; he might list the company on a stock exchange, drive up the price of shares, and sell out. In the style of the veteran "bonanza king" that he was, Gillespie now pursued variations of all three.

His first step was to construct a processing plant. The claim presumably had large bodies of ore running from 5 to 20 ounces of silver to the ton. The problem for Gillespie was to mine these ores at a profit. The same issue confronted the other mines on Smuggler Mountain. What he proposed was to build a mill and concentrator. The latter would "concentrate" the ores of the Mollie Gibson—probably on a ratio of ten to one, that is to say, process ten tons of 20-ounce ore into a single ton of 200-ounce ore. What he did not tell anyone, and what only gradually found its way into the local mining currency, was that he sold a minority interest in the Mollie Gibson to Jerome B. Wheeler in order to raise capital for the processing plant. Wheeler's involvement seemed to ensure Gillespie's success, or at least access to sufficient capital to complete the plant. The mill and concentrator began operations in January 1889. They had cost $25,000. This was exactly Wheeler's investment. Gillespie announced that the Mollie Gibson would produce forty tons of ore a day to feed the new mill and concentrator.[4] In order to do so, he had to confront the issue of finding more capital. Miners had to be paid to bring forty tons to the surface every day, and thus far the Mollie Gibson was all cost and no income.

In mid-February 1889, just as things looked bleak, Gillespie reported a fabulous strike in the Mollie. At a depth of one hundred feet, at the end of a distant drift, Superintendent Ira Batchelder had discovered a streak of ore that ran from 10,000 to 15,000 ounces per ton. Over the next several days, reports of the "bonanza" in the Mollie Gibson dominated the mining news of the city. Residents read daily stories about Gillespie and Batchelder at the head of a brave band of miners who chased the elusive eight-inch vein to and fro under Smuggler Mountain. While Gillespie gave daily interviews to the press with details about the progress of the hunt, Aspenites collectively sighed at the silver streak's disappearance and rejoiced at its rediscovery. At the same time, the city's boosters used the strike to publicize Aspen's mines to the outside world and potential investors. The Mollie Gibson was Gillespie's—or most of it was—but as a success it also belonged to the city of Aspen.[5]

Gillespie had more practical matters on his mind. He sacked quantities of the ore and took the train to Denver. By this time, the assays had sunk to 5,000 ounces, but this was still a "bonanza" in mining terms. That the local newspapers found "the news from the MOLLIE GIBSON . . . too astonishing to publish" did not keep them from counting every sack, describing cars on the D&RG train that took the riches to the Omaha and Grant works in Denver, or reporting the numbers of armed guards. Speculations on the value of the single carload ranged up to $75,000. The Denver newspapers now picked up the story, reporting that the first four tons shipped had assayed out to $50,000. The Aspen *Rocky Mountain Sun* modestly called the strike "the richest ever known in any part of the world." Gillespie organized a ceremony to reward his superintendent. At a presentation attended by the Aspen press corps, he gave Batchelder a gold watch engraved with these sentiments: "Presented to Ira Batchelder, superintendent of the Mollie Gibson, by his employers."[6]

Over the next six months, the city settled down to daily bulletins proclaiming the Mollie Gibson as the continuing wonder of the mining world. Batchelder sank the main shaft down two levels, to two hundred and later three hundred feet, and then sent out drifts in search of the bonanza vein. Gillespie supervised the sacking of the "rich ore" and accompanied the shipments—generally four or five tons—to Denver, where he briefed the press on the continuing riches of the Mollie Gibson. The assays had settled in around 5,000 ounces of silver to the ton, according to the Colonel, which would make the Mollie one of the richest mines in the history of American silver mining.

Interspersed with the shipments to Denver, which went about every two or three weeks, came extraordinary specimens from the underground treasure caverns of Aspen's most publicized mine. As a climax, Gillespie put on exhibit in the company's Aspen office a 300-pound chunk, assaying at 10,000 ounces to the ton. The *Aspen Daily Times* headlined the whole display "WEALTH! WEALTH! The Mollie Gibson Produces the Most Wonderful Specimen of Ore Ever Seen." On May 1, 1889, Batchelder unveiled a single piece of ore, three feet by two feet by two feet, weighing 1,700 pounds, estimated to assay at 6,000 ounces to the ton, valued at nearly $4,000. And through it all moved Henry B. Gillespie, generously giving of his time and the company's resources to exhibit these specimens. It was a wonderful tribute to the city and its mineral treasures. The total production of such an extraordinary property was described in superlatives—"bonanza," "wealth," and "fabulous wealth." Specific numbers were never mentioned.[7]

Actually, Gillespie's public displays of mineral wealth were designed not to benefit the city of Aspen but to further his own plans. When he accompanied the Mollie Gibson's shipments to Denver, he pursued his third option—"stocking the mine." The selling of shares to the public at a good price would meet his continuing financial obligations, and the rising value of the stock would increase his equity in the mine. In early June 1889, the Denver Mining Stock Exchange elected him a member. Gillespie had been an early advocate of a Denver exchange, and in promoting an exchange when he had no property, he had shown extraordinary foresight. More likely, he simply demonstrated his own conviction that mines might be made profitable in many ways, including the sale of shares to a public eager to participate in the fabulous profits in mining that people read about in the daily press.

Membership in the exchange seemed to make Gillespie qualified to speak about the value of mining stock generally. Added to nine months of unending publicity about the Mollie, it left him in an ideal position to promote the mine under the guise of making the profits associated with this wonder available to a wider cross section of the public than simply the five original stockholders. He increased interest in the company by making its public stock issue the subject of uncertainty. He tempted the public with the prospect that the exchange stood in the way of fantastic investments by the nation's citizens. Surrounded by reports of the mine's extraordinary riches, many of which he had authored, Gillespie archly promised to list the mine on the Denver exchange "if by any means he [could] bribe the listing committee into accepting it."[8]

Gillespie was as good as his word. On September 1, he and the five other owners of the mine organized the Mollie Gibson Mining and Milling Company, with capital of $2,000,000, or 1,000,000 shares at $2 each. The officers included Henry B. Gillespie, president, and on the board of directors, Byron Shear. Ten days later, Gillespie returned from Denver on the evening Midland train and, interviewed by the local press, confirmed that the company's stock would soon be listed on the Denver exchange. Asked to characterize the newly "stocked" company, President Gillespie responded, "It has enormous bodies of low grade concentrating ore and there is a rich chute of mineral running through at least one portion of the property." His description seemed curiously muted, indeed modest by comparison with the public statements that had made the mine out to be scarcely inferior to the Seven Wonders of the World. Perhaps, as the stock sales of the company unfolded, Gillespie had reason to be modest. On Monday morning, September 23, brokers on the Denver exchange called the name of the stock for the first time, and very shortly the value of its shares was pegged at fifty cents. Over the autumn months, the shares fluctuated between forty-four and fifty-five, closing at fifty cents at the end of the year.[9]

In the little more than one year that he had controlled the Mollie Gibson, Henry B. Gillespie had made it the most talked-about mining property in a city with some seven thousand claims and half a dozen major producers. How he had done this was no mystery. He had pursued the option of modest development work and production while publicizing the discovery of a highly rich ore streak only one hundred feet underground. The accessibility was important, because Gillespie had so little capital that without appeals to investors like Jerome B. Wheeler he could not afford to sink a main shaft much deeper. In his plans, he had willing accessories, people like newspaper editors, real estate promoters, and mine brokers, all of whom needed something to capture the public's attention.

In a short time, the Mollie Gibson had become more than Gillespie's mine, or Gillespie's in conjunction with his five partners; it was a public resource. It was a vehicle for calling renewed attention to Aspen. For the city and its boosters, the Mollie Gibson might be used to promote the good of the whole. The editor of the *Aspen Times* suggested that a railroad car "decorated with banners and streamers" filled with the Mollie's fabulous ore visit Denver, Kansas City, St. Louis, and other cities. The object was a practical one: "In connection with the shipment a large quantity of printed matter describing Aspen could be sent out, and when the ore was finally sampled and sold, the returns, properly certified, could be published in every prominent paper in the country."[10]

The celebration of the Mollie Gibson served another vital function for the city: it re-created the rags-to-riches drama that was a foundation of Aspen (and every other mining camp) and that had faded from view with the emergence of an industrial city with a few immensely wealthy entrepreneurs who controlled so many of the resources. The Mollie proved, once again, that pluck, luck, and get-ahead drive could still produce a fortune. And, it was evidence that similar results awaited mineowners who would expend modest sums to develop their properties. The *Times* asserted "its belief that every 1500 feet of this contact [vein], for a long distance, contains paying ore bodies" and that no one can argue to the contrary without thorough exploration. The transformation of a mine with low-grade ore to a "producer of the richest ore in the camp may well be regarded as a guarantee that the contact may be fearlessly explored in any claim in full confidence. . . ." That the mine had so long had an indifferent reputation and "could have been bought for a mere song within a comparatively short time," as the

Times continued to remind its readers, made the riches flowing out of a shaft almost within the city limits so significant for other claim owners.[11]

The Mollie Gibson projected a wonderful vision of mining wealth—ores so valuable that they were sacked rather than loaded in cars by the ton, the owner riding with his treasure trove to Denver, the prospect of hundreds of thousands raised to the surface and several millions "in sight" underground. Behind the images, however, what might be discerned of reality was a mine in its early stages of development, struggling to raise capital to meet ongoing expenses, burdened with debt and operating expenses for a mill and concentrator that were losing money, and actual production figures that fell far short of the numbers suggested by expansive newspaper columns. The mill and concentrator, built to treat ores from the Mollie Gibson, could not do so, because the mine did not raise enough ore to keep the plant busy. Shear—he directed the milling operations and Gillespie the mining—ran the mill with ores from the Smuggler through the spring. Eventually, the milling operations closed down, idling machinery and a plant that had cost $25,000.

For those who read them, the first production figures might have been a shock. The press had claimed and Gillespie confirmed in early May that the Mollie Gibson had already produced $100,000 since the first great strikes. In its summary of the output of Aspen's mines for the first six months of 1889, the *Times*'s charts showed that the Mollie's "total output" was $52,500.68. By comparison, the properties of Wheeler's Aspen Mining and Smelting Company (especially the Spar and the Emma), the Aspen, and the Compromise Mining Company each exceeded half a million dollars. The daily output of the Mollie was a meager ten tons, or about half a railroad carload. The work force of twenty-eight men made the mine one of the smallest employers among producing mines. According to these figures, the Mollie Gibson was in a class with the Last Dollar and the O.K. mines, which were not household names in the mining world. When Gillespie at last put the stock on the market, only five thousand shares could be sold and these at fifty cents a share or less. The stock that had opened at fifty cents soon fell below forty cents. The company had not paid a dividend. Gillespie was in debt, and by fall he could no longer meet the payroll. On September 1, the president of the most publicized mine in the most publicized silver-mining city in the nation sought help. He went quietly to Jerome B. Wheeler and James J. Hagerman.[12]

The result of these negotiations was the reorganization of the company, its consolidation with the Contact Mining Company (J. J. Hagerman, president), with its capital of $5,000,000 divided into 1,000,000 shares at $5 each. The announcement provided details about the difficulties of the parent company, as the rich ore chute had given out and the deep workings covered by an inrush of water. The name of the new company remained the Mollie Gibson Mining and Milling Company, but the new president was James J. Hagerman. Hagerman immediately put $50,000 into the treasury for work; he also paid $20,000 in debts incurred by Gillespie.[13]

The administration of James J. Hagerman contrasted in virtually every respect with that of his more flamboyant predecessor. First came changes in personnel, as Hagerman replaced Batchelder with his own superintendent, C. E. Palmer. The new management now began systematic exploration and development of the mine. Palmer drove the incline to a third level (three hundred feet below the surface) and then a fourth (four hundred feet below). This work took a full six months. At each level, including the first and second, miners extended drifts north and south in search of ore bodies. This continuing development work cost about $6,000 a month. To assist in the exploration for paying ore bodies, the company began to use diamond drills. The contact vein in the Mollie Gibson was so small that it could not be thoroughly prospected by drift and crosscuts without enormous expense. The diamond drills took small but useful samples at close intervals. Drilling a seven-eighths-inch core at the rate of sixty feet a day, the new drills rapidly disclosed the mineral composition of large sections of the mine. The diamond drills were expensive, but Hagerman's capital gave the whole operation a long-range businesslike air that contrasted with the hand-to-mouth operations of Gillespie, who had to depend on high-grade ores immediately brought to the surface to pay monthly operating expenses.[14]

Water was Palmer's most difficult problem. Below the 200-foot level, the incline and drifts took in an estimated 150 gallons a minute. If the water flow could not be slowed, the other improvements were irrelevant as far as productive mining was concerned. Palmer's solution was to close the mine for three months, while he dealt with the water problem. The Knowles pump and plant that Palmer installed at the bottom of the incline of the fourth level had the capacity to raise 1,000 gallons a minute through an eight-inch pipe over a vertical lift of 300 feet. In addition, two smaller pumps in other parts of the mine delivered water to the main pump, where it could be moved rapidly to the surface. Work on the pumping station was completed on November 15, 1890, almost exactly one year after Hagerman and his man

Palmer took control of the Mollie Gibson. For the first time, actual mining operations could begin under the new management.[15]

The first mineral strike in the Mollie Gibson under Hagerman and Palmer took place on December 9, 1890, on the third level, south. One week later, miners found the rich ore chute that had been the basis of the Gillespie strikes on the fourth level. The management said nothing about these discoveries; when rumors began to circulate in the city, Palmer and Hagerman deliberately downplayed the significance of the finds. "The statements are very conservative," noted the *Times*. "Not the whole truth is told." Palmer even denied that the new discoveries were important, although the wide smile on Byron Shear's face—he was still a major shareholder—served to alert the press. As the high quality of the strikes became more apparent, Palmer threatened to discharge any miner who talked to the press. He had reason to fear a breach in his tight security, for the weeks after the first discovery saw an almost unending series of strikes, each richer than the last.[16]

By early February 1891, sixty days after the initial discoveries, the Mollie Gibson had once again become the principal topic of conversation in Aspen. In spite of the continuing reticence of the officers, superintendent, and employees, enough was known of the strikes to lead the *Times* (which needed little encouragement to praise Aspen mining properties) to say, "[T]he developments in the MOLLIE GIBSON prove it to be one of the greatest silver mines the world has ever known." The paper went on, "It is no exaggeration that the equal of the MOLLIE GIBSON mine has never before been known in Colorado." Explorations had opened up an immense body of rich ore in the fourth level, north. Gillespie's earlier claims had been based on a vein eight inches thick; the new vein was four to six feet wide. "The key to the mine has been discovered and its vaults have been unlocked," concluded the *Times*.[17] It was an analogy to a bank. All that remained was to empty the vaults in systematic fashion.

The spring of 1891 was the season of superlatives in Aspen. While officials connected with the Mollie Gibson continued their policy of saying little or nothing, newspapers sought to give an eager public coverage of everything associated with the mine. The nature of the ore bodies, their assays and total value, the principal stockholders and their lifestyles, technical and miscellaneous details—all had become daily reading in the "Crystal City of the Rockies."[18]

In order to diffuse speculation, the company brought boxes and sacks of mineral under armed guard to the railroad depot after midnight and shipped the samples in express cars to the Omaha and Grant smelter in Denver. Such arrangements only intensified interest in the mine and its ores. Newspapers interviewed railroad employees and even acquired information about the assays from several men who had stolen ore from the mine. The result of this piecemeal assessment was that the Mollie had at least one thousand tons blocked out assaying between two and three thousand ounces to the ton. An educated guess declared that $3,000,000 in silver lay between the third and fourth levels of the Mollie Gibson. Through all the excitement, Hagerman secluded himself at his home in Colorado Springs, Palmer remained underground or inaccessible in the company office, and other large stockholders simply smiled.[19]

This time, production in the Mollie Gibson kept pace with the superlatives. With their characteristic caution and preparation, Hagerman and Palmer delayed shipping until they were satisfied that everything was in order and that ore might be raised to the surface as part of a long-range plan for efficient and continuous production. The first large-scale shipment of ore from the new strikes took place on March 1. By the middle of the month, the Mollie shipped daily forty tons of ore worth an estimated $1,500 a ton. Newspaper editors with quick pencils calculated that the mine could ship $1,000,000 in a month.[20]

In a production sense, this might have been true, but difficulties rapidly appeared in the smelting operations. Smelters did not welcome such rich ore; there was more profit in large quantities of average ore. Furthermore, the high assays and returns meant a continuous payment of tens of thousands of dollars for each shipment, and even the largest smelters were pressed to keep such cash flowing in and out. As a result, much of the Mollie Gibson's rich ores had to be mixed with poorer ores to reduce the silver content from 600 ounces to the ton to 250 ounces to the ton.[21]

The Mollie also had large fixed costs. In 1891, for example, the company dispersed $106,000 in debt payments, $171,000 for new property purchases, and $243,000 for operations and construction. Freight charges and treatment costs at the smelter represented additional overhead. Even with inconveniences in rich ores and substantial costs, the production record of the Mollie for 1891 was a remarkable one. Between March 1 and November 15, the mine produced ores valued at $1,645,000. Consider that the great Aspen mine had become the leading producer of the district by mining ores that assayed at 48 ounces of silver to the ton; for nine and a half months of 1891, the Mollie Gibson mined and shipped ore whose average value never fell below 600 ounces to the ton.[22]

At almost the same time when the Mollie Gibson began to ship ore, the officers took other steps to ensure the future of the company by purchasing the Silver King, a property immediately adjacent to the Mollie. Hagerman had to fight off other rapacious entrepreneurs, chiefly David H. Moffat, president of the Denver and Rio Grande Railroad. He paid $150,000 in cash, most of it to Captain George W. Thatcher, the principal owner. Hagerman also agreed to pay a royalty of 15 percent on all ore extracted from the ground of the former Silver King. Thatcher would prove a difficult man to do business with, but Hagerman needed the King, even if he had to deal with the devil. The Mollie Gibson now had sixty acres of ground, the King's apex contact vein, and an excellent mining plant. In its final form, the Mollie Gibson Consolidated Mining and Milling Company consisted of the original Mollie Gibson, the Lone Pine, the Silver King, a part of the Emma, and some other fractional claims.[23]

With the news of the strikes in 1891, and despite the silence of the officers and superintendent, Mollie Gibson stock began to move upward. As late as December 1890, the share price had been about thirty cents. By late January, it had risen to seventy-five cents, and after a pause, on March 1, shares reached $1.00 on the Denver exchange. Then, as the mine continued to ship ore at the rate of forty tons a day, the stock doubled to $2.00 by March 21, and on April 1 reached $3.00. In four months, the price had increased ten times. With the mine stocked at 1,000,000 shares, the book value of the Mollie Gibson was now $3,000,000. Throughout the summer and into the fall, propelled by the unending accounts of the riches pouring from the mines, the stock continued to rise, reaching $7.25 a share by October 1. Predictions that it would reach $10.00 by the end of the year seemed, if anything, conservative.[24]

Newspaper accounts, street gossip, and reports from the Denver smelters aside, the most powerful force driving the price of Mollie Gibson stock upward was the dividend. Dividend-paying silver mines—in Aspen or anywhere in the world, for that matter—were among the rarest of God's creations. Of the seven thousand mining claims in the Roaring Fork District, no more than fifty ever shipped ore commercially, that is to say, shipped ore for processing rather than for assaying. And of these fifty, no more than a dozen paid dividends to shareholders. And, finally, of those that paid such dividends, not more than six offered stock to the public at a price within the range of an ordinary investor. The great Aspen mine property, for example, was owned solely by a small group of investors headed by Jerome B. Wheeler. Although it was reputed to pay large dividends, as a private corporation—the mine was listed on the New York Stock Exchange, and shares occasionally changed hands at about $40 a share—the Aspen published no annual report.

The Mollie Gibson was one of those few mines that became available to the public before its great riches became known. That this happened was due in large part to the efforts of Henry B. Gillespie to raise money for operating expenses. The number of its shareholders never exceeded four hundred, and six men owned most of the stock, but the company was still a public corporation in the sense that the stock could be bought and sold by individuals. Management declared the first dividend of five cents a share April 10, along with a stock dividend of the 25,000 shares left in the treasury, prorated among the shareholders of record on April 15. It is ironic that these dividend shares languished in the treasury because they could not be sold when Gillespie first offered the stock to the public. Hereafter, the company paid fifteen cents a share, or a total of $150,000 each month. By mid-November, dividends totaled $700,000, and the treasury had a $425,000 surplus. Hagerman constantly had to deny rumors that he would increase the dividends. Given a dividend return of $1.80 per share projected over a year, it is little wonder that the stock rose to unprecedented levels in a record time.[25]

As the source of great riches, the Mollie Gibson not surprisingly also became the object of great litigation. The lawsuits that in a burst of symmetry filled the columns of the press adjacent to those detailing the wondrous production of the mine had a different character from much of the early conflict over Aspen mines. The great legal battles of the earlier periods had revolved around ownership of rights to the contact vein, as exemplified by the courtroom struggle over the apex principle. Or they hinged on the problem of location, the original location being pitted against conflicting claims or amended locations that had claimed the same vital few acres over the contact vein. The original litigation between the Mollie Gibson and the Lone Pine took place over this question, and here, and eventually almost everywhere (even in the celebrated apex suits), compromise proved the most common outcome.

The litigation over the Mollie Gibson that began in 1891 was different in nature. The issue was not conflict over area but conflict over ownership of shares of stock in the mine. The legal battles that developed were very personal, pitting the leading entrepreneurs of the mining district against one another in suits that rested not on legal principles (as in the case of the apex) but on personal integrity and charges of fraud.

The Mollie Gibson had had many owners and part owners since the driving of the first stakes on the original claim in 1880. The buying and selling of the mine reached a new level with the ascent to power of Henry B. Gillespie. Gillespie brought in various junior partners in his search for liquid capital to continue mining operations. He also "stocked" the mine and offered shares to the public through the Denver Mining Stock Exchange with the same object in view. In the end, he found water in the shafts and his own debts rising in like proportion. He accepted James J. Hagerman as controlling partner but retained a large block of stock. In early 1890, three months after the change in management, Gillespie sold Jerome B. Wheeler 145,000 shares for thirty cents a share. Later, he disposed of a block of 50,000 shares to Hagerman for $1.25 a share, a very considerable advance over the price to Wheeler. In spite of these sales, Gillespie continued to demand the rights due a major shareholder, although his holdings were minimal and he had not paid assessments on the stock when he owned it.[26]

Then came the strikes of December 1890 and the bonanzas of January and February 1891. These events represented a watershed in the ownership of stock in the Mollie Gibson. Earlier, stock had changed hands with regularity, most of the transactions involving the purchase of shares by Hagerman to consolidate his claim to the property; thereafter, little or no stock changed hands, except for ever-increasing prices. In May 1891, Gillespie announced that he would bring suit against Hagerman on the grounds that, after disposing of his 50,000 shares for $75,000, Gillespie was told by informants that Hagerman was aware of the large bodies of rich ore and had deliberately kept the discoveries a secret in order to acquire the shares at a nominal price. In short, the issue was fraud and misrepresentation. The difference in the stock's prices would be about $250,000, a sum that Gillespie now sought in the courts.[27]

Gillespie's legal action was only the first. In March 1892, while the Gillespie-Hagerman suit still awaited trial, Jerome B. Wheeler filed suit against Hagerman, J. E. Boles, and C. E. Palmer, the major stockholders of the Mollie Gibson, charging that fraud had been used to inveigle him to sell his shares in the mine below market value. The legal activities of the several present and former shareholders soon exceeded in interest and newsprint the continuing remarkable production of the Mollie Gibson Consolidated Mining and Milling Company. In May, the *Aspen Times* ran the headline "THE KINGS AT WAR. The Mollie Gibson and Her Suitors Before the Courts."[28] With the stock over ten dollars a share and dividends holding steady, the stakes of the two parties were increasing while the cases rested idle on the docket.

The saga of the Mollie Gibson marked a high point in the mining experience of Aspen. The city had its celebrated mining claim, a mine of fabulous wealth to compare with any other in the nation, legal conflict between the leading entrepreneurs of the day, a rising stock, and regular dividends. Yet we should take note that, though the Mollie was the most publicized of Aspen's mines from 1887 to 1893, it was far from being the only mine that drew the admiring attention of press and public. A score of others regularly found their way into the public eye, with strikes, stock schemes, rumors of sales (generally to Wheeler or Hagerman), and improvements. Throughout these seven years, Aspen mining moved to ever more remote places, spurred by the riches of the Aspen, the Compromise, and the Mollie Gibson, with the thought that other claims just as wealthy might lie just over the next creek or valley, only awaiting the owner with capital and pluck, who would take a risk.

The Mollie Gibson illustrated most of the themes of mining Aspen in these years. It brought into the same arena the two entrepreneurial styles that opened up the mines (and the camp) on the Roaring Fork. Henry B. Gillespie was the "boomer," the man who made up for lack of capital by taking risks, trusting to instinct, benefiting from the investments of others in projects that he had the foresight and luck to begin. His successor, James J. Hagerman, was a successful businessman, with a record of achievements as head of the Milwaukee Iron Company, who came west to Colorado Springs for his health. He was responsible, more than any other individual, for the successful operations of the Colorado Midland Railroad (whose appearance on the scene spurred the D&RG to plan to build a line to Aspen after years of ignoring the camp on the Roaring Fork). In their activities with the Mollie Gibson, Gillespie and Hagerman acted very much like themselves. Gillespie treated the mining operation like an exercise in publicity and marketing; Hagerman saw it as simply another aspect of industrial production, where large investments of capital and careful planning produced a suitable reward. That such skills and important achievements only made him the object of legal action by less successful colleagues-turned-rivals was very much in the mining tradition.

The Mollie Gibson was enormously important to the city of Aspen. The strikes in the mine earned it notoriety in Denver and eventually throughout the nation. For Aspen, the presence of the Mollie was a sign of legitimacy. The mine proved the reality of the optimistic declarations of the preceding ten years. In its infancy, it was ignored; in middle age, it was the object of several suitors, who used the mine in different ways; in maturity, it was a prototype mining operation— conservative and careful in management, stable in production, generous in dividends, extraordinary in the rewards that it offered owners and investors.

The story of the Mollie Gibson added to the legend of Aspen's silver riches. Hagerman and Wheeler added to their wealth. Gillespie made a nest egg for further adventures. Palmer made his first fortune, moving from superintendent to stockholder. But the most dramatic story was that of Byron Shear, Gillespie's old partner in the Spar and his first partner in the Mollie. When Hagerman reorganized the company in the fall of 1889 and emerged as president, Shear held on to his stock. Between winter 1890 and spring 1892, the price of shares went from thirty cents to $10 a share. When Shear sold out to Hagerman, in February 1892, his sixty thousand shares were worth $600,000. In the interval, he had also earned another $200,000 in dividends. On the occasion of the transaction, the *Times* noted that Shear had come to Aspen without a penny in May 1880, and B. Clark Wheeler gave him a job for $2.50 a day plus board. Now Shear was headed to Washington, D.C., where he was building a house that would cost $150,000. In the style of mining camaraderie, the *Times* saluted his departure and re-joiced "in his prosperity, and pray[ed] that every old timer and all newcomers may strike it as rich." When the editor observed that the owners of the Mollie Gibson would "take up their positions in life as bonanza kings," he was only confirming what was expected and accepted behavior. Men and women did not seem to begrudge others success and the displays that came with it. They wished only to emulate them.[29]

14

"It Is Useless to Say That Here All Have an Equal Chance": Working and Living in Aspen, 1887–1893

In the burst of growth and prosperity that engulfed Aspen from 1887 to 1893, its boosters referred to the transformation of the mining camp with such phrases as "metropolitan life" and "metropolitan airs."[1] With its new urban condition, however, Aspen had a new character. What had been a simple mining camp ten years earlier had by 1893 been transformed into a modern (by nineteenth-century standards) industrial city. Into the Eden-like valley of the Roaring Fork came all the by-products of late-nineteenth-century American industrial life: the noises associated with machinery and railroads, smoke from the concentrators and the Holden Works, dirt and grime from the industrial processes carried on within the limits of the city itself, the growing residue of waste products of mining and its industrial by-products, and the systematic cutting of timber on the sides of the mountains to meet the ravenous appetites of the mines (the Smuggler mine alone used 100,000 board feet a month in its underground operations) that left the surrounding hillsides as bare as a stretch of arctic tundra.

These physical manifestations aside, the emergence of Aspen as an industrial city brought a large work force of professional mines to the valley of the Roaring Fork. They replaced the early mix of prospectors, small merchants, and teamsters, occupations associated with a mining camp, not a city. The new arrivals gave Aspen an appearance and character similar to those of mining cities like Butte (Montana) and eastern industrial cities like Homestead (Pennsylvania) and Lowell (Massachusetts). Their growing presence transformed the character of Aspen as finally and irrevocably as maturity succeeded adolescence and large corporations came to dominate small mining operations. Aspen industrial workers, like their counterparts elsewhere, now toiled for daily wages in a dingy, impersonal workplace for long hours and under conditions over which they had no control. These new citizens generated fears among more-established Aspenites about the lifestyles and patterns of leisure of the newer arrivals, but they also became objects of pride for civic boosters, who saw their presence as symbolic of the rise of Aspen and the opportunities for work and advancement inherent in American industry. "Who would not rather be a miner in the hills of Colorado than the Czar of all the Russians?" asked the *Sun*.[2] It was a rhetorical question intended to be answered in the affirmative, but given the choice, some Aspen miners might have seriously pondered the option.

Between 1887 and 1893, with the emergence of half a dozen large mines that laid the basis of Aspen's growth and prosperity, there came a work force of professional miners—skilled men who worked for a daily wage in the mines and whose duties fell within a narrow range of options. The numbers of these miners increased from 650 in 1885 (the year for which we have census returns) to 2,500 in 1893. In addition, by 1893, probably another 500 men worked for wages in the samplers, concentrators, Holden Works, and the sawmilling operations connected with Aspen's mining enterprises. Because most of these wage earners arrived in the city after 1887 in response to the growing demand for their services, much of the increase in population of these years is accounted for by the appearance of these men, their families, and those who came to support them with housing, food, clothing, and recreation.

Mining companies in Aspen were not social service organizations. They were designed to make large profits for their owners and stockholders, and they were run within the context of complete control that characterized American industrial organization in the 1880s and 1890s. In short, the authority of the owners and their appointed representatives in the form of general managers and superintendents was complete. This new group of professional miners who worked deep in the drifts and stopes of the Aspen or the Smuggler or the Mollie Gibson did not share the visions of El Dorado and great mineral wealth associated with the popular image of western mining. Theirs was simply another industrial occupation in which more and more Americans worked in the factory and not on the farm, for wages and not as independent tradesmen, and at specific hours and in a specific place dictated by someone else. Mining was an occupation probably dirtier and certainly more dangerous than most. In 1891, the *Sun* dropped the mask of civic boosterism to remark, "It is useless to say that here all have an equal chance."[3]

The work lives of these professional miners were remarkably similar. The daily wage was $3.00. Mining wages were generally standardized within a mining district. The wage in the Comstock Lode was $4.00; in Leadville, $3.50. The differences were probably the result of the longer-established mining activities at the other two camps and of the more-difficult physical conditions of the work (mining in the Comstock was already down to three thousand feet beneath the surface). Other aspects of the work were as standardized as the wage. Professional miners in Aspen (and elsewhere) did what they were told to do by their supervisors, who set the terms and conditions of employment. The employer, whether owner, superintendent, or foreman of the shift, had complete authority over the work force. The company assumed no liability in the case of death, injury, or disability. Men might be hired or fired by the arbitrary decision of superiors; mines might be shut down for retimbering, drainage, shortage of railroad cars, or any other reason, during which time miners would be laid off. These conditions were not peculiar to Aspen; they were the same in American industrial society generally and the mining industry in particular, whether gold, silver, copper, or lead.

Actually, conditions at Aspen were better than those in many mining camps. Companies paid miners in cash rather than in scrip redeemable only at the company store. The peonage aspects of the company store and company housing were unknown. Miners and their families bought food and clothing for cash, traded where they liked, and made their own living arrangements. The reasons for this degree of economic independence were historical ones: the slow pattern of the camp's development produced a full panoply of independent services within the town and no single mining company that came to dominate competitors. Aspen and its mines were free of most of these exploitive features that characterized much of the American mining experience in the late nineteenth century. The major grievance against Aspen's wage system was that miners were paid only once a month, with the result that much of their purchasing in the intervening thirty days had to be done on credit.[4]

The physical circumstances of life above ground were almost as standardized as work below. Single men lived in one of the numerous boardinghouses scattered throughout the city. Boardinghouses were significant because, among other things, their management provided a gainful employment for women. For single miners, home was a tiny room, a bed, a washstand, meals in a communal dining room, and a lunch packed for the shift. Laundry cost extra. For men with families, the city offered a range of houses to rent, uniform in nature and varied only by location. Investors built these houses in great numbers beginning in 1888, as part of the rush of investment capital to the city. Constructed to a standard plan on the vacant lots that rapidly filled in, these houses measured twenty-eight feet by thirty feet and were divided into five rooms: a parlor (with bay window), sitting room, kitchen, bathroom, and porch. They had no indoor running water and used the outhouse for sanitation. Mass-produced by Aspen's carpenters and mechanics at the rate of four a day, this family house, plastered, painted and ready for occupancy, cost $1,000 to build, plus another $200 for the lot. It could be rented for $25 a month, or $300 a year, a substantial return on the investment.[5] For the miner and his family, it was home. And so the families poured into these clapboard dwellings the energy and love necessary to make it a special place with flowers, curtains, paint, and whatever furnishings the tight budget would allow.

Life above ground in these standardized clapboard houses was important because life below ground was hard, monotonous, and dangerous. Miners worked eight-hour shifts—ten hours in some mines for proportionately higher wages—which began at seven in the morning, three in the afternoon, or eleven at night. Speed was considered necessary, because at the change one shift must be brought to the surface and the next shift into the working mine quickly and efficiently. The major producers in Aspen were deep mines, and so, after reporting to the shift boss, the miner would be lowered down the shaft in a cage, jammed with ten or so others on a five-by-five-foot platform, dropped at high speed into pitch blackness. The image of a descent into hell must have been inescapable.

Mines in Aspen (and those in the West generally) had a shaft sunk down or at an angle, off which tunnels called levels would be run every hundred feet. Numbers would identify the levels and their depth: thus, level four would be at four hundred feet, five at five hundred feet, and so forth. At the individual levels, drifts would be run out from the shaft; in these, miners would probe for silver contact veins—an elusive thread of wealth from six inches to six feet in width—in an endless search for the silver needle in the haystack of bedrock, assisted by modern geology in the form of maps and charts and by modern technology with its diamond drills. When the miner arrived at his assigned level, he would find his candles and other tools (pick, shovel, hammer, drill) and go to the spot assigned him.

Aspen miners worked at two basic tasks. Exploration and development involved the endless extension of shafts and drifts, with the continuing probes for mineral. When the vein was exposed to a degree to make actual production of ore profitable, miners would open a stope, an ever enlarging room, where the ore would be blasted down from the ceiling (the force of gravity was used wherever possible in dealing with heavy rock), shoveled into cars, and run out to the shaft, where it would be hoisted to the surface. Whether in extending the shaft for exploration or in cutting out ore for the surface, the procedures were much the same. Miners would hand drill (by drill and hammer) a three-quarter-inch hole to the depth of four or five feet into the rock wall, load the hole with explosives, attach a blasting cap, and, after taking precautions to warn their fellow workers in the vicinity, fire the charge.

After the smoke settled, "muckers" would clear out the debris, and the process would be repeated. In large mining operations with heavy ore production, all the firing would be done at the end of the shift, in order to allow the dust to settle while shifts changed. The new shift would start out by cleaning up after the last. The exacting physical labor and the periodic use of explosives both continued throughout the entire shift. With these two qualities also went the ongoing necessity to produce. Like others engaged in mechanical work in industrial America, miners were judged by how much they did on the job, and the number of feet blasted at the head of a drift or the number of tons produced in a stope might form the basis of continued employment.

Throughout his working day or night (it made no difference eight hundred feet underground), the Aspen miner was exposed to a variety of discomforts and dangers, immediate and long-run. To begin with, mines were unpleasant places to work, restricted in space, dark, and sometimes wet. As shafts sank deeper and deeper into bedrock, they were also increasingly hot places where men worked stripped to the waist, their forms lit by flickering candles hung on the wall, their nostrils filled with the dust of their labors and the odor of their own perspiration. Inconveniences ranged from bruised and battered hands, chronically wet feet, and the steady irritation of working in close quarters with heavy tools to lungs that gradually became lined with dust particles, a condition known as the "miner's consumption" or simply the "miner's disease."

Work in the Aspen mines produced more than inconveniences. Mining—whether for gold, silver, copper, or coal—was extremely dangerous. Mining in Aspen was no different. The physical beauty of the valley of the Roaring Fork did not disguise the dangers below ground, certainly not for those who labored there or for their wives and families. The monotonous nature of the job, with the continuing physical effort necessary, served as an anesthetic that induced carelessness. Death and permanently disabling injury lay on every side, but most serious accidents came from the presence of deep shafts and the continual use of explosives.

The trip into the mine by means of cages loaded with human cargo, the continued use of the shaft to bring ore to the surface and move tools and supplies from one level to another, and the existence of other shafts for ventilation constantly exposed miners to the hazard of falling into an open shaft. Any such fall was almost surely fatal. One of the most common forms of accident (to judge by newspaper reports) occurred when a miner pushed a loaded ore cart to a shaft for raising to the surface but when, unknown to him, the platform had been moved to another level to perform some chore. The luckless and careless miner—his vision obscured by the ore cart and the semidarkness—would dump the cart into an empty shaft and find himself pulled in after it. He would fall at least a hundred feet, landing on the cage at the level below, and he might fall a thousand feet to the bottom of the shaft. The recovery of his mangled body from the bottom of a main shaft might take several hours.[6]

Explosives in the form of powder, dynamite, and blasting caps were in constant use. As a result, miners were continually exposed to accidents, in moving explosives, in preparing them, or through faulty charges that did not fire and had to be retrieved. The result was a lost hand, mangled arm, blindness, or death. Sometimes, miscalculations in the setting of charges could lead to cave-ins that buried miners under tons of rock. Aspen miners shared these hazards with miners throughout the mining West. During the period of heavy mining operations in Aspen—in 1891 and 1892—miners died at the rate of about one a month. Injuries and disabilities occurred in proportionately larger numbers.[7]

The similarity of the work and of the various dangers associated with the workplace gave Aspen's miners much in common. Their response resembled that of other western miners: they formed a union. The first Aspen union, organized in the summer of 1884, had a strong social and cultural side. The annual "Miners' Union Ball" was among the more prominently featured of the camp's winter social events. The *Sun* vigorously supported the union as "a great benefit and protection to the crafts." Indeed, the center of strong union sentiment apparently rested in the crafts and not in the mines. A chapter of the Knights of Labor participated in various social and benevolent events, including a ball on Washington's Birthday. One of the few labor conflicts that attracted public attention was a strike by printers against the *Aspen Times*, owned and edited by B. Clark Wheeler.[8]

With the growth of Aspen from 1887 to 1893, and the parallel emergence of a large cadre of professional miners, union activities also changed direction. The Aspen Miners' Union, organized (or reorganized) in 1890, reflected this transition, the larger numbers involved (2,250 miners in 1893), and a labor solidarity that was expanding across the nation. By 1892, the Aspen Miners' Union claimed some 1,300 members.[9] Its benevolent focus on mutual benefits, such as accident and burial insurance and continued support for widows and orphans, recognized the dangers of mining as a profession. In negotiations, it was generally undemanding.

The union had a supporting newspaper, the *Aspen Union Era*, published from August 1891 to August 1892 under the editorship of Davis H. Waite, a local reformer. The *Union Era* emphasized union solidarity, publicized meetings of the local, sponsored outside speakers from the Knights of Labor, and talked increasingly of the connection between labor and politics. With its broad array of issues and its increasing emphasis on injuries, wages, and strikes, the paper was extremely cautious about advocating direct action on the part of Aspen miners. By the summer of 1892, the focus of the *Union Era* had shifted to the price of silver, an issue that gave it much common ground with mine owners.[10]

The Aspen Miners' Union knew well the arbitrary forces that governed the lives of its members. Some of these reflected the monotony of hard labor and the hazards of the workplace; others acknowledged the vagaries of silver mining. Whatever the sources, these circumstances seemed beyond the influence of any individual or organization. Usage over a generation had fixed conditions within the mines. The periodic layoffs that characterized the mining industry—even in a city as generally prosperous as Aspen—continued throughout these years. Mines might be shut down because of water in the works, scarcity of railroad cars, cleanup and retimbering, or the declining price of silver.

Between 1888 and 1893, Aspen mines closed for varying periods for all these reasons.

The two important local variables were wages and hours. Local mineowners or their representatives made decisions in these areas, and these issues were the source of negotiations between miners and owners. The first big push to raise wages coincided with the organization of the miners' union in the fall of 1890. In response to the passage, in July 1890, of the Sherman Silver Purchase Act, which required the Treasury Department to buy specific amounts of silver each month at the market price, silver prices began to edge upward. The price of silver was common knowledge. Aspen newspapers—and those in other silver communities throughout the West, for that matter—carried it on the editorial page every week. It was, perhaps, the single most important number in the city.

As the price of silver began its steady rise after 1890, miners quickly observed that their wages had not changed. They signed petitions for an increase in wages and presented them to the superintendents of individual mines. Each side took a unified position. The miners pointed to wage rates that were lower than those of the Comstock and of Leadville and argued that they should share in the rising profits of the mines. The mineowners responded that mining had been unprofitable or only marginally profitable under the depressed silver prices of previous years, that the higher prices of silver at last gave them a reasonable return on their investment. The wages stayed the same.[11]

The second major period of negotiations began when the price of silver started a gradual decline in the fall of 1891. Rumors circulated that mineowners would increase hours or cut wages. The *Sun* commented in May 1892, "The question of more hours of a day's work in this eight hour camp is a serious one which if really considered at all will be regarded as a painful sequel to the long continued low price of silver." When Jerome B. Wheeler telegraphed from New York City that hours and wages would remain the same in his Aspen mine, the city breathed a sigh of relief and the miners rejoiced. Still, an estimated eight hundred men appeared at a meeting called by the union. With wages and hours holding as other mines followed Wheeler's policy, and Aspen's mines continuing their high rate of production (led by the Mollie Gibson and the Smuggler), the miners adopted a policy seeking to maintain the status quo. For the moment, the mineowners agreed; wages and hours stayed the same.[12]

Miners needed housing, clothing, and food. They also required leisure activities and forms of recreation. In public and private aspects alike, recreation saw variations on traditional patterns. Sports was the most prominent of the public exhibitions. Among the most popular activities was baseball. "The people of Aspen are fond of good baseball," remarked the *Aspen Daily Times*, in an understatement.[13] The people of Aspen were baseball fanatics. Baseball was an old interest, but the growth of a working class had changed its appearance. In Aspen's first years as camp and town, baseball had been a sport of active participation. After 1888, it became a spectator sport.

The original Aspen teams had an amateur, casual air about them and played against nines from Independence and Ashcroft. Now Aspen's team of semiprofessionals (there was only one) competed in a league that included Leadville, Denver, Pueblo, and Grand Junction. Crowds of fifteen hundred for a weekend game were common. Aspen's newspapers lavished almost as much attention on its baseball team as on the Mollie Gibson. The success of each was considered vital to the city. While mining news covered page three, baseball dominated page two. The details ranged from players' records to their current form and health, as well as a detailed account of all games, including those on the road. Victories over larger cities—over Denver, most of all—were especially gratifying and taken as further evidence of Aspen's emergence to urban prominence. The close of the season in September left a substantial void in the city's recreational life and in the columns of its newspapers.

Baseball shared the spectator spotlight with horse racing and boxing. Local horse races drew as many as a thousand spectators. The contests were generally match races between local horses, with side bets. Strictly amateur in their organization, Aspen races were characteristically delayed. It would often take the better part of an afternoon to run four or five races, while the crowd milled around the grandstand. Delayed or not, the races were free and gave Aspenites something to do on the weekend. For those who could afford a wager, and probably for many who could not, a side bet heightened the level of interest.[14]

Aspen's fascination with boxing was new. It centered on the heavyweight champion John L. Sullivan. Sullivan won the championship from Ryan in 1882, and thereafter he fought all comers across the nation, to a rising chorus of publicity that reached the most remote mining cities. Part of the intense interest in Aspen reflected the local Irish influence; part, the establishment of national wire services, which described the smallest detail of his private life and public career, especially his bouts. Sullivan's loss to Jim Corbett in 1892 created shock waves in the Branch Saloon that spread through the city. Interest in

Sullivan carried over into local boxing contests, in which local fighters (called "pet pugilists") attracted as many as four hundred fans for outdoor matches.[15]

This growing fascination with spectator sports reflected the increased sports coverage in local newspapers. It also served as a reminder that a large male work force had traditional entertainment needs and leisure patterns that provided opportunities for profit or moral outrage for others. There was a private as well as a public side to these patterns of leisure, and it was often a controversial one. The enormous enlargement of this working population in the years 1887–93 brought more drinking, gambling, and prostitution and more demands for moral reforms. The number of Aspen's saloons expanded to keep pace with the mining population. The city council generously granted licenses, being more concerned about the prosperity and growth of the city and the opportunities for revenue than about the moral issue of drinking. Churches and their ministers led the drive for reform.

To the traditional campaign to repress or discourage drinking—with counterparts elsewhere in the nation—came demands for enforced moral standards peculiar to Aspen. Part of the impulse to reform came from the haphazard physical arrangements of the city. It has always been a cardinal principle of American city planning to lay out a metropolitan area in such a way as to segregate various groups by their interests. In this fashion, affluent families could live together, in neighborhoods with similar values. Allowing for periodic outbursts of reform, it was easier to share the city with morally outrageous behavior if the miscreants lived out of sight at a goodly distance. Aspen's random growth as a city lacked such planning, and groups with very different values sometimes intersected in their daily routines. Most of the saloons lay along Cooper Avenue, where they did business in their own private world. The houses of prostitution had been established by custom and convenience on Durant Avenue, where they led a similarly isolated but notorious—a newspaper once referred to "the jungles of Durant Street"—existence.[16]

The arrival of the railroad changed this pattern. The Colorado Midland built its railroad terminal on Deane Street, one block south of Durant, and the citizenry of Aspen now had to pass through Aspen's "red light district" on the way to and from the station. Because the railroad was Aspen's most prominent transportation service, access to it was essential. Furthermore, the more affluent citizens of the city were the ones most likely to use the railroad. "Ladies and children cannot be expected to pass through such scenes," the *Aspen Times* noted of the physical arrangements of the city. The cry arose not to abolish prostitution but "to compel the courtesans to move away from Durant Avenue."[17] Presumably, the entertainment industry—a recognized part of a mining city—might continue on a less visible thoroughfare. The prostitutes moved, and the uproar died down.

Gambling remained a part of the miner's entertainment pattern, generally in the form of card games. "Tinhorns," or "the sporting fraternity," as they were known in respectable circles, did a good business among the miners and other wage earners. They operated out of saloons (where drink no doubt encouraged the victim) or places of business known as "sure thing joints." The gambling business was something that the city accepted as a necessary evil, to be controlled by taxation and confined to certain places. Periodically, reform elements organized to drive the gambling element out of town. They never succeeded.

With a large group of workingmen in an industrial setting where the saloon was a traditional site of recreation and leisure, an elected city council, and a small but vocal reform element made up of some of the wealthiest and most socially prominent people in the city, reform in Aspen had a curiously cyclical cast to it. In September 1891, the ministers of the city petitioned the city council to tighten up on the enforcement of local ordinances that dealt with the Sunday closing of saloons. Aspen's civic leaders, public officials, and editors found themselves in an awkward position. The hundreds of miners who had arrived between 1887 and 1893 formed the basis of the city's prosperity for mineowners and merchants alike. Furthermore, saloons and houses of prostitution had been accepted parts of the mining frontier since the first gold rushes to California. The compromise that emerged took the form of periodic bursts of law enforcement in selective areas. In response to the petition to close the saloons, the authorities launched a drive to expel known gamblers from the city. The argument was that gamblers lived off the hard-earned wages of miners and that their presence was thus a moral affront and dispensable. Houses of prostitution were moved to locations away from the daily traffic in the city. The saloons remained undisturbed.[18]

American cities of the late nineteenth century had unattractive qualities, from which Aspen was not exempt. Poverty and pauperism were the most talked about, perhaps because they existed amid much prosperity. Those who analyzed these social manifestations agreed that organized charity was a disgrace to recipients, a blot on the record of public officials, and an affront to taxpayers. The *Sun* argued, "The saloon, the brothel, the gambling table are all supported indirectly by the donations of charity." What the editor and others reflected was a tendency to make a clear distinction between public and private charity. Public charity was morally reprehensible, but private charitable acts to those who suffered from special problems, by contrast, demonstrated the kindheartedness of the city. The widows and orphans of those killed in mine accidents and the families of those so injured and disabled became appropriate objects of the benevolence of the citizens of the city. "In a mining camp like this unfortunate instances of poverty and distress frequently come to notice," wrote an editor. "It is to be expected, and when help is solicited the response is most liberal always."[19] Charity in Aspen had no institutional framework under which the destitute automatically received assistance. Rather, those in need had to throw themselves on the benevolence of the city in a public declaration of their impoverished condition. And such an act offered an opportunity to scrutinize the petitioner and deliver homilies on the moral dangers of getting something for nothing.

In spite of a continual flow of warnings against the moral implications of charity (synonymous, presumably, with idleness) and the parallel burden for the taxpayer, the city of Aspen had an overseer of the poor, an appointed public official, whose duty was apparently to discharge the city's minimum responsibilities to its citizens at the smallest cost. Aspen and the overseer had developed a standard technique for dealing with paupers. The overseer simply bought each a one-way railroad ticket out of town. Under ideal circumstances, this ticket would carry the unfortunate man or woman to family and friends. In actual practice, what was important was to send the individual to any distant location from which he or she would be unable to return. Thus, the biggest item in the budget of the overseer was for "transportation" and "tickets."[20]

Violence and a rising crime rate had already become a part of America's expanding cities, increased by the impersonality of the new industrial world and the millions of immigrants who poured into the cities, adding to the confusion and tension. Such urban places produced dramatic contrasts between affluence and poverty. Aspen escaped some of the most obvious examples of wealth because the very wealthy mineowners—and there were several who could lay claim to the title "bonanza king"—lived and displayed their wealth elsewhere. Jerome B. Wheeler lived in New York City and in Colorado Springs; David M. Hyman had an elaborate residence in Cincinnati and a summer home on Long Island; James J. Hagerman owned a mansion in Colorado Springs. Still, the city of Aspen had some prominent "mansions," of which the stately homes of the D. R. C. Browns, the H. P. Cowenhovens, and the Alfred Lambs were among the most ostentatious examples.

Opinions differed on the amount of crime in the city. The popular perception of Aspen as a safe and pleasant place to live underwent a change between 1887 and 1893. By 1889, the new mineral strikes had made ore-stealing one of the most common crimes, as the richness of the ores made it possible to profit from several pounds instead of tons. The theft of rich ore was also one of the best ways to publicize the richness of the mines. Henry B. Gillespie constantly talked about mine thefts from the Mollie Gibson, and he built Aspen's first mine dressing room, where miners changed after shifts, presumably with a view to cutting down on his losses.[21]

More-traditional crimes against property drew much public notice. Newspapers periodically ran a spate of editorials about robberies. "Stay at home nights with wife and baby, or go out and get held up," the *Sun* commented in March 1892. The police statistics did not support these dramatic charges. Aspen's police force of seven men made about one hundred arrests each month. The number was somewhat higher in the summer months, which saw an influx of transients and more out-side activity, and lower in the wintertime, when the changing weather provided its own solution to talk of a crime wave. Most of the arrests were for drunkenness, disorderly behavior, and assault and battery. The weekends were busy in police headquarters and the jail. Those arrested and charged were fined and released. Almost no one was held for any length of time.[22]

Certainly, there were the usual brawls outside saloons. Sometimes men used knives—a "cutting affray" the press called it—and inflicted more-serious injury. More commonly, it was scrapes and abrasions, followed by a night in the jail, a fine, and a headache. Most of those who participated in these activities were back at work on Monday morning. Crime consisted of petty theft and vandalism, punctuated by an occasional armed robbery. A shooting that left one man dead in June 1890 drew the observation that it was Aspen's first murder in two years. The man indicted for murder escaped from the county jail within a week and was never heard of again, suggesting that the local law enforcement agencies had little experience in or machinery for dealing with such serious crimes. In January 1892, a local grocer was killed in a holdup attempt. In spite of an intense investigation, the crime was never solved. Yet, the impression persists that the incidence of crime and violence fell well within the range found in any American industrial city. A comparison of the figures reported in the newspapers suggested that any Aspenite was much safer on the streets of the city or in a saloon at any hour of the day or night than he was working in the mines.[23]

The anguished cries of the Protestant churches against drinking, smoking, gambling, and prostitution had an ill-disguised class-consciousness about them. These were vices of the working class, people who labored with their hands during the week and sought physical outlets on Sunday in sports or other forms of recreation. The attack of the churches was a moral judgment against others in the city and against their lifestyle. As such, it aroused ambivalence in some and hostility in others.

The drive for reform in patterns of alcohol consumption, the concern about paupers, the attacks on charity, and the uneasiness about crime and violence were signs of deep concern about the direction of American life. Floods of immigrants were pouring into American cities (at the rate of one million a year from 1880 to 1914); most of them came from southern and eastern Europe, spoke incomprehensible languages, and brought with them strange values and customs. They were often Roman Catholics, Jews, or Greek Orthodox, but clearly not Protestant. At the same time, millions of men and women born in America had begun their own migration from the countryside and small towns to the cities, where lay the new economic opportunities in the factories. Independent farmers and craftsmen had become wage earners on assembly lines. Along with changing values went an impersonality and anonymity associated with life in large urban areas. The traditional stable features of American life—the family, the workplace, the trust and shared values of an intimate world—seemed threatened or gone.

A growing ethnic consciousness became evident as early as 1887 and 1888. The first object of concern was the Italians. Italians symbolized the new immigrants: southern European, non-English-speaking, Roman Catholic. They had first appeared in the construction crews that built the railroads up the valley of the Roaring Fork in the fall of 1887, to the accompanying cheers of the town. After the railroad arrived, Aspenites decided that they did not like Italians, who seemed to embody all those qualities associated with the new immigration and, in a more immediate sense, with cheap foreign labor. "Too much cannot be said on the subject," commented the *Sun*. "The miners, and in fact all laboring men must be made to see their danger and stop the influx of pauper labor by some means in the near future or it will be too late." Regarding the differences in values and behavior, it noted "One needs but to look upon a newly arrived lot of immigrants, dirty, ragged, ignorant, depraved and vicious, to see what the manners of our own people will be a few generations ahead if this be not stopped."[24]

Another kind of hostility developed against black Aspenites. Aspen had a small black population. The census of 1885 recorded 29 blacks and 19 mulattos in a total population of 4,484 in Pitkin County. The black population probably grew at the same rate as the county and the city, and in the years 1887–93 the blacks of Aspen became the target of racial slurs. Newspapers reveled in details about peculiar black customs such as the "cake walk," practices that marked blacks as different from the other Aspenites. Petty crime and conflicts within the black community, particularly "scandals" involving "colored preachers," received special attention. The implication was that such behavior was foreign to white Protestant congregations. Another item of interest was any relationship between a black man and a white woman. The constant emphasis was on the "differentness" of black Aspenites and on their separation in values from the rest of the community. At the same time, there was no suggestion (as in the case of the Italians) that the blacks constituted an economic threat; nor did the newspapers indicate that drinking, prostitution, or gambling were more prevalent in Aspen's black population than in its dominant white population. The impression emerges that Aspenites had simply adopted the growing national view that black Americans were irreconcilably different from white Americans and that such differences presumably justified restrictions on civil rights and economic opportunity.[25]

The virulent hostility toward American Indians generated by the Aspen newspapers in this period was typically western in its contempt for eastern reformers. "The sickest thing in the whole country on this Indian question is the sickly sentimentalism of a few dudes on the eastern coast who never saw a red devil in all his glory," commented the editor of the *Sun.* A certain basis for the hostility existed in the participation of the "Aspen Volunteers" in a campaign against the Utes. Amid rumors of Indian hostilities in the White River, Aspen's volunteer military organization set forth as "wives and sweethearts shed tears," "Indian excitement rose to the highest pitch yet reached," and "the company was off for the war." In the skirmish that followed, three Aspen men were killed. After 1887, Aspen's newspapers (and presumably its citizens) displayed unremitting hostility toward American Indians generally and the Utes in particular.[26]

When a Denver correspondent called Aspen "cosmopolite, a true child of the Rockies," he provided a brief but sufficient explanation: "Aspen is a mining camp pure and simple, the second largest in size in the state, at the same time she affords comforts and luxuries that many a larger eastern city has not yet begun to dream of."[27] The reporter had struck a familiar chord. Aspenites thought of themselves as enjoying the best of two worlds: the economic growth and opportunity associated with the new America of cities, industrial complexes, and modern technology mixed in the right proportions with traditional American virtues of push, grit, hard work, and talent. On the other side, Aspen also eschewed the negative aspects of the changing nation (urban squalor, political corruption, hordes of ignorant immigrants of different values) and maintained the values of the old America of family, hard work, and reward.

These characteristics, combined with the beautiful natural setting of the Roaring Fork Valley, gave the city much to boast about. Yet it was also a city whose lovely natural environment had suffered the imposition of industrial complexes that left slag heaps in full view on mountainsides, smokestacks whose product overhung the camp, and streams polluted by the waste products of a series of giant mining enterprises. In its socioeconomic character, too, the city had changed—from a town with a wide range of occupations and interests to a city in many ways dominated by a large work force that labored for daily wages in mines deep underground or in supporting industrial complexes. And not even Aspen could escape the by-products of modern industrial America and the sense that the several societies emerging within the city were not all equal.

15

"A Great Crisis Is at Hand": Aspen and the Collapse of Silver in 1893

With the arrival of the railroad in the fall of 1887 and the ensuing years of mining prosperity, Aspen made the transition from town to city. The change was not something new. Every American agricultural frontier, from the first settlements at Jamestown in 1607 to the Oklahoma land rush in 1889, moved from a subsistence to a market economy. The prosperity and affluence that came with the sale of crops brought a degree of dependence on factors beyond local control. Farmers in the Ohio and Mississippi valleys found themselves dependent on steamboats, river levels, and crop prices at the wharves in New Orleans; planters in the antebellum South had their lives circumscribed by cotton prices in Liverpool and Manchester and by the interest rates of a shipping agent in New York or London; Texas cattlemen drove their herds a thousand miles through heat, drought, and Indian dangers to railheads in Kansas only to sell their beef at a price sent over the telegraph wire from Chicago.

Aspen also felt an array of outside influences. By 1892, it had become a great mining city. Yet its prosperity seemed curiously fragile in the face of forces from across the range, forces over which Aspenites—however powerful their local reputations—had little control. The city's continuing growth and prosperity depended on impersonal policies and distant people: corporate boardrooms in New York City, railroad rates set in Denver and Colorado Springs, smelter charges in Salt Lake City, Denver, and Kansas City, and, above all, the price of silver. The great natural resources of the Roaring Fork Valley needed capital for their development, and the call went out for investors, as it had from a hundred other mining camps. Eastern capitalists responded. Thus, Aspen prospered through the mining ventures of David M. Hyman and Charles A. Hallam of Cincinnati, the investments of Jerome B. Wheeler and Albert E. Reynolds of New York City, and the railroad construction work of William Jackson Palmer of Denver and James J. Hagerman of Milwaukee and Colorado Springs. These circumstances gave to Aspen's economy a colonial aspect that the city resented as soon as it had finished welcoming its investors.[1]

At the height of its mining prosperity, in 1891 and 1892, Aspen shipped almost four thousand tons of ore a week, or thirty cars a day (Sundays included), each holding the standard load of twenty tons. The ore cars that rumbled out of Aspen on the tracks of the D&RG and the Colorado Midland down the valley of the Roaring Fork went to large industrial complexes for refinement and processing—to Durango, Pueblo, and Denver, in Colorado; to Salt Lake City, Utah; and, increasingly, to Kansas City, Missouri. The products of the mines might be identified, separated out, and brought to the surface by self-contained mining operations, but their shipment, sale, and processing depended on others. The little camp of a decade ago had joined Leadville and Denver as the leading metropolitan centers of the state of Colorado, but the new status was a mixed blessing. Self-sufficiency declined, to be replaced by participation in a national economy that experienced cycles beyond the control of any mineowner, however influential he may have been in Aspen. Aspen had become a part of the nation— economically, technologically, and, as time would show, politically.

Silver mining was a more complex enterprise than agriculture, and the several ingredients of investment, assaying, mining operations, transportation, smelting, and marketing involved a broad range of industries, often in widely scattered places. The railroad itself was the most obvious example. Rates and the availability of cars on demand had much to do with profit and loss for Aspen's mines, from the smallest to the great "bonanza" producers. No mine and no mineowner—up to and including Jerome B. Wheeler, James J. Hagerman, or David M. Hyman—was free of this dependence. That the use of the railroad also produced enormous profits provided sufficient compensation for such outside influence. Examples of the profits generated might be found in the monthly dividend figures of the large producers, in the quarterly production of the Aspen or the Mollie Gibson, or in the annual output of the mining district itself.

Other examples of outside influences revealed a negative side. In the fall of 1890, for example, a strike against the Denver and Rio Grande Railroad by a union of Denver switchmen brought Aspen mining to a standstill. Cars filled with ore sat on the sidings of the D&RG and the Colorado Midland in the Roaring Fork Valley. In Aspen, a contemporary account noted, "to-day its merchants are crippled and its miners idle, every sampler full of ore, every mine with crowded bins, unable to send its minerals down." Several of Aspen's largest mines closed down. The *Sun* estimated the payroll loss of the Aspen mine alone at $40,000 a month—"this amount of money accrues directly to the benefit of the miners of Aspen, their families and the merchants."[2] The Aspen newspapers vented their collective wrath on the railroad union, but, whatever the merits in the issue of the strike, no one in Aspen, from the most vitriolic of the editors to the most influential and wealthy of the mineowners, could solve the problem. When the strike finally ended after thirty days, every mining camp in the state needed cars, which were in short supply. It took another month to straighten out the confusion and return to normal mining operations. In this interdependent world, Aspen's miners-merchants-mineowners found themselves without recourse except the editorial pages of the local papers.

Aspen mining enterprise also depended on the state of the local ore market. Railroad cars full of silver ore streamed to smelters not only from Aspen but also from half a dozen other major silver producers in the Rockies. When shipments suddenly increased as a result of new mineral strikes, the coming into production of new mines, or simply the scheduling of ore cars, the smelters would find themselves unable to process the silver ore and would refuse to accept further mineral product. As cars filled with ore waited on sidings outside the smelters, the impulse would quickly pass back along the lines, up the valley of the Roaring Fork, and into the mines on Aspen and Smuggler mountains, where single jackers and muckers in the drifts and stopes of the Aspen, the Compromise, and the Smuggler mines would be laid off. Such a condition followed the resumption of railroad shipments in December 1890, as a flood of ore poured into the plants with the end of the strikes. No sooner had the problem of transportation been solved than the problem of too much ore arose.[3] The production of ore had a wide range of variations, but the capacity of the industrial plants that processed the ore was fixed. It was difficult to balance the two.

Of all the distant influences that affected life in all its forms in Aspen the most important was the price of silver. Silver was a complicated question that engaged the attention of miners and owners and, eventually, of drought-striken farmers of the Middle West and the Plains; finally, as the most important political issue of the day, it captured the attention of the nation itself. The issue of the price of silver had been around as long as large-scale silver mining in the Rockies. Indeed, the two were closely connected, in the sense that the great and growing success of mining threatened to unhinge the price of the mineral product.

In 1873, Congress omitted the standard silver dollar from the coinage act passed that year, leaving the white metal (as it was affectionately known to silverites) to find its value on the open market. Although there is no evidence that such omission was a conspiracy or "crime," as silver supporters later charged, the demonetization of silver left gold the only monetary standard. Silver found itself in a world of increasing production and falling prices. Strikes by 1878, in Leadville and soon thereafter in Aspen, enormously increased the production of silver. In 1872, Colorado's mines produced 1.5 million ounces of silver; in 1892, at the floodtide of Aspen's prosperity, the production figure was 24 million ounces, a sixteenfold increase. As supply dramatically outstripped demand on the open market, the price of silver began to fall, from $1.32 an ounce in 1872, to $1.10 in 1887, and to $0.93 in 1888.[4]

In the same two decades, hundreds of thousands of people rushed to the mining frontier of the Rockies and the Sierra Nevada to participate in this search for riches. This massive (if uneven) increase in population led, among other things, to new states in the Union and to political influence in Congress. Growing congressional representation in the silver states blended with rising agrarian discontent on the Plains in a series of political maneuvers designed to increase the amount of money in circulation, a scheme that would satisfy both groups. As a direct result, Congress passed legislation to subsidize silver prices—very much as Congresses in the twentieth century would find it politically expedient to support prices of agricultural commodities.

The first such law, the Bland-Allison Act of 1878, passed over the veto of President Rutherford B. Hayes, required the secretary of the treasury to make monthly purchases between $2 million and $4 million at the market price and convert the silver into standard dollars. The law produced an artificial demand that supported silver for a decade, but with the great increase in silver production in the late 1880s—by which time Aspen was among the leading producers—the price again began to fall. The new city on the Roaring Fork depended not only on absentee boards of directors on Wall Street and on the charges imposed by railroads and smelters but also on fluctuating silver prices. The most important news of the day in Aspen was no longer strikes in new mines, production of older mines, or construction of new civic improvements. It was the number that came over the telegraph about ten o'clock in the morning and rapidly spread through the city. This figure exercised a direct influence over the lives of all Aspenites, however important or anonymous.

The struggle to support the price of silver was a political and economic issue; the fight was increasingly centered on the Congress, the president, and the secretary of the treasury. Accordingly, after 1890 the focus of Aspen's attention began to shift from local concerns to national and state politics. After all, at a certain point it made no difference which party controlled the offices in Pitkin County if the price of silver was falling. The "silver question," as it was known in Aspen and elsewhere, came to dominate the attention of Aspenites, whatever their political persuasion. The concern to protect local mining enterprise spilled over into other areas, too. Newspapers and politicians began to agitate against the importation of duty-free Mexican lead as a threat to the nation, which was another way of saying a threat to Aspen's interests.[5]

From 1887 to 1893, Aspen's history mirrored these outside influences, especially that of silver prices. Thus, though the city enjoyed growth and prosperity, both were cyclical. In the best of times, Aspen's economic condition responded to silver prices set by decisions made in Washington, D.C., strikes by union switchmen in Denver, and smelter charges in Pueblo and Kansas City. Even as the railroad arrived in November 1887 and Aspen's production of silver ore increased six times to $6 million a year in 1888, the price of silver was falling, from $1.10 in 1887 to $0.93 in 1888, in a cycle that forced Aspen's mines—like farms faced with similar overproduction—to produce more each year in order to stay even.

Complaints about economic hard times could be heard in the fall of 1889, even as the city celebrated its greatest season of construction and physical growth. In December 1889, the Aspen and the Compromise mines closed, laying off more than one hundred miners, because of the "unsatisfactory state of the ore market." Both resumed mining operations within thirty days, but the Smuggler then shut down because of flooding in the mine shafts. A year later came the economic disruption of the railroad strike, during which most of the leading producers in the camp were shut for two months. In the face of such economic uncertainty, the cry arose for the mines to pay weekly rather than monthly, because miners suffered a lag of up to thirty days between work and wages. But the real issue was the closing of the mines. Their reopening at the end of the year coincided with the failure of two of Aspen's best-known merchandising firms, Lone Star Merchandise and the E. L. Haskins Company. The reason was "hard times." In the midst of massive growth and prosperity lay a vein of uneasiness about the future.[6]

The year 1890 was one of mixed economic news in Aspen but of political triumph in distant Washington. The coalition of determined mining interests and farmers angry about a prolonged depression won a significant but incomplete victory. While advocating the free and unlimited coinage of all silver produced throughout the nation (and, some said, around the world), the two groups accepted a compromise under which the secretary of the treasury would purchase 4.5 million ounces each month at the prevailing market price and issue treasury notes payable in gold. The figure agreed upon was the estimated total production of American silver mines. The act generated fear and anxiety among eastern business groups that saw the gold reserve depleted; it soon bred renewed dissatisfaction in inflation and silver camps because it did not guarantee unlimited coinage. The immediate effect, however, was a steady rise in the price of silver, as mandated government purchases supported the market.

In the city of Aspen, the year 1891 was an exceptionally prosperous one. The numbers of employed miners and of producing mines and the amount of ore shipped all rose to record levels. The shadowy crises of the preceding year seemed forgotten in the face of renewed prosperity. The Holden Works opened, giving reality to Aspen's search for a greater degree of economic independence by reducing the high freight and treatment charges associated with the shipping of ores to Denver and Pueblo. The Mollie Gibson had become one of the most profitable mines in the West—in the world, many said—and the Aspen and a handful of others were "bonanza" producers. In closing the year, the *Sun* could confidently remark, "As a city, we may be proud of the past and contemplate the future with a great deal of contentment."[7]

Guided by the instinct of self-preservation, Aspen had become worldly and cosmopolitan. It had done so because it recognized that the world east of the mountains controlled the present and shaped the future. The evidence of this concern was not a growing interest in cultural affairs, or a society associated with an urban metropolis, but rather an overriding concern with politics. News from Washington, D.C., was more significant than news from the state capitol in Denver, and Aspenites, accordingly, began to immerse themselves in questions of national politics.

Like other frontier communities, Aspen had an early political history that reflected the backgrounds of its first settlers. The first prominent Aspen political figures had been Democrats with southern antecedents. Early politics was largely nonpartisan. As the camp grew, more men from the West and Middle West appeared, and elections soon called forth salutes to Abraham Lincoln, the Union, and the fallen heroes of Gettysburg and Vicksburg. The dominant interests of the city lay not in the past, however, but in the future, specifically in mines, in town lots, in merchandising, and in transportation. The city and the county became nominally Republican, as so much of the area north and west of the Ohio River was Republican after 1865. Politics in Aspen had an old-fashioned quality about it: the most qualified men did not campaign but were swept into office by the spontaneous outburst of support on the part of the community and, once in office, proceeded to govern on principles of business and efficiency, with the efforts of all individuals and parties directed toward the growth of the city.

The falling price of silver and the focus on national politics changed this political scene. The most dramatic variation had to do with the traditional two-party system. Like other Americans, Aspenites had grown up amid two political parties, with an unstated assumption that at least one party would provide views compatible with their own. After 1890, this did not prove to be the case. Part of the crisis over silver in the decade of the 1890s was the attitude of the major parties toward the white metal. The Republican positions ranged from indifference to hostility, the party relying instead on the traditional appeals to the memory of the late war; the Democrats divided into gold and silver wings, but Grover Cleveland, the man most likely to be the party's candidate for the presidency in 1892, was on record as being against silver.

The failure of the two parties to find meaningful relief for the continuing agricultural depression on the Plains led to the organization of a new political party, the People's, or Populist, party. Silverites in Aspen and other mining camps of the West now examined the new party to see what it would say about the silver issue. Populism immediately attracted the allegiance of one of Aspen's long-time civic reformers, Davis H. Waite, who was also editor of the *Aspen Union Era*. He became the first chairman of the infant Pitkin County Populist party, organized in September 1891. Waite was B. Clark Wheeler's father-in-law. Aspenites would have called them a well-matched pair: Waite invested the same frantic energy in reform that Wheeler poured into endless entrepreneurial schemes. At the same time, each had instincts in the other direction. Waite, amid his fulminations against corporations, served on the boards of several of his son-in-law's companies; Wheeler had his own political ambitions, which he pursued with sufficient energy through his paper, the *Aspen Times*, to be elected mayor of Aspen in 1890.

The appeal of the Populist party grew with the reappearance of the crisis over silver. After a steady rise in response to the Sherman Silver Purchase Act of 1890 and an exceptionally prosperous year in 1891, the price of silver began to fall. By spring 1892, its steady decline had changed concern into alarm. The *Sun* observed in March, "The difference in the price of silver between this time and a year ago is great enough in this camp to equal the expense now incurred in operating the producing mines." On the heels of the news that Aspen (with 8,474,300 ounces in 1891) had at last overtaken Leadville (6,114,526 ounces) as the leading silver producer of the state came word that the Best Friend, one of Aspen's leading mines, had shut down "owing to the extremely low price of silver." Perhaps even more serious in the public eye, in March 1892, the price of Mollie Gibson shares fell for the first time since its meteoric rise had begun, thirteen months earlier. The *Sun* claimed that the low price threatened all Colorado silver mines—even the richest—and concluded, "A great crisis is at hand."[8]

Aspenites wanted to mobilize for silver, and to this end they organized the Silver Club. Probably, they ignored the Populists because many of the party's reform principles—a graduated income tax and government ownership of railroads, for example—aroused controversy. Silver was the one issue that everyone in the city could agree on, and although some regarded the Silver Club with suspicion because it might be a vehicle for political action, citizens flocked to the silver standard. By the end of April 1892, some 1,796 men had signed their names on the membership rolls, and a month later the figure had reached 2,000. Other mining camps followed suit (although Aspen always claimed that its Silver Club was the first), and suddenly silver clubs were "all the rage in Colorado." In Denver, the members of the Denver Mining Exchange formed the Silver Club in that city, suggesting that it was not viewed as a radical organization. The fifty-eight silver clubs in the state now established the State Silver League, with a total membership in excess of 25,000. Aspen and the state had organized, and they proceeded to join other silver supporters at a national silver convention in Washington D.C. One of the keynote speakers was B. Clark Wheeler of Aspen.[9]

The people of Aspen had reason to worry. On April 1, 1892, the price of silver fell two cents in twenty-four hours. With silver hovering in the low nineties, knowledgeable mining people predicted that silver in the eighties would close most of the mines in Colorado. A miners' union meeting drew eight hundred for speeches that stressed the themes of indignation, helplessness, and fear. In early June, D. R. C. Brown's mining property, the Deep Shaft, closed. The legendary Dave Brown, Aspen's most remarkable self-made man, had "busted." The word sent a shiver of alarm through the city.[10] Brown had other mines and a range of other profitable economic activities, but this failure gave the impersonal economic crisis a personal aspect.

It was in midsummer that Aspen turned to the Populist party. As recently as April, the Populists had failed to generate either interest or votes in the city election. The continuing fall in the price of silver and the indifference of the two established political parties propelled the Populists to the forefront in the silver interests' search for relief. At the July convention in Omaha, delegates nominated James B. Weaver of Iowa for the presidency and wrote into the platform, besides a bundle of reforms for workingmen and women and relief for American agriculture, a plank for the free and unlimited coinage of silver at the old, pre-1873 rate of sixteen to one. The statement appeared the more decisive because both the Democrats and the Republicans at their national conventions refused to satisfy delegates from the silver states on the silver question.

The series of political surprises in 1892, already a substantial one, had only begun. Many of Colorado's Democrats and Republicans now began to drift toward the Populists and free silver. In July, at the Populist state convention in Denver, the new party made an alliance with the State Silver League. It was an awkward amalgamation of radical reformers and conservative businessmen with silver interests, and it demonstrated, if nothing else, the degree to which the silver issue had become the overriding political question in Colorado. After difficult deliberations in the search for candidates who would satisfy the Populists and appeal to independent Republicans and Democrats, the convention nominated for governor Davis H. Waite of Aspen. It was the greatest political shock in the seventeen-year history of the young state. Six weeks later, Waite received the endorsement of a badly divided Democratic party.[11]

Silver supporters around the state greeted the choice of Waite with enthusiasm; those in Aspen, with something between amusement and alarm. Waite was an old-time reformer, whose fulminations on behalf of labor and the working class had covered the front pages of his paper, the *Union Era,* from August 1891 to August 1892. Many of those in Aspen who supported the cause of free silver and the Populist party found Waite's nomination curiously inappropriate. The *Sun* commented that Waite was "a good, quiet, peaceable citizen, but erratic in his ways and garrulous in the extreme." The editor concluded that "the mention of his name in connection with the chief executive office of this great state [was] something too preposterous for serious consideration." As for the aspiring Populist party, the comment continued, Waite's nomination was "the worst political blunder that could have been committed by the convention."[12]

Whatever their views on Davis H. Waite, Aspenites found themselves in the middle of a vigorous political campaign, in which the issues fought out at the national and state levels promised to affect the future of the city. General Weaver, the Populist party's presidential nominee, and Mary Elizabeth Lease, the Kansas reformer, came to Aspen to a tumultuous welcome. There they joined with Waite in invoking the memory of the Republicans a generation earlier in founding another new national party devoted to reforms. As the speakers castigated large corporations and the "Gold Bugs" of Wall Street, thousands of men and women shouted their approval.[13] That Aspen's mines were themselves large corporations and that some of them, at least, had headquarters on Wall Street did not bother the people of Aspen. Jerome B. Wheeler, James J. Hagerman, and David M. Hyman were *their* bonanza kings, men who had supplied the capital to raise the city to its present level of prosperity and whose entrepreneurial skills and generosity toward the city could be relied on to protect Aspen and its citizens in the future.

In November, the voters of Colorado and Aspen carried their enthusiasm for the Populist party to the ballot box. "Weaver and the Populist State Ticket Scoop Up All in Sight," read the headlines. James B. Weaver rode a floodtide of silver sentiment to victory in Colorado, winning 57 percent of the popular vote; it was one of only two states that he carried. Davis H. Waite won with a plurality of 47 percent in a three-way race. The center of his political strength was in the silver-mining region of the state. In Pitkin County, Weaver took 84 percent of the vote; Waite, 77 percent. The Populist landslide carried B. Clark Wheeler, Waite's son-in-law, into the state senate. Buoyed by a sense of political accomplishment, Aspenites waited to see whether new political leadership would make things better for silver.[14]

A deceptive quiet now descended on the city. Silver stood at eighty-two cents an ounce, teetering on the brink of a further collapse that might endanger the whole mining industry. Yet old-timers knew and recent arrivals soon learned that Aspen had confronted difficult times before, and that it had come through them to survive and prosper. Nothing suggested that the present crisis was any more serious or more permanent than the original search for capital (ended by Jerome B. Wheeler), or the prolonged court conflict over the apex principle (resolved by compromise), or the endless struggle for a railroad (ended by the arrival of two railroads within six weeks of one another).

Throughout the winter of 1892–93, Aspen remained confident. Mrs. D. R. C. Brown hosted a party in the armory for two hundred guests. The "big bonanzas" continued to pay their usual dividends. Figures for 1892 showed that the city on the Roaring Fork had once again led the state and the nation in silver production, with 182,118 tons. But the fall in the price of silver from an average of ninety-nine cents an ounce in 1891 to eighty-seven cents in 1892 had cost Aspen mineowners an estimated $3,825,000. Still, $9,000,000 was a good year's work. The price of Mollie Gibson stock had stabilized. Interviews with a cross section of citizens demonstrated continuing confidence in the city and the future of silver. The realtor R. H. Wood announced that he would not trade the riches of Smuggler Mountain for the state of Massachusetts. "Wealthy as the old Bay State is," he proclaimed, "the undeveloped wealth of the Smuggler in my opinion can discount it." Rumors circulated that president-elect Grover Cleveland had modified his anti-silver views and begun negotiations with Congress for legislation to support the white metal. Tax collections for January and February 1893 were up substantially over the the same month a year earlier. And common sense supported the general mood of optimism. How could a city that stood astride a thirty-mile mineral belt of unparalleled riches, emerging from five years of virtually uninterrupted growth and prosperity, fear for the future?[15]

With the coming of spring, signs of business-as-usual continued. The mining work force remained at about 2,250 men. News of mineral strikes dominated mining news. Newspapers and civic leaders turned to pressing local issues: the pollution of the Roaring Fork by a slaughterhouse, paving the streets, a schoolboard election in which the *Sun* backed the woman candidate (she lost). A group of real estate developers bought the Old Athletic Park racetrack and subdivided it into lots. The usual cast of leading characters appeared before the public eye playing their customary roles. D. R. C. Brown went to Europe; Jerome B. Wheeler, David M. Hyman, and Charles Hallam visited Aspen to attend to their business interests, which, indirectly at least, were the interests of everyone. Within the city of Aspen, the business of mining and all the auxiliary occupations went on as always.[16]

The dangers to the city and its people lay not within but without, in a vast arena of national and international finance that few in Aspen understood and no one could influence. In late 1892 and early 1893, economic uneasiness in Great Britain dampened continuing investment in America. The failure of two major Philadelphia companies early in 1893—the Philadelphia and Reading Railroad Company and the National Cordage Company—triggered an economic crisis. This growing panic now blended with the obvious decline in the nation's gold reserves to feed a gnawing fear that the nation might be forced off the gold standard. To many responsible public officials, the failure of the gold standard was comparable to the failure of Western civilization. Each formed the basis of an orderly, civilized life.

These developments reinforced the long-held views of President Grover Cleveland and his advisers that the drop in the gold reserves might be traced directly to the Sherman Silver Purchase Act of 1890, with the subsequent inflation of the currency by silver money at the expense of gold. Furthermore, at a time when the economic condition of the entire nation worsened almost daily, the silver subsidy became a useful scapegoat for bank failures and unemployment lines. Accordingly, Cleveland announced his intention to call a special session of Congress to repeal the Sherman Silver Purchase Act. Additional bad tidings for the silver supporters came in the form of news that the British Indian Mint had suspended operations. Western Europe seemed to have turned its back on silver as a circulating medium.

In the spring of 1893, economic depression rolled west, leaving in its wake business failures, bank closings, and lengthening unemployment lines. It reached Chicago in May and the agricultural Middle West almost immediately thereafter. This tidal wave of economic disaster struck Colorado in late June. Within thirty days, every silver mine in the state closed. "THE CRISIS AT HAND," proclaimed the *Sun*. "The dreaded emergency is now upon us . . . a situation as deplorable as the imagination has ever conceived. The mines have been ordered shut down. At least 200,000 in Colorado alone are made destitute. . . ."[17]

Whatever the imagination had conjured up, reality was devastating. Within a week, the mining work force in Aspen dropped from 2,250 men to 150. The unemployed were on the streets, their families without support. "The once flourishing mining camp of Aspen is now badly prostrated by a crushing blow to its great industry," the *Sun* reported. A run on the banks immediately began, as panicking miners and merchants alike tried to rescue their hard-earned savings from fearsome economic dangers. On July 22, the Wheeler Bank suspended operations. The shock was almost as great as the closing of the mines itself. "The name of J. B. Wheeler is held in the greatest esteem and veneration by the people of Aspen," observed the *Sun* in a kind of obituary.[18]

Almost literally overnight, the nature of the city changed. Miners who had been gainfully employed—some of them for many years— searched the garbage behind hotels for food scraps to feed their families. Others hung around the woodyard, to pick up discarded sticks for fuel, or the railroad line, where they gathered pieces of coal. The city of Aspen found its attention abruptly diverted from civic improvements to relief for the hungry and homeless. It was a role that it was ill equipped to play, conditioned as it was by a national philosophy of self-help and half a dozen years of continuous growth and prosperity. Much of the assistance came from the outside, as earlier investment had come from beyond the limits of the city. Flour mills in Alamosa contributed two thousand pounds of flour; a commission company of Denver gave one thousand pounds of potatoes. Colorado Midland Railroad officials brought in three carloads of coal without charges.[19]

The Aspen Chamber of Commerce, heretofore the principal vehicle for advertising the growth of the city, established a central relief committee with subordinate committees in the districts. Notices went up around the city that applicants for relief should apply in person to the appropriate local committee. A charity concert raised $262.15, much of it from a few large contributors. Livery stables reported a run on ponies and jacks as miners prepared to leave the city. Many intended to head for Cripple Creek, where the gold mines produced around the clock and where ongoing economic opportunity mixed with incipient labor-owner violence.[20]

Through the rapid and complete change in the fortunes of the city ran a persistent theme: that what had happened was inconceivable and that some sort of solution must be forthcoming. Everyone, from miners to managers and merchants, rehearsed the same argument. The stakes were too great, for mineowners, for businessmen, for the railroads, for smelters, for influential people around the state and the nation. Under the circumstances, these men of power and influence would resolve the crisis. Men like Jerome B. Wheeler, James J. Hagerman, and David R. C. Brown, who had transformed Aspen from a camp to a thriving city, had enough insight and authority to resolve the problems at hand. They would make the trains run, help the Holden Works to belch smoke, fill the streets with crowds of busy shoppers, and fill the tunnels and stopes of the mines with energetic workingmen.

President Cleveland's special session of Congress convened on August 7. The struggle over the repeal of the Sherman Silver Purchase Act was long and bitter, involving as it did elements of a class conflict, sectional division, and a massive split within the Democratic party itself. Resistance was most protracted in the Senate, where the silver forces had a large representation. Although mining spokesmen praised the vigorous defense, likening it to a small band of heroes fighting to the death against the overwhelming forces of evil, the bill passed the Senate on October 30. Cleveland signed it on November 1, 1893. The price of silver was sixty cents an ounce.

It was scant consolation to Aspenites that the struggle over silver caused a permanent split in the Democratic party and that Cleveland's signature became the first step in a realignment of Democratic party politics that would lead to the nomination of William Jennings Bryan in 1896 on a platform pledged to silver. Bryan's famous statement "You shall not crucify man upon a cross of gold" resonated through the once-booming silver-mining camps of the Rockies. Aspen was one of these. It was still a mining camp, and would remain one at least through World War I. The mines would reopen, on a smaller scale and with reduced wages. But things would never be the same again.

IV

THE TOWN AND THE CAMP

Aspen, 1893–1930

16

"The Old Site Is Here as Beautiful as Then"

Loud cries, many voices, soaring superlatives, and extravagant claims all celebrate growth and prosperity—those characteristically American frontier qualities. Prolonged silences, empty buildings, and solemn notices accompany stagnation and decline. Mining camps intensified these contrasts, for the growth was spectacular, the reversal of fortunes abrupt, and the decline precipitous. That such cycles occurred frequently was demonstrated by the large number of camps established and the few that achieved permanence. Mining camps turned out to be fragile creations, susceptible to lasting damage to their economic health by richer strikes across the range, by minerals that played out, or by uncontrollable fluctuations in the price of the product.

Aspen now found itself caught in this downward spiral. In 1893, at the age of fourteen years, the mining city on the Roaring Fork—long a favored child of the mining world, seemingly immune to the influences that strangled other camps—stumbled and fell. And as the camp had grown to a town and the town to a city with twelve thousand (some said fifteen thousand) people, the decline was the more unexpected and paralyzing. As the heartbeat of silver mining slowed and then stopped, the lifeblood of the city ceased to circulate. One day the mines teemed with workers and the streets with shoppers; a week later, both lay silent. In their place were unemployed men who walked the railroad tracks in search of coal; at home, women and children who continued their varied duties amid dramatically changed circumstances. Yet this condition could not last. People had to eat and be sheltered. If Aspen and its mines could not provide the means, then its citizens had to go elsewhere. They had to reenact the cycle of out-migration that had come to hundreds of mining camps in the American West.

Many left. No one knew how many, and local editors did not want to know. The new object of their interest was the gold camp at Cripple Creek, twenty-five miles west and south of Colorado Springs. As recently as September 1891, gold production from the collection of tents known as the Cripple Creek diggings was less than $25,000; by the summer of 1893, the incorporated town of Cripple Creek had a population of five thousand, and the district was producing gold at an annual rate of $6,400,000. With the destruction of the silver market in 1893, mining men from silver districts, especially Aspen and Leadville, poured into Cripple Creek. An Aspenite wrote from the town, "Every other person you meet is either from Leadville or Aspen. Nine of our ten best business houses are conducted by Aspen merchants. . . ."[1] He might have added "former" Aspen merchants.

The key to Aspen's survival was the mines, for if they remained closed, the corps of professional miners and their families would disappear. Attempts to reopen them produced deep fissures in the economic and social fabric of the "Crystal City of the Rockies." In the autumn of 1893, Aspen's mineowners proposed to reopen the mines with a new wage scale of $2.00 for eight hours (a reduction from $3.00) or $2.50 for ten hours. The proposal immediately brought the companies into conflict with the Aspen's Miners' Union. The confrontation was an unequal one. The miners and their families had to eat; virtually every mineowner had other sources of income. The miners quickly capitulated and returned to work—where they could find it—at the compromised wage of $2.25 for eight hours. In the spring of 1894, half a dozen of the strongest properties resumed ore production on a limited scale. By autumn, perhaps as many as one thousand men were at work in Aspen's mines, but the numbers were misleading. The only wage employers were the Smuggler (96), the Mollie Gibson (116), the Aspen (65), and the Cowenhoven Tunnel (61).[2]

The rest of the miners worked as lessees. More than two of every three miners returned to the risky business of working alone or in small partnerships for scanty returns on a leasing basis. Lessees contracted to work in the smaller mines, hoping to scratch out enough sackfuls of valuable ore to put food on the table and pay the rent. As they worked, they also did exploration and development work for the mineowners, for it was only through finding new bodies of rich ore that the lessee could make a substantial sum. The mining cycle in

Aspen for a majority of the miners and the owners had assumed the shape of a very small circle. The owners, who had insufficient capital to pay regular wages, watched passively while lessees worked their mines. The lessees, on the other hand, threw themselves into an economic gamble in which they staked their work and the risk of injury against the long odds of a strike that would let them reap a substantial profit in the time before their leases expired. The mineowners had lost authority over the development of their own mines; the miners had lost the shield of regular, guaranteed wages.

By the autumn of 1894, with the aspen leaves turning gold on the sides of Aspen and Smuggler mountains, the city had begun to function again. Aspen resembled someone who had survived a prolonged illness of such gravity that no one wished to talk about the patient's condition. It was enough that the invalid had survived. So Aspen continued to pursue its normal economic, social, and cultural activities, but the fragility of its health meant that they had to be reduced in number and intensity.

Whatever the lower levels of mining enterprise, Aspen was still a mining city. The annual production for the year 1894 was about $4,000,000, less than half of the figure for 1892. Of the shippers, the Smuggler had produced more than $1,000,000 (more than a quarter of the total output of the district); the Della S., $748,000; the Mollie Gibson, $450,000; the Aspen Mining and Smelting Company, $260,000; and the other mines, only bits and pieces. Except for the four major mines, lessees dominated mining activity. The stock of every Aspen mining company, even of the strongest, was below par—that is, below the price at which it had originally been put on the market. If production and stock prices were indices of Aspen mining, then mining was alive but hardly prospering. The Smuggler and the Mollie Gibson had resumed paying dividends. They were small dividends, five cents a share instead of fifteen, but dividends nonetheless. Silver was fifty-nine cents an ounce.[3]

The devastating crisis of the summer of 1893 and the partial recovery of 1894 enlarged the distinctions in Aspen between those who had considerable wealth, those who continued to do well, and those who operated on the margins of mining or who worked for wages. These latter groups found the economic bases of their existence largely wiped out. Yet, amid the individual economic crises that confronted a thousand families, the Smuggler declared a dividend of $50,000 a month, or $600,000 a year, on an annual production of $1,000,000. And it did so at a time when David Hyman, a principal shareholder, used the argument of low silver prices and hard times to reduce the wages of miners

227

from $3.00 to $2.25 per day. The Wheeler Opera House had entertainments scheduled almost every night. Mrs. D. R. C. Brown held a reception at the "palatial residence on Hallam Street" in September 1894 that brought together seventy-five ladies, the cream of Aspen society. The hostess wore "a striking dress of black satin with profuse diamonds." The *Sun* noted, "It was as if a crowd of richly plumed humming birds had alighted among a thicket of honey-suckle."[4]

The initial spurt of production in 1894 could not be sustained. In spite of ceaseless public exhortations and newspaper editorials calling for more work and enterprise to return Aspen to its former greatness, the crippled mining city on the Roaring Fork continued to slide. When the Smuggler reduced its work force in January 1895, the *Sun* chastised the "calamity howlers" and proclaimed in a spirited tone, "This camp has a glorious future which will burst upon us shortly with a brightness all the more enjoyable by comparison with the hardships we have endured."[5] The declaration, made in the face of a sharp economic setback, had a note of irrational defiance about it. During the years 1895 and 1896, mining news gradually disappeared from the newspapers, to be replaced by impassioned editorials on the national and international implications of the demonetization of silver.

Stocks fell steadily. By December 1895, shares in the Mollie Gibson had sunk to thirty-five cents a share, and Aspen mining properties generally no longer attracted attention as either investments or speculations. Instead, Aspenites poured their speculative energies into the inexpensive stocks of Cripple Creek gold properties. Brokers called them "cheap Cripples," but, whatever the term, investment in them became a species of Aspen mania, very much as investment in its own mines had been five years earlier. Aspen's intense entrepreneurial and speculative activity now focused on mines in a distant and (in some respects) rival city. Aspen had ceased to attract outside investment capital. One observer commented in December 1895, regarding the absence of eastern capital, "I do not think a dollar has gone into the camp in the last two years." Aspen began to talk not about eastern capital but about eastern tourists. The town's mineral production had dropped to a level of $2 million by the end of 1896. In the same year, the output of gold in Cripple Creek reached $20 million. The mineral output of Pitkin County (that is to say, Aspen and its mines) dropped steadily over the next ten years, dipping below $1 million in 1908. Population declined in the same proportion. In 1900, the census enumerators counted 3,303 people in Aspen city; ten years later, a mere 1,834.[6]

In the fifteen years from 1893 to 1908, Aspen changed from a city into another small mining town on the Western Slope of the Rockies.

During this time, one dramatic economic initiative broke the silence on the Roaring Fork—a major new mining venture under the leadership of D. R. C. Brown. In a context of national disaster for silver and the end of outside investment, only a local figure of economic independence could have launched such an enterprise. Dave Brown was such a man, and his attempts to revive Aspen's mining in this period testify to his strong commitment to the town.

In May 1894, workmen broke ground northwest of the Smuggler and the Mollie Gibson mines for a new shaft for a new company. The Free Silver Mining Company was made up of shareholders from the two older mines, with D. R. C. Brown as president and principal new investor. The company intended to drive a shaft that would intersect the rich ores of the Smuggler and the Mollie Gibson at a depth of fifteen hundred feet. A special feature of the new mining company was its planned widespread use of electricity. Pumps, drills, and hoisting machinery would all be operated by electric power. The work proceeded steadily over the next three years, as the Free Silver became the symbol of Aspen's mining revival and its new policy of self-help. In August 1897, as the project neared completion, miners cutting two drifts out from the bottom of the shaft stopped work because of rising water. Two months later, the shaft house on the surface burned. The company now faced damage to its surface works and the prospect of flooding in the deep shaft.

In the summer of 1909, the principal mineowners of the Mollie Gibson, the Smuggler, and the Free Silver made a last, determined effort to "dewater" (to use the technical phrase) the Free Silver shaft. The solution was a series of powerful electric pumps, installed with the intention of drying the shaft to the fifteenth level (fifteen hundred feet below the surface). The pumping continued vigorously for several months, interspersed with failures of equipment, and the water gradually receded. All Aspen watched the struggle to empty the lower levels of the Free Silver with the same intensity that it had followed the search for bonanzas in the Mollie Gibson twenty years earlier.

In November 1910, the pump at the twelfth level failed, and the company contracted with a New York firm for the services of deep-sea divers to make repairs. As a result of this agreement, two divers came from New York to Aspen, where they descended into the cold, dark shaft. George Patterson and Fred Johnson became local Aspen heroes. Pictured in the local newspapers with full diving equipment, they formed a remarkable contrast to the image of the early prospectors arrayed in western attire and leading burros. Thirty-one years had passed since the first prospectors had crossed Independence Pass into the valley of the Roaring Fork, a full generation from jack train to diving suit and air hose. The divers succeeded in repairing the pumps, and through their intervention the water level continued to recede, until on November 21, 1910, it was down to within sixty-five feet of the bottom of the shaft. The *Aspen Democrat-Times*, noting their achievements, commented, "Divers with diving suits and other paraphernalia may soon be considered a necessary part of a mine's equipment."[7]

The continuing work in the shafts and drifts of the Free Silver, the Mollie Gibson, and the Smuggler kept Aspen a mining town. As men continued to labor underground in pursuit of silver ore, their presence (however minimal) served as a constant reminder of the town's years of glory, the period from 1890 to 1892, when the arrival of the railroad and the bonanzas of the Mollie Gibson put the finishing touches on what Aspenites thought was the greatest mining town in the nation if not the world. Nowhere else, so the litany ran, did economic prosperity combine in such perfect proportions with natural beauty and the presence of a pleasant, informed, and progressive people. The inspirations of the past helped to preserve the expectations of the present. J. W. Deane evoked both in 1916 when he wrote, "The old site is here as beautiful as then. By less than a handful of millions have the stored riches been taken from the hills. Again we shall see the loaded wagons and the burdened trains, and a flood of riches flowing on iron wheels to be converted at the smelters."[8]

The decline of Aspen in its varied economic, social, and cultural forms was paralleled by the dispersion of the characters who had played such a crucial role in its rise to prominence. Some moved their entrepreneurial operations to more-promising fields; others retired to distant residences. A few simply passed from the scene. Henry P. Cowenhoven died on January 1, 1896. At his bedside were his wife, Margaret, his daughter, Katy, his son-in-law, D. R. C. Brown, and two grandchildren. The *Sun* saluted Cowenhoven as one of Aspen's "foremost and most progressive citizens, whose enterprise had much to do with the advance of Aspen from a little mining camp to a prosperous city." Cowenhoven was indelibly associated in the public mind with the great days of Aspen's prosperity and growth. He epitomized the American dream of self-made achievement in conjunction with the mining fantasy of enormous wealth created through pluck and luck. His estate included a dozen of the best-known Aspen mines (the Aspen, the Della S., the Franklin, the Deep Shaft, the Free Silver, the Cowenhoven Tunnel, and others), several city lots in Aspen and Denver, the Roaring Fork Electric Company, and the Aspen Water

Works. The Aspen press reckoned that the estate of the man who came
to Aspen in the summer of 1880 with two wagon loads of trade goods
would "run into millions."[9]

Henry B. Gillespie took his considerable promotional talents to
ever-more distant lands. In the winter of 1895–96, he journeyed to
London to promote the Gold Valley properties in Routt County, Colorado. Over eighteen months, he was unable to interest any substantial
investors in that remote northwestern corner of Colorado, and he returned to the luxury ranch that he and his wife had built down the
valley of the Roaring Fork, some twenty-four miles south of Aspen. Yet
it was not Gillespie's style to remain passive. In the winter of 1901–2,
he returned to Aspen to manage the Star group of mines for an anonymous investor, rumored to be W. S. Stratton, the man who had made
millions in Cripple Creek gold mines. The Spar did not pay, the investor withdrew his support, and Gillespie once again retired from active
life. He reemerged in December 1902, when he left for Dutch Guinea.
Rumor had it that he "stood in a fair way to realize an immense
fortune" when he contracted malaria and died after a brief illness in
April 1903. In his obituary, the Denver *Rocky Mountain News* called him
the "Father of Aspen." Gillespie would have been pleased. He would
also have thought the title no more than his due.[10]

If Henry B. Gillespie was the father of Aspen, then Jerome B.
Wheeler was the rich uncle. Wheeler came into camp as an anonymous
wealthy relative. His anonymity did not last. Within ten years, he had
left his name on the new city's most prominent buildings and on the
lips of most of its citizens. The crash of 1893 did not treat Wheeler
kindly. Unlike Gillespie, who had removed himself to a safe distance
from the mining enterprises of Aspen, Wheeler was intimately involved in both mining and banking. Both failed. The closing of the
Wheeler Bank was an especially serious blow to the city and to
Wheeler himself. The bank failure seemed to symbolize the power and
impersonality of an economic crisis that did not spare Aspen's foremost benefactor, in either pocketbook or reputation. Nor did the subsequent years give Wheeler consolation. Although he lived the life of a
retired "bonanza king" in Colorado Springs (the gathering place of
wealthy mining entrepreneurs), endless litigation swirled around him.

In 1901, Wheeler filed for bankruptcy. It was a legal move that
shocked Aspen and the whole Colorado financial community almost as
much as the crash of 1893 had. Interviewed at home, he blamed "de-
signing and unscrupulous persons who claimed equities in silver mines
which were fairly and honestly purchased by me." Wheeler vowed
that he would "eventually be able to pay them [his debts] in full,

principal and interest." He also noted that while silver prospered, he had been able to pay the necessary legal fees and settlements, but that when silver prices plummeted, so did his income, while the fees and other costs of litigation remained constant. Whatever the legal reason and the accompanying assurances, bankruptcy was a drastic step. Wheeler spent the rest of his life trying to put his affairs in order. He died in Colorado Springs on December 1, 1918.[11]

David M. Hyman continued his close and successful relationship with the city on the Roaring Fork that was slowly changing back into a town. His was the only story of continued entrepreneurial success. During the heady years of 1891 and 1892, Hyman's Smuggler pressed forward with extensive development work that uncovered large bodies of rich ore. The bonanzas of the Mollie Gibson overshadowed these discoveries (and virtually everything else in the city), but the Smuggler's new discoveries proved of lasting importance. The crisis of silver in 1893 and the accompanying economic depression coincided with the playing out of the rich veins in the Mollie. By contrast, the Smuggler had uncovered its richest deposits ever. Hyman now led the fight to reopen the mines with reduced wages, and the Smuggler, the Aspen, and the Durant (also showing excellent ores) were soon back in production. Within a few months, the Smuggler again declared a dividend.

Hyman divided his time among homes in New York City, Cincinnati, and Denver, eventually moving to New York City. He maintained his close connection with interests in these three Aspen mines through 1910, interspersed with a period of several years when he was directly involved with the affairs of the American Refining and Smelting Company, a giant trust with headquarters in New York City. Hyman's continued interest and financing kept the Smuggler group in operation, and in a very direct way he helped to preserve Aspen as a mining town.[12]

One individual remained closely identified over half a century with Aspen, spanning the range of its birth, youth, growth and prosperity, decline, and struggle for survival. David R. C. Brown came across the mountains with the Cowenhovens in 1880. He prospered in the merchandising business and, like others, used his economic base as a merchant to move into mining enterprise. His mining properties transformed him from a substantial citizen into a rich man. He became, with his father-in-law, Aspen's most prominent millionaire. Brown was also closely associated with the improvements in the town itself. People often referred to him as the "Landlord of Aspen," because he owned most of the electric light company and the waterworks. Although the

Browns spent increasingly long periods away from Aspen, they continued to be identified in the public mind as Aspenites who kept a residence in town and financed a wide range of public benefits.

Brown's life was not without its sad interludes. Henry P. Cowenhoven died in 1896 and Margaret Cowenhoven the following year. Katherine Cowenhoven Brown died in 1898, leaving a grieving widower
and two small children. Brown moved to Paris in 1900, where he devoted himself to the education of his two daughters and kept in touch
with his Aspen mining interests by cable. In 1907, Brown married Ruth
McNutt, the daughter of a San Francisco physician. The Browns traveled extensively, usually spending their summers in Aspen. David R.
C. Brown became ill in 1929 and died in his Aspen home on June 29,
1930. He left an estate of $1.5 million. A group of friends formed an
honor guard to accompany the casket to the top of Independence Pass,
whence it was conveyed to a cemetery in Denver.[13]

David R. C. Brown had come to Aspen in 1880, when the mining
camp on the Roaring Fork had a business district of twenty tents on
five dirt streets and when Aspen probably had five hundred people,
most of them spread out across the sides of Aspen and Smuggler
mountains. When he died half a century later, Aspen had a larger
business district of wooden and brick buildings interspersed with numerous empty stores and vacant lots. The population, according to the
census taker of 1930, was 705. The camp had come full cycle in the
lifetime of Brown, and he had seen most of it. He had certainly been
present in the heady days of growth and prosperity. And in the days
of stagnation and decline, he never lost his intimate connection with
the city that had reverted to a town and, by 1930, to a camp.

Brown's death coincided with the appearance of another group of
entrepreneurs. Like their earlier models, they were from the East. Like
their mining predecessors, they were few in number, but their impact
was enormous. And like the first entrepreneurs interested in silver
mining, they set out to reproduce a cycle of prosperity and growth
based on a natural resource.

It was snow.

Notes

This history of Aspen is written in the context of other scholarly histories of mining camps. The best of these (listed alphabetically) are Paul Fatout, *Meadow Lake: Gold Town* (Bloomington, 1969); Don L. and Jean Harvey Griswold, *The Carbonate Camp Called Leadville* (Denver, 1951); W. Turrentine Jackson, *Treasure Hill: Portrait of a Silver Mining Camp* (Tucson, 1963); Watson Parker, *Deadwood: The Golden Years* (Lincoln, 1981); Duane A. Smith, *Silver Saga: The Story of Caribou, Colorado* (Boulder, 1974); and Marshall Sprague, *Money Mountain: The Story of Cripple Creek Gold* (Boston, 1953). Throughout, I have intended comparisons with these studies, for I have talked about many of the same things. I have not made reference to these volumes in every case where appropriate, for such citations would be constant. Instead, I have relied on the reader's initiative in looking to these works for useful comparisons and contrasts.

I have abbreviated the citations to some newspapers. Thus, the Aspen *Rocky Mountain Sun* is listed as *RMS*; the *Aspen Times* is *AT*; the *Aspen Daily Times* appears as *ADT*.

CHAPTER 1

1. Frank Hall, *History of the State of Colorado*, 4 vols. (Chicago, 1889), 4:272–73. For Hayden's survey, see F. V. Hayden, *Annual Report of the United States Geological and Geographical Survey of the Territories, Embracing Colorado, Being a Report of Progress of the Expedition for the Year 1873* (Washington, 1874).

2. Rodman Wilson Paul, *Mining Frontiers of the Far West, 1848–1880* (New York, 1963), analyzes the first generation of the mining frontier. William S. Greever, *The Bonanza West: The Story of the Western Mining Rushes, 1848–1900* (Norman, 1963), covers the whole mining West. Rodman Wilson Paul, *California Gold: The Beginning of Mining in the Far West* (Cambridge, 1947), is the standard work on the California gold rush. For a discussion of historians and the American mining frontier, see Clark C. Spence, "Western Mining," in Michael P. Malone, ed., *Historians and the American West* (Lincoln, 1983), 96–122.

3. Among the several histories of the Comstock Lode, the most complete is Eliot Lord, *Comstock Mining and Miners*, U.S. Geological Survey Monographs, vol. 4, (Washington, 1883), a work by a contemporary who collected an enormous amount of information from newspapers, state and county records, and mining companies. He also interviewed many of the most important figures associated with the Comstock. The

best study setting the Comstock Lode in the context of nineteenth-century American industrialization and urban growth is Hans Muessig, "The Impossible Dream? Economic Stability on the Mining Frontier: The Comstock Lode, 1860–1900" (master's essay, University of Iowa, 1978), in possession of the author.

4. Leadville and its bonanza kings have many histories. Don L. and Jean H. Griswold, *The Carbonate Camp Called Leadville* (Denver, 1951), and Edward Blair, *Leadville: Colorado's Magic City* (Boulder, 1980), are two of the best. Duane A. Smith, *Horace Tabor: His Life and the Legend* (Boulder, 1973), is a good biography.

5. Aspen has been the subject of a wide range of historical treatments. Those deserving mention are (in order of publication) Frank L. Wentworth, *Aspen on the Roaring Fork* (1935; reprint, Denver, 1976), a collection of documents, newspaper clippings, and personal reminiscences; Robert F. Bartlett, "Aspen: The Mining Community, 1879–1893," *The Westerners Brand Book: The Denver Posse of the Westerners*, vol. 6 (Denver, 1951), is based on research for the author's master's thesis, "The Early History of Aspen" (Denver University, 1951), a copy of which is in the Denver University Library; Manuel Hahn and Andrew J. Buesch, "Aspen over the Divide—Its Past and Present," *The Westerners Brand Book: The Chicago Corral of the Westerners*, vol. 8 (Chicago, 1951), a popular treatment emphasizing the emergence of Aspen as a ski resort; Len Shoemaker, *Roaring Fork Valley* (Denver, 1958), is a series of vignettes of the towns in the Roaring Fork Valley, arranged chronologically from 1879 to 1905, by a Forest Service employee who collected materials while he lived and worked in the vicinity; Len Shoemaker, *Pioneers of the Roaring Fork* (Denver, 1965), is an unsystematic collection of sketches and documents sent him by Roaring Fork Valley pioneers and their descendants in response to the publication of his earlier volume; and Thomas John Kimmell, "A History of a Rocky Mountain Silver Camp: Aspen, Colorado, 1879–1910" (bachelor's thesis, Harvard College, 1975), a copy of which may be found in the Aspen Public Library.

CHAPTER 2

1. Warner A. Root, "Aspen: The Men Who Led the Way over the Divide," *Aspen Times*, April 23, 30, 1881; 14 Stat. 251 (July 26, 1866).

2. Duane A. Smith, *Rocky Mountain Mining Camps: The Urban Frontier* (Bloomington, 1967), chap. 4, is a good account of the founding and first weeks of the Rocky Mountain mining camp. Compare W. Turrentine Jackson, *Treasure Hill: Portrait of a Silver Mining Camp* (Tucson, 1963), 23–27, a study of an eastern Nevada camp, where the first arrivals lived in caves.

3. "Hon. H. B. Gillespie" and "Colorado Mining Towns—Aspen," *Colorado Mines: A Souvenir of the New Mining Exchange Building* (Denver, 1891), and an article on Gillespie in the *Illustrated Weekly*, Nov. 7, 1900, 7, all exaggerate Gillespie's contributions to Aspen mining. His obituary, "Father of Aspen Dies in Dutch Guinea," Denver *Rocky Mountain News*, April 21, 1903, is equally excessive.

4. Materials on B. Clark Wheeler are virtually endless, in part because Wheeler was the sort of character that everyone remembered and wrote about, such as in "B. Clark Wheeler," in Frank L. Wentworth, *Aspen on the Roaring Fork* (Denver, 1976), 9–24; in part, because Wheeler later purchased the *Aspen Times* and loved to write about himself. His customary interest in self-promotion received added impetus with rising ambitions for a political career. He served as mayor of Aspen from 1890 to 1892, and in the general election of 1892 he was elected state senator on the Populist ticket, at the same time that his father-in-law, Davis H. Waite, was elected governor of Colorado.

5. David R. C. Brown, "My Trip from Black Hawk to Aspen," MS in Aspen Public Library. Cowenhoven's obituary in the Aspen *Rocky Mountain Sun*, Jan. 25, 1896, mentions a fifth member of the party, Samuel Flemming; Brown's account does not.

6. Once again, compare Smith, *Rocky Mountain Mining Camps,* chap. 4. On the rise and fall of rival camps in the Roaring Fork Valley, such as Independence, Roaring Fork, Scofield, Ashcroft, and Elko, see Len Shoemaker, *Roaring Fork Valley* (Denver, 1958), chaps. 5–11. The federal census of 1880 for Gunninson County shows Aspen with 108 residents.

7. William M. Dinkel, "A Pioneer of the Roaring Fork," *Colorado Magazine,* 21 (1944): 138.

8. Root, "Aspen," *AT,* April 23, 30, 1881. For immediate comment, see letters to the editor and editorials, ibid., May 21, 28, 1881.

9. "Letter Books of the Roaring Fork Improvement Company," MS in Colorado Historical Society, is informative on company activities. See especially letters from William Balderston, the company's Aspen agent, to W. Henry Sutton, treasurer, dated April 21, 25, 1881.

10. Root, "Aspen," *AT,* April 30, 1881.

11. Ibid.

12. *AT,* April 23, 1881. On the procedure for incorporating a "town" and on the powers of the town as exercised through the council and boards of trustees, see "An Act in Relation to Municipal Corporations," *General Laws of the State of Colorado* (Denver, 1877), 874–919. The law contains 104 sections, including separate parts on General Powers; Ordinances, Fines and Suits; General Taxes; Officers; Classes of Municipal Corporations; Cities; Cities of the First Class; Cities of the Second Class; and Incorporated Towns.

CHAPTER 3

1. On the initial construction of the Clarendon Hotel, see J. W. Deane, "Aspen's First Christmas," MS in the Aspen Historical Society; *AT,* April 23, 1881.

2. *AT,* April 23, 1881.

3. See "General Taxes" and "Officers," *General Laws of the State of Colorado* (Denver, 1877), 901–4.

4. *AT,* April 23, 1881. Thomas John Kimmell, "A History of a Rocky Mountain Silver Camp: Aspen, Colorado, 1879–1910" (bachelor's thesis, Harvard College, 1975), 15–17, analyzes elections and officeholders in early Aspen.

5. *AT,* May 7, 1881.

6. *AT,* May 14, 21, 1881. For a general discussion of ordinances, see Duane A. Smith, *Rocky Mountain Mining Camps: The Urban Frontier* (Bloomington, 1967), 151–53.

7. *AT,* May 21, 1881.

8. *AT,* June 4, Oct. 15, 1881.

9. *RMS,* July 1, 1882.

10. *RMS,* July 30, Aug. 20, 1881.

11. *AT,* June 25, 11, 1881; *RMS,* Aug. 13, 1881. On the services available in western cities in 1880—e.g., street surfacing and maintenance, waste disposal, water systems, police protection, and schools—see Lawrence H. Larsen and Robert L. Branyan, "The Development of an Urban Civilization on the Frontier of the American West," *Societas—A Review of Social History,* 1 (1971): 33–50.

12. *AT,* Aug. 20, 1881.

13. *AT,* May 28, June 25, Dec. 17, 1881. On schools in other camps, see Smith, *Rocky Mountain Mining Camps,* 111–17.

14. *AT,* May 21, 1881.

15. *RMS,* Aug. 27, 1881. On the strategies of the company, see Balderston to Sutton, July 6, 20, Sept. 2, Oct. 21, 1881, "Letter Books of the Roaring Fork Improvement Company," MS in Colorado Historical Society.

16. Comments on the dispute over the townsite are in almost every newspaper over the two years from summer 1881 to summer 1883. For representative selections in just

the first year, see *RMS*, July 9, Aug. 6, Sept. 10, Nov. 19, Dec. 17, 1881; *AT*, May 21, 28, Dec. 10, 1881.

17. *AT*, May 28, 1881; *General Laws of the State of Colorado* (Denver, 1877), 913–14.
18. *AT*, Aug. 13, Sept. 3, 1881; *RMS*, April 1, 15, 1882.
19. *RMS*, Oct. 26, 1881.
20. *AT*, Oct. 22, 1881.
21. *AT*, May 6, 27, 1882.
22. *AT*, Sept. 10, Oct. 22, 1881, June 10, 1882.
23. *AT*, Dec. 24, 1881, Oct. 7, 1882.
24. *RMS*, July 1, 1882.
25. *RMS*, Jan. 7, 1882.
26. *RMS*, Nov. 19, 1881.
27. *AT*, July 30, 1881; *RMS*, March 25, April 15, 1882.
28. *RMS*, June 24, 1882.
29. *RMS*, May 19, 1883.

CHAPTER 4
1. Duane A. Smith, *Rocky Mountain Mining Camps: The Urban Frontier* (Bloomington, 1967), chaps. 4–6, gives the general characteristics of mining camps. For a comparison with early Leadville, see Edward Blair, *Leadville: Colorado's Magic City* (Boulder, 1980), chap. 4.
2. *AT*, Sept. 17, Nov. 26, 1881; *RMS*, Nov. 26, 1881. See also Smith, *Rocky Mountain Mining Camps*, 106–11.
3. *AT*, July 16, 1881.
4. *AT*, May 6, 1882.
5. *AT*, Aug. 20, 1881. On politics in mining camps generally, see Smith, *Rocky Mountain Mining Camps*, 154–58.
6. *AT*, April 30, Dec. 17, 1881. Don Harrison Doyle insightfully analyzes "the voluntary community" on the frontier in *The Social Order of a Frontier Community: Jacksonville, Illinois, 1825–70* (Urbana, 1978), 156–93. Doyle's subject is an agricultural community, but the parallels are nevertheless useful.
7. *AT*, Nov. 19, 1881.
8. *AT*, Jan. 14, 1882. J. W. Deane, "Aspen's First Christmas," MS in Aspen Historical Society, contains an account of the Literary Society.
9. *AT*, Oct. 8, Dec. 31, 1881.
10. *AT*, June 17, 1882; *RMS*, July 1, 1882.
11. *AT*, July 23, Aug. 20, Oct. 1, 1881.
12. *AT*, Dec. 31, 1881, Feb. 11, 1882.
13. *AT*, Jan. 14, 1882, Jan. 27, 1883.
14. *AT*, Feb. 25, April 8, 1882.
15. *RMS*, July 8, 1882.
16. *AT*, May 6, 1882. On the enormous freighting enterprise necessary to keep Aspen supplied, see William M. Dinkel's memoirs, where he describes a freighting train in these terms: "There would be from sixty to one hundred burros in a large train; two mounted drivers and a couple of shepherds." "A Pioneer of the Roaring Fork," *Colorado Magazine*, 21 (1944): 137.
17. *AT*, July 9, 1881.
18. *AT*, Dec. 30, 1882.
19. *AT*, June 25, 1881, June 3, 1882. Smith, *Rocky Mountain Mining Camps*, 213–15, notes the widespread popularity of baseball.
20. *AT*, June 24, 1882.
21. *AT*, Aug. 6, 1881. Every historian who writes about mining towns deals with the issue of the law and its enforcement. See, for example, Smith, *Rocky Mountain Mining*

Camps, 80–83, 122–23, for a general description; Blair, *Leadville*, chap. 9, deals with a single camp notorious for its wide-open qualities.

22. *AT*, July 16, 1881, June 17, 1882.
23. *AT*, June 17, July 15, 1882.

CHAPTER 5

1. 17 Stat. 91 (May 10, 1872). J. W. Deane, "How to Locate Claims," *AT*, May 14, 1881, provided instructions for those in Aspen who had not yet mastered the basic details of making a claim.
2. *RMS*, July 9, 1881.
3. Ibid. On large-scale mining operations generally—the kind to which Aspenites aspired—see Rodman W. Paul, *Mining Frontiers of the Far West, 1848–1880* (New York, 1963), chap. 5, which contrasts mining in California and Nevada, between 1859 and 1880. Otis E. Young, Jr., *Western Mining: An Informal Account of Precious-Metals Prospecting, Placering, Lode Mining, and Milling on the American Frontier from Spanish Times to 1893* (Norman, 1970), is detailed and technical.
4. *AT*, Oct. 1, 1881; *RMS*, Oct. 22, 1881; *Mining and Scientific Press*, Jan. 28, 1882. On July 2, 1881, the *Aspen Times* called Independence the "Leading Gold Camp in the State."
5. *AT*, June 25, July 2, 1881; *RMS*, April 15, 1882.
6. *RMS*, May 13, June 3, Oct. 7, 1882.
7. *AT*, May 14, June 25, July 2, 1881; *RMS*, Nov. 12, 1881.
8. *AT*, Aug. 5, 1882, is a complete history of the Spar.
9. *RMS*, April 15, 1882.
10. James E. Fell, Jr., *Ores to Metals: The Rocky Mountain Smelting Industry* (Lincoln, 1979), chap. 1, is an account of the European origins of Rocky Mountain smelting. Young, *Western Mining*, contains much useful material on smelters and smelting.
11. *AT*, June 11, 25, 1881; *Denver Mining Review*, quoted in *AT*, Sept. 17, 1881.
12. *AT*, Sept. 23, 1882.
13. *AT*, Dec. 30, 1882.
14. *RMS*, Dec. 30, 1882.

CHAPTER 6

1. Ralph M. Hower, *History of Macy's of New York, 1859–1919: Chapters in the Evolution of the Department Store*, Harvard Studies in Business History, vol. 7 (Cambridge, 1943), 157–60, 169–73, is the best source on Wheeler's marriage and New York business career. Wheeler was the object of constant newspaper attention in Aspen and in Denver. A good summary of his entire career is in his obituary in the *Denver Post*, Dec. 3, 1918.
2. Liston E. Leyendecker, "Roaring Fork Hustler: Harvey Young's Career in Aspen," in Patricia Trenton, *Harvey Otis Young: The Lost Genius, 1840–1901* (Denver, 1975), 115–25. Trenton's chaps. 1 and 2 cover Young's early artistic career. Several color reproductions of Young's best-known works are found in this volume. See also an interview with Young in 1886, Bancroft Collection, Western History Collection, University of Colorado, in which he states that he "will return to Europe in the Spring, and will devote the remainder of his life to the study of art." Young actually hung on in Aspen until 1891, when he retired, burdened by debts that he spent his artistic career (1891–1901) trying to pay off.
3. *AT*, June 30, 1883; *RMS*, July 14, 1883.
4. *RMS*, July 7, 14, 1883.
5. *AT*, Oct. 20, 1883.
6. *RMS*, March 1, Aug. 23, 1884; *AT*, Dec. 12, 1884.

7. Len Shoemaker, *Pioneers of the Roaring Fork* (Denver, 1965), 116–23, based on information apparently supplied by Devereux's son, Alvin. Devereux introduced polo to Glenwood Springs, building a polo field on the south edge of town.

8. *AT*, Jan. 1, 1884. These production figures are probably inflated. See *AT*, Jan. 5, 1885.

9. *AT*, Jan. 19, 1884; *RMS*, Jan. 26, 1884.

10. *AT*, May 3, July 5, 1884; *RMS*, May 10, Aug. 23, 1884.

11. *AT*, May 3, 1884.

12. *AT*, July 12, 1884. For an explanation of the production of concentrate, see Otis E. Young, Jr., *Western Mining* (Norman, 1970), 136–39.

13. *AT*, Nov. 22, Dec. 20, 1884; *RMS*, Jan. 3, 1885. Hyman called the process through which the claim passed into control of Cowenhoven and Brown an example of "how grand prizes are drawn in this lottery of mining." David M. Hyman, "The Romance of a Mining Adventure," 61, MS in the American Jewish Archives (Cincinnati), a typed copy of which is in the Western History Collections, Denver Public Library.

14. *AT*, Oct. 11, 1888, Aug. 23, 1884.

15. *AT*, July 12, Oct. 4, 1884.

16. *RMS*, June 7, 1884.

17. *RMS*, Dec. 13, 1884.

18. *RMS*, Aug. 25, Sept. 22, 1883, May 24, Nov. 29, 1884; *AT*, Aug. 11, 1883, Nov. 29, 1884.

19. *AT*, Nov. 29, 1884.

20. *RMS*, Sept. 6, 1884; *AT*, Sept. 6, 1884.

CHAPTER 7

1. David M. Hyman, "The Romance of a Mining Adventure," 1–10, MS original in the American Jewish Archives (Cincinnati), typed copy on permanent loan in the Western History Collections, Denver Public Library. After I read this manuscript, it was published under the same title by the Larchmont Press, Cincinnati (1981). Citations here are to the typescript version in the Western History Collections. I should add that my account of David Hyman's activities in Aspen mining in no way does justice to the complexity of the problems he and other mineowners faced, but it does suggest the range of these issues: financial manipulation at several levels, innumerable questions concerning law, and uneasy partnerships—the whole surrounded by a certain loose attitude toward ethics. His account may be supplemented by reference to the Aspen newspapers, where his name, like Wheeler's, appeared constantly, commensurate with the town's perception of his importance.

2. Hyman, "Romance," 11–12.

3. Ibid., 13.

4. Ibid., 13–15.

5. Ibid., 17–18.

6. Ibid., 19–23.

7. Ibid., 23.

8. Ibid., 25–27.

9. Ibid., 39–40.

CHAPTER 8

1. David M. Hyman, "The Romance of a Mining Adventure," 47, MS in Western History Collections, Denver Public Library (original in American Jewish Archives, Cincinnati).

2. Charles H. Shinn, *Mining Camps: A Study in American Frontier Government* (1885; reprint, New York, 1948), is the standard study. On litigation in Colorado mining,

see Joseph E. King, *A Mine to Make a Mine: Financing the Colorado Mining Industry, 1859–1902* (College Station, 1977), 142–49.

3. 14 Stat. 251 (July 26, 1866); 16 Stat. 217 (July 9, 1870).

4. 17 Stat. 91 (May 10, 1872).

5. Hyman, "Romance," 36; Hague's comment from the *Engineering and Mining Journal*, Oct. 20, 1904, is quoted in King, *Mine to Make a Mine*, 142.

6. For the place of this strike in the development of Aspen mining, see above, p. 75.

7. Hyman, "Romance," 37.

8. Ibid., 41–42.

9. *ADT*, Feb. 24, 1885. See also *RMS*, Feb. 14, 1885. Wheeler purchased the Times Printing Company and inaugurated the *Aspen Daily Times* on Feb. 19, 1885, with the words "To direct capital and labor to the best avenues for expenditure, a daily paper becomes a necessity."

10. *ADT*, Feb. 24, May 29, 1885. See also *RMS*, Feb. 28, July 18, 25, Aug. 8, 1885.

11. *RMS*, May 16, 1885.

12. *RMS*, May 30, 1885.

13. *RMS*, June 6, 1885; *ADT*, June 5, 1885.

14. *RMS*, April 14, 1885; Hyman, "Romance," 41.

15. Hyman, "Romance," 40.

16. Hagerman to Wheeler, June 10, 1885, J. J. Hagerman Papers, Western History Research Center, University of Wyoming Library.

17. Hyman, "Romance," 43–44. John D. W. Guice, *The Rocky Mountain Bench: The Territorial Supreme Courts of Colorado, Montana, and Wyoming, 1861–1890* (New Haven, 1972), 96–111, describes Hallett's place in the court system and his reputation.

18. McEvoy and others v. Hyman, 25 *Federal Reporter*, 600. Complete newspaper accounts are in the Denver *Rocky Mountain News*, Nov. 25, 27, Dec. 8, 1885. On the reaction in Aspen, see *RMS*, Dec. 12, 1885.

19. Hyman, "Romance," 56.

20. Ibid., 57–58; *New York Times*, Dec. 24, 1886. In June, during preparation for the trial, Walter B. Devereux, Wheeler's metallurgist, hatched a scheme "to buy out a lot of mines belonging to those who are making the apex fight." Nothing came of the plan. J. J. Hagerman to T. M. Davis, June 7, 1886, J. J. Hagerman Papers.

21. *RMS*, Oct. 23, Dec. 18, 1886.

22. *RMS*, Dec. 4, 1886.

23. The coverage of the trial by the Denver newspapers was detailed. See, for example, *Denver Tribune-Republican*, daily from Dec. 3–28, 1886; and Denver *Rocky Mountain News*, daily summaries of evidence and testimony, Dec. 3–29, 1886.

24. Hyman v. Wheeler and others, 29 *Federal Reporter*, 347–57. Judge Hallett's condemnation of Thompson is on 350–51; his charge to the jury, on 351–57.

25. *Denver Tribune-Republican*, Dec. 24, 1886; *RMS*, Dec. 25, 1886.

26. *RMS*, Oct. 15, 22, 1887.

27. Hyman, "Romance," 63.

28. Ibid., 64–65.

29. Ibid., 66–67.

CHAPTER 9

1. *AT*, July 7, 1883, Jan. 1, 1884; *RMS*, Oct. 13, 1883.

2. *AT*, Oct. 11, 1884; *RMS*, Aug. 23, Oct. 25, Nov. 8, 1884.

3. *RMS*, Aug. 23, 1884.

4. *RMS*, March 21, May 2, 1885; *ADT*, March 20, 1885.

5. *RMS*, April 11, July 18, 1885; Colorado Census of 1885, Schedules for Pitkin County.

6. *RMS*, Oct. 9, 1886. Lawrence H. Larsen, *The Urban West at the End of the Frontier* (Lawrence, 1978), analyzes the common needs of all western cities in the frontier

period, principally problems of sanitation, health, fire, and police protection, and the rapid transition of technology from eastern cities to the West. Aspen fits this model in everything except size, a condition that Aspenites intended to remedy at the earliest possible moment. Larsen defined the "city" as a place with a population of 8,000 or more (to conform to the federal census of 1880). Aspen's population reached 8,000 about 1890.

7. *RMS*, May 12, 1883, June 7, 1884, May 9, 1885.
8. On fire and fire protection, see Duane A. Smith, *Rocky Mountain Mining Camps: The Urban Frontier* (Bloomington, 1967), 93–98, and Larsen, *Urban West*, 77–79. *AT*, May 12, 1883; *RMS*, Feb. 2, 1884.
9. *RMS*, May 2, 9, 16, 1884.
10. *RMS*, Feb. 16, 1884.
11. *RMS*, July 19, 1884.
12. *RMS*, Nov. 22, 1884.
13. *AT*, March 3, 1885; *RMS*, Nov. 7, 1885.
14. *RMS*, Feb. 6, 1886.
15. *RMS*, March 6, Feb. 13, 1886.
16. *ADT*, Feb. 28, 1885; *RMS*, May 23, 1885.
17. *RMS*, Jan. 16, 1886.
18. *RMS*, April 4, May 2, 1885, Feb. 27, 1886.
19. *RMS*, May 30, 1885.
20. *RMS*, March 27, April 24, 1886.
21. *RMS*, March 13, 1886; *General Laws of the State of Colorado* (Denver, 1877), 912–13. Section 79 specified that voters should elect an alderman from their ward to hold office for two years.
22. *RMS*, Feb. 6, 1886.
23. *RMS*, April 3, 1886.
24. Ibid.
25. *RMS*, Jan. 10, March 21, 1885.
26. *RMS*, Aug. 6, 1887, March 4, 1885, July 31, 1886. Mining camps that had advanced to the status of town or city often used the word "camp" as a term of endearment. Perhaps it also served as a reminder of the humble origins of the town/city and reinforced thereby the high level of achievement.
27. *RMS*, June 25, 1887.
28. Ibid.

CHAPTER 10
1. *RMS*, March 12, 1887.
2. *RMS*, March 19, 1887.
3. Richard H. Peterson, *The Bonanza Kings: The Social Origins and Business Behavior of Western Mining Entrepreneurs, 1870–1900* (Lincoln, 1971), offers some useful comparisons.
4. "David Brown came to Aspen in 1880 to make $100,000. He has now raised his star to $1,000,000." *ADT*, March 22, 1885.
5. *RMS*, Jan. 12, Dec. 13, 1884; *AT*, Dec. 13, 1884.
6. *RMS*, July 11, Aug. 15, 1885; *ADT*, Aug. 29, 1885.
7. *RMS*, March 27, 1886; Sept. 26, 1885.
8. *RMS*, Sept. 26, 1885.
9. *RMS*, July 18, 1885.
10. *RMS*, Jan. 23, Feb. 13, 1886.
11. *RMS*, Aug. 22, 1885.
12. *RMS*, Sept. 12, 1885, Nov. 13, 1886, Nov. 21, 1885.
13. *AT*, May 31, 1884.

14. *RMS*, March 5, 1887.
15. *RMS*, Feb. 26, 1887.
16. Colorado Census of 1885, Pitkin County, "Population Schedule." The census taker told a reporter, "Sporting women of the town are all adverse to telling their real names, or where they were born." Instead, they identified themselves as governesses, dressmakers, milliners, or music teachers. *ADT*, June 13, 1885.
17. *RMS*, June 14, 1884; Sept. 19, 1885.
18. *RMS*, July 3, 1886.
19. *RMS*, April 18, 1885, Feb. 20, Oct. 16, 23, 1886.
20. Colorado Census of 1885, Pitkin County, "Population Schedule" *RMS*, March 12, 1887.
21. *RMS*, Feb. 13, 1886.
22. *RMS*, July 19, 1884, Oct. 29, 1887. John R. Morris, *Davis H. Waite: The Ideology of a Western Populist* (Washington, 1982), chap. 8, is a history of women's suffrage in Colorado.
23. *RMS*, April 23, 1887.
24. *RMS*, Dec. 11, 1886.
25. *RMS*, Aug. 23, 1884.
26. *RMS*, Aug. 23, Sept. 27, 1884.
27. *RMS*, Nov. 15, 1884, June 27, 1885.
28. *RMS*, Dec. 19, 1885.
29. *RMS*, Oct. 1, 1887.
30. *RMS*, Oct. 16, Jan. 2, 1886.
31. *RMS*, Oct. 16, 1886, gives a history of Aspen's churches.
32. *RMS*, May 29, Oct. 16, 1886; *AT*, Jan. 24, 1891.
33. *RMS*, May 16, Aug. 1, 1885.
34. *RMS*, Aug. 15, Sept. 4, 1886.
35. *RMS*, Oct. 17, 1885.
36. *RMS*, June 26, 1886.
37. *RMS*, June 6, 1885, May 29, 1886, June 4, 1887.
38. *RMS*, June 5, 1886, June 4, 1887.
39. *RMS*, July 23, 1887.
40. *RMS*, Sept. 25, 1886.

CHAPTER 11
1. *RMS*, Jan. 2, 1886.
2. Rodman Wilson Paul, *Mining Frontiers of the Far West, 1848–1880* (New York, 1963), 125; Edward Blair, *Leadville: Colorado's Magic City* (Boulder, 1980), 150–56.
3. Robert G. Athearn, *The Denver and Rio Grande Western Railroad: Rebel of the Rockies* (Lincoln, 1977, orig. pub., 1962), chaps. 1–5, esp. pp. 1–22, 84–90, 98–101.
4. *AT*, Jan. 7, 1882.
5. *AT*, Sept. 6, 1884; *RMS*, Sept. 6, 1884.
6. "Memoirs of John James Hagerman," written in Roswell, New Mexico, June 1908 (J. J. Hagerman Papers, Western History Research Center, University of Wyoming Library), is a complete account of Hagerman's early business career. On Hagerman's connection with the Colorado Midland, see John J. Lipsey, "J. J. Hagerman: Building of the Colorado Midland," *The Westerners Brand Book: The Denver Posse of the Westerners*, vol. 10 (Denver, 1955), 95–115.
7. J. J. Hagerman to Henry T. Rogers, Jan. 19, 1886; Hagerman to D. R. C. Brown, Oct. 6, 7, 1885, Hagerman Papers. Hagerman to Mr. Van Dyke, July 29, 1885, is a prospectus of the Colorado Midland and probably summarizes the arguments that he presented to prospective investors during his New York trip.
8. Athearn, *Denver and Rio Grande Western Railroad*, 146–50, 153–54; J. J. Hagerman to S.

S. Sands, March 22, 1886, Hagerman Papers, is an account of Hagerman's negotiations with Jackson.

9. Quoted in Athearn, *Denver and Rio Grande Western Railroad*, 160.
10. Ibid., 140, 150, 160–65.
11. *RMS*, June 6, 1885.
12. *RMS*, July 17, 1886.
13. Jackson C. Thode, "To Aspen and Beyond," *The Westerners Brand Book: The Denver Posse of the Westerners*, vol. 23 (Denver 1968), 175–223, is excellent on the technical problems of constructing a railroad to Aspen.
14. For a corporate view of the race of Aspen, see Athearn, *Denver and Rio Grande Western Railroad*, chap. 8.
15. *RMS*, Oct. 29, 1887.
16. *RMS*, Nov. 5, 1887.
17. *AT*, Nov. 5, 1887; *RMS*, Nov. 5, 1887.
18. *RMS*, Oct. 15, 1887.

CHAPTER 12
1. *RMS*, Dec. 10, Nov. 5, 1887.
2. *RMS*, Jan. 7, 1888.
3. Ibid.
4. *RMS*, May 13, 1893.
5. U.S. Census, Eleventh Census (1890), "Population Schedule."
6. *RMS*, May 26, July 14, Nov. 24, 1888. Wheeler owned 112,000 of 200,000 shares. See *AT*, July 23, 1887.
7. *RMS*, Dec. 22, 1888, April 6, 1889.
8. *RMS*, March 23, 1889, July 2, 1892, Sept. 15, 1888; *AT*, June 21, 1890.
9. The listing of the mines is in the Pitkin County Court House, under "Index to Lodes, Pitkin County." My count was in excess of 7,150. The most popular initial letter for a mining claim was "O" (780), the least popular, "X" (7). It is a tribute to the creativity of the mining claimants of Pitkin County that they could produce more than 7,000 different names.
10. *AT*, Aug. 15, 1891; *RMS*, April 2, 1892.
11. *RMS*, Dec. 22, 1888, Aug. 17, 1889, May 15, Aug. 23, 1890; *AT*, Nov. 14, 1891.
12. *AT*, Dec. 19, 1891, Feb. 13, 1892.
13. Rodman Wilson Paul, *Mining Frontiers of the Far West, 1848–1880* (New York, 1963), 74–75, 79–80. Joseph E. King, *A Mine to Make a Mine: Financing the Colorado Mining Industry, 1859–1902* (College Station, 1977), describes in detail the promotional activities and stock manipulations typical of much of the Colorado mining scene.
14. *AT*, Oct. 1, 1889. Marian V. Sears, *Mining Stock Exchanges, 1860–1930: An Historical Survey* (Missoula, 1973), is a good introduction to the varieties of mining exchanges.
15. *AT*, May 10, 1890; Jan. 16, 1892. An "Aspen Mining Stock Exchange" organized in 1890.
16. *AT*, Nov. 14, 1891.
17. *RMS*, Feb. 16, 23, 1889.
18. *AT*, Sept. 20, 1890. The term "lixiviation" meant simply the process of leeching.
19. *RMS*, Nov. 28, 1891; *AT*, Feb. 13, 1892.
20. *RMS*, Feb. 25, 1888.
21. *RMS*, Dec. 1, 1888, March 23, 1889.
22. *RMS*, Nov. 30, 1889.
23. *RMS*, Sept. 6, 1890.
24. *RMS*, Dec. 15, 1888, April 4, 1889.
25. *RMS*, March 9, 1889.

26. *RMS*, Sept. 1, 8, 1888. See also Rodman Wilson Paul, "Colorado as a Pioneer of Science in the Mining West," *Journal of American History*, 47 (1960): 45–50.
27. *RMS*, June 1, 1889.
28. *RMS*, Nov. 16, 23, Dec. 7, 1889.
29. *RMS*, Sept. 21, 1889.
30. *RMS*, Jan. 2, 1892.
31. Ibid.
32. Ibid.
33. *RMS*, March 19, 26, May 7, 1892.
34. *RMS*, Jan. 28, 1893.
35. *RMS*, Feb. 6, 1893.

CHAPTER 13
1. *RMS*, Feb. 27, 1892, is a complete history of the mine to that date.
2. *RMS*, April 6, 1889.
3. *AT*, Jan. 2, 1892, recounts Gillespie's career in Aspen. See also his obituary in the Denver *Rocky Mountain News*, April 21, 1903.
4. *RMS*, Feb. 16, 23, 1889.
5. *ADT*, Feb. 13, 15, 16, 20, 1889; *RMS*, Feb. 23, March 2, 1889.
6. *RMS*, March 2, 1889; *ADT*, March 5, 1889.
7. *ADT*, Feb. 24, May 1, 1889.
8. *RMS*, Aug. 31, 1889. Marian V. Sears, *Mining Stock Exchanges, 1860–1930: An Historical Survey* (Missoula, 1973), describes the stock exchanges in Colorado, where twenty-five were established but few survived more than a few years.
9. *AT*, Sept. 11, 1889.
10. *AT*, Feb. 16, 1889.
11. *AT*, April 4, 1889.
12. *RMS*, May 4, 1889; *ADT*, June 25, 1889; *AT*, Jan. 2, 1892.
13. *AT*, Nov. 23, 1889, Jan. 2, 1892.
14. *AT*, April 12, May 17, July 19, 1890.
15. *AT*, Nov. 15, 1890, Nov. 21, 1891.
16. *AT*, Jan. 17, 1891.
17. *AT*, Feb. 7, 1891.
18. *AT*, Feb. 28, 1891.
19. *AT*, March 7, 14, 1891.
20. *AT*, March 14, 1891.
21. *AT*, Feb. 14, 1891.
22. *AT*, Nov. 21, 1891.
23. *AT*, April 4, 1891.
24. *AT*, Feb. 14, March 21, April 4, Nov. 21, 1891.
25. *AT*, April 4, Nov. 21, 1891.
26. *AT*, Jan. 2, 1892.
27. *RMS*, May 23, 1891; *AT*, July 11, Aug. 22, 1891, Jan. 9, 1892.
28. *AT*, May 7, 1892.
29. *AT*, Feb. 20, 1892.

CHAPTER 14
1. *RMS*, March 23, 1889.
2. *RMS*, April 5, 1890.
3. *RMS*, Feb. 28, 1891.
4. James B. Allen, *The Company Town in the American West* (Norman, 1966), is a comprehensive study of this aspect of the mining frontier.

5. *RMS*, Jan. 28, May 26, 1888.
6. My account of mining in Aspen is drawn from Richard E. Lingenfelter, *The Hardrock Miners: A History of the Mining Labor Movement in the American West, 1863–1893* (Berkeley, 1974), 3–30, and Mark Wyman, *Hard Rock Epic: Western Miners and the Industrial Revolution, 1860–1910* (Berkeley, 1979), 61–75, 118–26.
7. Numbers abstracted from the *Aspen Times* for 1891 and 1892 show twenty-three major accidents the first year, thirty-six the second.
8. *RMS*, Sept. 13, 1884, Sept. 23, 1886, Jan. 29, 1887, Nov. 5, 1892. Wheeler would find this incident embarrassing when he later sought political office as a friend of the workingman.
9. *Aspen Union Era*, July 7, 1892.
10. Ibid., April 21, May 19, 1892.
11. *AT*, Sept. 6, 1890.
12. *RMS*, May 7, 21, 1892.
13. *ADT*, July 2, 9, 1889.
14. *AT*, June 14, 1890.
15. *ADT*, July 9, 1889; *RMS*, June 4, Sept. 10, 1892, Feb. 18, 1893.
16. *AT*, Nov. 26, 1892, Feb. 2, 1882.
17. *ADT*, Feb. 20, 1889.
18. *ADT*, May 24, 1889; *AT*, Aug. 10, 1889.
19. *RMS*, Dec. 6, 1890, Dec. 17, 1892.
20. *AT*, July 12, 1890; *RMS*, Feb. 1, May 10, 1890.
21. *RMS*, June 1, 1889.
22. *RMS*, March 19, 1892.
23. *AT*, Nov. 14, 1891, June 7, 21, 1890, Jan. 1, 1892; *RMS*, Jan. 16, 1892.
24. *RMS*, Nov. 29, 1890.
25. *RMS*, April 16, 1892, Feb. 14, 1891.
26. *RMS*, Feb. 22, 1890; *ADT*, Aug. 17, 1887; *RMS*, Nov. 29, 1890.
27. Quoted in *RMS*, Dec. 10, 1892.

CHAPTER 15
1. *AT*, Nov. 14, 1891.
2. *RMS*, Nov. 29, Oct. 11, 1890.
3. *RMS*, Dec. 13, 1890, Jan. 24, 1891.
4. *RMS*, Feb. 16, 1889.
5. James Edward Wright, *The Politics of Populism: Dissent in Colorado* (New Haven, 1974), 133–35, gives an insightful introduction to the silver issue and its impact in Colorado.
6. *RMS*, Dec. 7, 1889, Dec. 20, 1890.
7. *RMS*, Nov. 28, Dec. 26, 1891.
8. *RMS*, March 12, 19, 26, April 2, 1892.
9. *RMS*, April 23, May 7, March 12, 1892.
10. *AT*, June 11, 1892.
11. On the early reform career of Davis H. Waite, see John R. Morris, *Davis H. Waite: The Ideology of a Western Populist* (Washington, 1982), chaps. 1 and 2, and Wright, *Politics of Populism*, 141–44.
12. *RMS*, July 30, 1892.
13. *AT*, July 30, 1892.
14. *RMS*, Nov. 12, 1892.
15. *RMS*, Dec. 31, 1892.
16. *RMS*, Feb. 11, 18, March 11, April 29, May 6, 1893.
17. *RMS*, July 1, 1893.
18. *RMS*, July 1, 22, 1893.

19. *RMS,* July 22, Aug. 12, 26, 1893.
20. *RMS,* July 29, Aug. 19, 1893.

CHAPTER 16

1. Quoted in *RMS,* Jan. 13, 1894. On Cripple Creek, see Marshall Sprague, *Money Mountain: The Story of Cripple Creek Gold* (Boston, 1953); a brief account is William S. Greever, *The Bonanza West: The Story of the Western Mining Rushes, 1848–1900* (Norman, 1963), 206–10.
2. David M. Hyman, "The Romance of a Mining Adventure," 80–81, MS original in the American Jewish Archives (Cincinnati), typed copy on permanent loan in the Western History Collections, Denver Public Library. Hyman notes that the owners of the Mollie Gibson split from the unified stand of the mineowners and made a secret agreement with the Aspen Miners' Union to pay $2.37 a day.
3. *RMS,* Dec. 29, 1894.
4. *RMS,* June 30, Sept. 22, Nov. 10, 1894.
5. *RMS,* Jan. 19, 1895.
6. *RMS,* Dec. 21, Aug. 3, 1895.
7. *Aspen Democrat-Times,* Nov. 30, Dec. 2, 1910.
8. "Aspen's First Christmas," written for the *Aspen Democrat-Times,* Dec. 1916, MS in Aspen Historical Society.
9. *RMS,* Jan. 25, 1896. See also his obituary in the *Denver Republican,* Jan. 23, 1896.
10. *RMS,* Dec. 21, 1895; Denver *Rocky Mountain News,* April 21, 1903.
11. *Denver Republican,* July 5, 1901; *Denver Post,* Dec. 3, 1908.
12. Hyman, "Romance," 80ff. James E. Fell, *Ores to Metals: The Rocky Mountain Smelting Industry* (Lincoln, 1979), chap. 9, is a full discussion of the organization of ASARCO.
13. Among the most useful biographical sketches of Brown are the *Illustrated Weekly,* 10, no. 47 (Aug. 15, 1900); John G. Canfield, *Mines and Mining Men of Colorado* (Denver, 1893), 38–40; Len Shoemaker, *Pioneers of the Roaring Fork* (Denver, 1965), 49–52.

A Note on Sources

The footnote citations to this book identify much of the secondary literature (books and articles) that bears on the subject. There is no point in listing these items again. At the same time, it might be useful to note briefly some works that place Aspen in the larger context of mining history and to mention several of the primary sources that are at hand.

The materials available for a history of Aspen are a microcosm of the varieties of sources available for the history of small towns in general and of mining camps in particular. While Aspen has more than the usual number of secondary accounts for a small town—a tribute to its enduring interest for residents and visitors, even before it became one of the premier ski resorts in the world—at the heart of the sources are manuscript collections, newspapers, federal and state censuses, and city and county records. Taken together, this body of material is sufficient to offer us an outline of the early history of the camp, its remarkable growth, its transition to a town and then to a city, and its subsequent decline. At the same time, we are left with important parts of the story that we know all too little about. I think particularly of the lives of the twenty-five hundred miners and their families. These people formed the core of the city, both in numbers and in occupational structure, yet they left few written records. Only through the census, the anonymous faces in photographs, and occasional references in the newspapers do we get a sense of their significant presence.

The starting point for a history of Aspen is the context of the development of western mining after 1848, for Aspen appeared in the midst of half a century of continuous mining excitement that stretched from John Marshall's California mill race in 1848 to the Klondike in 1898. As such, the camp on the Roaring Fork emerged surrounded by the techniques, strategies, and values both in building a town and in exploiting its mines. The best place to begin such a large-scale examination is the definitive survey of the literature in Clark C. Spence, "Western Mining," in Michael P. Malone, ed. *Historians and the American West* (Lincoln, 1983). In spite of its prejudices and eclectic quality, I like Thomas A. Rickard, *History of American Mining* (New York, 1932), for its flavor of the mining world as perceived by an engineer and editor. Of the modern scholarly overviews, Rodman Wilson Paul, *Mining Frontiers of the Far West, 1848–1880* (New York, 1963), is clear on the technical aspects of mining, especially in the silver mines of the Comstock Lode, where engineers and superintendents through trial and error developed the techniques that would come into use in later silver districts such as Aspen.

On the history of individual camps (gold and silver), I have profited from the work of Larry Barsness (Virginia City and Alder Gulch), Paul Fatout (Meadow Lake), Watson Parker (Deadwood), Don and Jean Griswold (Leadville), Edward Blair (Leadville), Duane A. Smith (Caribou), Marshall Sprague (Cripple Creek), and W. Turrentine Jackson (White Pine). I have full citations to these studies at the opening of the notes, and I will not repeat them here.

On the intriguing problem of frontier communities and how they evolve in the midst of internal and external pressures, I have learned much from Robert R. Dykstra, *The Cattle Towns* (New York, 1968). A recent microcosmic study, Ralph Mann, *After the Gold Rush: Society in Grass Valley and Nevada City, California, 1849–1870* (Stanford, 1982), has adapted the techniques of the new social history to the study of two gold-mining towns in California.

For a history of Aspen, the best place to start is the manuscript collections in the western depositories. The Colorado Historical Society (Denver) has the "Letterbooks of the Roaring Fork Improvement Company" (1881 and 1882), correspondence that shows the influence of an absentee (Philadelphia) corporation on the life and development of the camp on the Roaring Fork from the very beginning of its unofficial life. Charles Ruter's "Letterpress book, 1885–1895" is the correspondence of a man who owned sampling works in Aspen and Pueblo. E. Dunbar Wright, "Manuscript Collection," is about one of Aspen's self-made mining entrepreneurs who began as an employee in the general offices of Denver and Rio Grande Railroad at a salary of $100 per month, invested in Aspen mines, and ended up general manager and substantial stockholder in the Park-Regent mine. His was an experience that editors loved to review before an admiring public, with statements that praised him as "the nerviest investor who ever struck this camp." The implication was, of course, that others could do likewise. The Charles E. Kuhn "Diaries" are marginal on mining, but their focus on ranching in the valley of the Roaring Fork reminds us that agriculture had an important place in Pitkin County (although not as important as the newspapers claimed) and one that survived long after the repeal of the Sherman Silver Purchase Act and the depression after 1893 had reduced the economic significance of silver mining. Of the oral histories of Colorado mining deposited in the Historical Society, only the interview with R. W. Thaler, "Reminiscences of Aspen and Victor," covers Aspen.

The Western History Department of the Denver Public Library has a copy of David M. Hyman's "The Romance of a Mining Adventure" (original in the American Jewish Archives, Cincinnati), written in 1918 for his sons. It also has a large number of important photographs of the mining camps in Colorado.

Western Historical Collections of the University of Colorado Library (Boulder) house the David R. C. Brown Papers. The Letterbooks of the Aspen Mining and Smelting Company cover the years 1884 through 1909, and they are indispensable for a history of silver mining in Colorado, especially of its economic aspects. They are less useful for a history of Aspen itself. Unfortunately, several of the volumes hold copies of letters in purple ink, much of it badly faded, a condition that makes reading a heavy task and reproduction almost impossible. Some of the pages are so faded that they can be read only when held up to the light. The Historical Collections also contain copies of interviews with Colorado mining men (originals in the Bancroft Library, University of California, Berkeley), and four of the interviewees (Edwin Arkell, J. W. Atkisson, J. R. Williams, and Harvey Young) are Aspenites. The chance to hear the words of someone under the spell of Aspen's boom year of 1886 should not be missed, even strained through a Bancroft interviewer.

The Aspen Public Library has a copy of David R. C. Brown's "My Trip from Black Hawk to Aspen."

The Archives of the Aspen Historical Society hold copies of several of these manuscripts (including Hyman and Brown), as well as some things that no one else has.

Among the latter are two Hyman manuscript letters and his "Journal." The Louise Berg tapes contain details about the town. J. W. Deane's "Aspen's First Christmas" is an exaggerated account celebrating the hardy pioneers of the Roaring Fork (he uses ancient Carthage as a basis of comparison) and the virtues of the white metal, which will eventually rise again. The Archives have an outstanding collection of photographs, which are exceptionally useful in establishing the flavor of Aspen's past.

The Western History Research Center at the University of Wyoming has the John J. Hagerman Papers. These include the "Autobiography," written for his children at Roswell, New Mexico, in 1908, and correspondence (transcribed by John J. Lipsey) concerning the construction of the Colorado Midland Railroad, which vitally involved Aspen.

Among the newspapers, I found useful the *Aspen Times* (1881–91) and the *Aspen Daily Times* (1885–93), edited by B. Clark Wheeler. Wheeler was opinioned and self-serving but never dull. His main rival, the Aspen *Rocky Mountain Sun* (1881–93), pursued a less personal approach to life in the "Crystal City of the Rockies." Both editors and their newspapers shamelessly boosted the camp/town/city. Davis H. Waite's *Aspen Union Era* (1891–92), of lasting interest because of its editor's subsequent political career, emphasized consensus on silver coinage, an issue on which all Aspenites, of whatever economic persuasion, could unite, rather than confrontation between miners and owners. Of the mining journals, the *Mining & Scientific Press* (San Francisco, 1879–93) seemed oriented toward California in its coverage. The *Engineering and Mining Journal* (New York, 1884–93) is technical.

Of the federal and state documents, the most directly useful are the Colorado State census of 1885 (modeled after the federal census of 1880), the federal census of 1890 (which lacks individual schedules), and the federal census of 1900. F. V. Hayden, *Annual Report of the United States Geological and Geographical Survey of the Territories, Embracing Colorado, Being a Report of Progress of the Expedition for the Year 1873* (Washington, 1874), provided the marching orders for Aspen's pioneering prospectors. Josiah Edward Spurr, *Geology of the Aspen Mining District* (Washington, 1898), is a useful reference point. Adolph Knopf, *Recent Developments in the Aspen District, Colorado* (Washington, 1926), demonstrates how far into the twentieth century Aspen thought of itself as a mining town. Charles W. Henderson, *Mining in Colorado: A History of Discovery, Development and Production* (Washington, 1926), is a good summary.

Aspen emerged in the context of a legal structure that directly influenced all aspects of its history. *General Laws of the State of Colorado* (Denver, 1877) and *Laws Passed at the 2nd Session of the General Assembly of the State of Colorado* (1879) are necessary reference works.

The Pitkin County Court House contains a wide range of records relating directly to Aspen, from its earliest official beginnings to the present. Among the records that deserve mention are County Commissioners' Records, Minute Books, #B (May 27, 1881, to Dec. 16, 1888), #1 (Dec. 12, 1888, to Oct. 4, 1893); Records of Deeds Filed, Pitkin County; Court Documents, General Record, #J (July 30, 1881, to May 2, 1889), Deed Record, #K (May 4, 1888, to May 18, 1912); Lien Records, #L (July 27, 1882, to March 9, 1898); Location Certificates, Deed Records [from Gunnison County], #W (1879–81); General Records, #Z (July 31, 1880, to March 4, 1881); Title Bonds for Mining Property, #1 (June 2, 1881, to Nov. 4, 1911); Tax Sale Record Book, vol. 1 (1884–94).

The "Ordinances of the City of Aspen" (1886) are helpful, although the individual ordinances were regularly printed in the local newspapers as they become law. The *Aspen City Directory* for 1889 and that for 1892 are standard references.

The list of unpublished theses and dissertations for Aspen is brief. It consists of Robert F. Bartlett, "The Early History of Aspen," (M.A. thesis, University of Denver, 1951); Thomas John Kimmell, "A History of a Rocky Mountain Silver Camp: Aspen, Colorado, 1879–1910" (bachelor's thesis, Harvard College, 1975); and Bertha Louise Shaw, "History of the Wheeler Opera House, Aspen, Colorado, 1889–1894" (M.A. thesis, Western State College of Colorado, 1965).

A Note on Sources

Of the contemporary accounts, pamphlets, and descriptions, I liked Arkell, MacMillan, and Stewart, comps., *Aspen, Pitkin County, Colorado: Her Mines and Mineral Resources* (Aspen, 1892), which modestly describes Aspen as the "richest five acres on earth"; *Aspen: Where and What is Aspen and How to Get There* (n.p., 1892); William Willard Howard, "The City of Aspen, Colorado," *Harper's Weekly*, Jan. 19, 1889; and John G. Canfield, *Mines and Mining Men of Colorado* (1893), which shows Aspen at the peak of its mining production, its reputation established, its future unlimited.

Index